# Praise for *The Journey Within*

"Radhanath Swami is a towering spiritual figure of our time. He is a masterful teacher and a wise leader whose knowledge inspires me. Don't miss the gems of wisdom and courage that comprise this powerful book."

— Dr. Cornel West

PHILOSOPHER, ACADEMIC, ACTIVIST, AUTHOR

"In *The Journey Home*, Radhanath Swami gave us a gripping account of his geographical and spiritual itinerary. Now, in *The Journey Within*, he summarizes the content of the wisdom he has achieved. The book will be an inspiration to his many followers, and no doubt also attract new ones."

— Edward Mortimer, CMG

COMPANION OF THE ORDER OF ST. MICHAEL AND ST. GEORGE (CMG); FORMER DIRECTOR OF COMMUNICATIONS TO UNITED NATIONS SECRETARY; AUTHOR; JOURNALIST; FELLOW, ALL SOULS COLLEGE, UNIVERSITY OF OXFORD

"Radhanath Swami is one of today's foremost exponents of India's spiritual wisdom and has practiced bhakti yoga for over forty years. Based on the deep spiritual knowledge of ancient scriptures and supported with examples from Radhanath Swami's own life, *The Journey Within* blends the eternal wisdom of India with practical advice for the spiritual seekers of our modern age."

— His Holiness Indradyumna Swami

"Radhanath Swami has conveyed the Divine Light through his writing with the gentle and seductive effortlessness that he does in person. This book is a joyful way to move closer to the truth within you."

— Russell Brand

COMEDIAN, ACTOR, AUTHOR, ACTIVIST

"*The Journey Within* is a modern-day exploration of a diverse range of age-old issues, including the self, wealth, divinity, materialism, adversity, illusion, and consciousness. Radhanath Swami's second book is as revealing and fascinating as his first and is destined to become one of the seminal texts on enlightenment."

— Matthew J. Offord, PhD

MEMBER OF PARLIAMENT, UK

"Radhanath Swami, one of the most beloved and revered spiritual leaders of our time, is an accomplished storyteller and masterfully weaves all of the essential teachings found in the world's great religious scriptures into his newest book. *The Journey Within* takes us on the most important journey of our lives—the journey to that eternal place of love and happiness."

—SHARON GANNON

CO-FOUNDER, JIVAMUKTI YOGA; AUTHOR, *YOGA AND VEGETARIANISM*, *JIVAMUKTI YOGA*, AND *SIMPLE RECIPES FOR JOY*

"Drawing from personal anecdotes and on religious insights derived from the Vedic traditions and folkloric wisdom, *The Journey Within* imparts inspiring devotional teachings for today's spiritual seekers."

—EDWIN BRYANT, PhD

PROFESSOR OF HINDUISM, RUTGERS UNIVERSITY; AUTHOR, *THE YOGA SUTRAS OF PATAÑJALI: A NEW EDITION, TRANSLATION, AND COMMENTARY*

"*The Journey Within* is a carefully crafted progression of practical directions illustrated by touching stories, many from the author's life experiences. In refreshingly lucid language, one whose entire life has been absorbed in the cultivation of authentic spiritual living shows how the bhakti path, well-traversed for millennia by sages and kings as much as the common folk of India, is perfectly accessible to us all."

—KENNETH R. VALPEY, PhD

RESEARCH FELLOW, OXFORD CENTRE FOR HINDU STUDIES, UK

"Through the anxiety, stress, and confusion of life, *The Journey Within* offers a road map to peace and tranquility. Radhanath Swami's use of personal stories and anecdotes leads readers on a pathway that illuminates what is truly important in life and how best to achieve it."

—DR. STEVEN ZODKOY

BEST-SELLING AUTHOR, *MISDIAGNOSED: THE ADRENAL FATIGUE LINK*

"*The Journey Within* conveys the same captivating and enlightening spirit that I've experienced in Radhanath Swami's personal presence. It combines the powerful wisdom of the East and the West, and I recommend this book to anyone who wants to feel authentic, lasting happiness!"

—MARCI SHIMOFF

#1 *NEW YORK TIMES* BEST-SELLING AUTHOR OF *HAPPY FOR NO REASON*, *LOVE FOR NO REASON*, AND *CHICKEN SOUP FOR THE WOMAN'S SOUL*

"Radhanath Swami's stories are filled with warmth and wisdom, and he has a way of writing that feels like he's speaking directly and very personally to the reader. This book is a must for anyone approaching or attempting to walk the very elusive path of devotional yoga! And don't forget to read his first book, *The Journey Home!*"

— JAI UTTAL

GRAMMY-NOMINATED MUSICIAN

"This book is yet another masterpiece from the author of *The Journey Home*. Radhanath Swami's characteristic humility, compassion, and wisdom shine through this impeccably written book. For adepts and novices alike, this book will serve as a faithful companion and guide for those on the path of bhakti."

—RAVI M. GUPTA, PhD

CHARLES REDD CHAIR OF RELIGIOUS STUDIES, UTAH STATE UNIVERSITY

"In his new book, Radhanath Swami deftly connects the ancient wisdom tradition of bhakti yoga—the yoga of love—to our busy modern lives. He eloquently persuades us, both through scriptural references from the world's major faiths and from his own life story, that to attain true happiness we don't need to change our externalities, we just need to change our consciousness. A very relevant and contemporary message drawn from timeless teachings."

—GOPI KALLAYIL

CHIEF EVANGELIST, BRAND MARKETING, GOOGLE; AUTHOR, *THE INTERNET TO THE INNER-NET: FIVE WAYS TO RESET YOUR CONNECTION AND LIVE A CONSCIOUS LIFE*

"Radhanath Swami has written a beautiful book that shows how the true journey in life—the journey that leads to the ultimate destination of peace, joy, understanding, and awakening—is a journey within ourselves. I am sure that all who read this book will be truly touched and transformed."

—HIS HOLINESS PUJYA SWAMI CHIDANAND SARASWATI

PRESIDENT, PARMARTH NIKETAN ASHRAM, RISHIKESH, INDIA

"My dear friend and brother Radhanath Swami has done it again. Just as with my experience when reading *The Journey Home*, I can't put down his new book. He writes so colorfully and with such inspiration. With every page I'm lifted higher and higher."

—GURMUKH KAUR KHALSA

CO-FOUNDER AND DIRECTOR OF THE GOLDEN BRIDGE YOGA CENTER; AUTHOR, *THE EIGHT HUMAN TALENTS* AND *BOUNTIFUL, BEAUTIFUL, BLISSFUL*

*"The Journey Within* is a remarkable recital of a soul seeking an answer to "Who am I?" and "What is my purpose in life?" The book honestly describes many journeys. The journey from Richard Slavin to Radhanath Swami. The fulfilling journey from a routine life to a life of bhakti yoga. The journey from an external world to an internal world. One senses an awakening after reading *The Journey Within*."

— LALIT KANODIA, PhD

FOUNDER AND CHAIRMAN, DATAMATICS GLOBAL SERVICES LIMITED; BOARD MEMBER, MIT


*"The Journey Within* reveals everything from an understanding of the real self within to an awareness of the inner nature of God, and from the actual meaning of yoga and how it's ideally practiced to how one might achieve spiritual fulfillment. Highly recommended for anyone with a thirst for the divine."

—STEVEN J. ROSEN (SATYARAJA DASA), PhD

EDITOR IN CHIEF, *JOURNAL OF VAISHNAVA STUDIES*; AUTHOR, *HOLY WAR: VIOLENCE AND THE BHAGAVAD GITA* AND *THE HIDDEN GLORY OF INDIA*


"In *The Journey Within*, Radhanath Swami opens up his devotional world to us. He shows readers his experiences and interactions with others through colorful anecdotes, explains his philosophical views and interpretations of life's challenges, and talks about his way of life and his own devotional practices. He affectionately extends all of these lessons to us, his readers, so that we, too, may join him on his insightful 'journey within.'"

—GRAHAM M. SCHWEIG, PhD

AUTHOR, *BHAGAVAD GĪTĀ: THE BELOVED LORD'S SECRET LOVE SONG*


"As someone who spent a lot of time in zones of war and famine, I didn't need anything that added to the weight of the world. Radhanath Swami writes wonderfully of true wisdom and makes the weight of the world feel lighter. I wish he had written this book many years ago so that I could have read it then."

— STEPHEN CHAN, OBE, PhD

PROFESSOR OF WORLD POLITICS, SCHOOL OF ORIENTAL & AFRICAN STUDIES, UNIVERSITY OF LONDON


"Radhanath Swami combines rich, eloquent storytelling with seeds of divine wisdom on each page, making *The Journey Within* a must-read for those seeking their true purpose in this world."

—ADAM OMKARA

FOUNDER, OMKARA WORLD; PRODUCER, INTELLIGENT FITNESS; COLUMNIST, COMMUNITIES DIGITAL NEWS (CDN)

"Radhanath Swami is such a pure, devoted, and inspirational being that whatever he chooses to share with us becomes a blessing. This book is an outpouring of wisdom, love, and great adventure."

— DEVA PREMAL & MITEN

MANTRA MUSICIANS; COMPOSERS, *SONGS FOR THE SANGHA*


"*The Journey Within* is a fascinating book that expresses the depth, vitality, and nonsectarian aspects of contemporary Indian devotional spirituality."

—FERDINANDO SARDELLA, PhD

ASSOCIATE PROFESSOR, HISTORY OF RELIGIONS, STOCKHOLM UNIVERSITY


"Radhanath Swami takes us through the uplifting journey of finding hope and meaning in a world confronting rapid change and ecological decay and offers readers a way to understand spiritual practice and how it can lead to planetary awakening and healing. Finding peace can be an adventure, and this collection of stories connects us profoundly with our deepest desire to be instruments of God's love."

— YEB SAÑO

LEADER, THE PEOPLE'S PILGRIMAGE;
FORMER MEMBER, PHILIPPINES CLIMATE CHANGE COMMISSION


"A must-read for all bhakti aspirants. Radhanath Swami delivers his message with concise and thorough prose. Rich in details of beauty, love, and compassion, *The Journey Within* is for those who want to dive deeper into their hearts and expand their true selves. I highly recommend this book."

— SRIDHAR SILBERFEIN

FOUNDER AND CREATOR, BHAKTI FEST; DIRECTOR, CENTER FOR SPIRITUAL STUDIES;
PRODUCER, *RIVER OF LOVE*


"By connecting us to the simplicities of life, Radhanath Swami brilliantly explains life's twists and turns. He generously shares his journey to help you on yours."

—SHOBANA MURATEE

EDITOR IN CHIEF, *VOICE OF ASIA*

"*The Journey Within* is the ripened fruit of the bhakti yoga tree. Radhanath Swami unravels powerful and timeless principles to help readers lead a more mindful life in these critical times, making it a must-read for one and all."

— N. Damodar Reddy

FOUNDER, CHAIRMAN, AND CEO OF SUTISOFT, INC.


"In this age of computerization and digitalization, Radhanath Swami's book *The Journey Within* brings that much-needed balance between high-paced work environments and our inherent needs as individuals with families within societies. In *The Journey Within*, the reader will learn the principles of a wholesome life of inner peace and joy, and how to share their wealth and wisdom with the world."

—Kinesh Doshi

CEO, ACCION LABS; ERNST & YOUNG ENTREPRENEUR OF THE YEAR 2015


"Here, at last, in one accessible volume, is an engaging, absorbing, clear, and sensible guide to bhakti (devotional) yoga. A must-read for all who seek to deepen their spiritual practices."

—Joshua M. Greene

AUTHOR, *SWAMI IN A STRANGE LAND; HERE COMES THE SUN: THE SPIRITUAL AND MUSICAL JOURNEY OF GEORGE HARRISON;* AND *GITA WISDOM: AN INTRODUCTION TO INDIA'S ESSENTIAL YOGA TEXT*


"The nature of bhakti is to see the harmony between understanding the greatness of the Lord and performing loving devotional service, and through such harmony we can experience our blissful nature. I hope this book will awaken the desire to connect with devotional service in society at large."

— Sri Vishvesha Tirtha Swami

PEJAVAR MATHA TEMPLE, UDUPI

# The Journey Within

# The Journey Within

## Exploring the Path of Bhakti

# A CONTEMPORARY GUIDE TO YOGA'S ANCIENT WISDOM

*Radhanath Swami*

MANDALA
PUBLISHING

*San Rafael, California*

**MANDALA**
PUBLISHING
PO Box 3088
San Rafael, CA 94912
www.mandalaeartheditions.com

Find us on Facebook: www.facebook.com/mandalaearth
Follow us on Twitter: @mandalaearth

Library of Congress Cataloging-in-Publication Data available.

ISBN: 978-1-60887-157-5


Mandala Publishing, in association with Roots of Peace, will plant
two trees for each tree used in the manufacturing of this book. Roots
of Peace is an internationally renowned humanitarian organization
dedicated to eradicating land mines worldwide and converting war-torn
lands into productive farms and wildlife habitats. Roots of Peace will
plant two million fruit and nut trees in Afghanistan and provide farmers
there with the skills and support necessary for sustainable land use.

Manufactured in the United States of America

10 9 8 7 6 5 4

*To my beloved teachers, family, and friends,*
*and to all seekers of truth and love*

# Contents

# INTRODUCTION

It was a cold and rainy day in London. As I walked down a long, elegant corridor in the British Parliament, my heart pounded. Here I was, a little monk with a meager education and no experience in politics, about to address a nation's leaders. Looking up at the hall's majestic stone arches, I felt small and so far away from the caves of the Himalayan jungle I had once called home.

My escort led me into an inner chamber of the House of Commons. The room, with its polished, hand-carved wood trim, plush wall coverings, and ornate paintings, was immaculate. Among those gathered in the hall were members of Parliament, lords and ladies, dukes and duchesses, mayors and esteemed priests and rabbis. Standing at the podium, I searched my heart for the words to begin.

Through an arched window on my right, I happened to glance at a familiar sight—the river Thames, flowing gracefully alongside the Palace of Westminster. My eyes sought and located the stone embankment across the river, where, forty-one years ago, I had sat alone late into many nights, staring in the deep current.

Back then, I was very young and very lost. I had come from the United States on a quest for meaning and purpose. I had no money and was sleeping on the stone floor of a church basement on Lambeth Road. Although I couldn't see it from where I now stood, I knew that church lay just behind the embankment wall.

It was in London that I had desperately begun to question everything. My emotions were at odds with the world around me. I was begging for answers to questions that sprang from a place so deep in me that they overshadowed all other concerns.

I passed through my teens in the turbulent 1960s. While in the States, I dove headlong into the idealism of the counterculture and the civil rights movement. Yet I was a shy boy, quite reserved with girls, moderate in my use of drugs, and mostly uninterested in mingling with the popular crowd. But in London at age nineteen, I cast my timidity aside and plunged unleashed and ravenous into the social scene. Crossing the ocean seemed to have freed me to enjoy myself as I had never dared to before, and the people I met praised and encouraged me.

But at the end of each day, if I was honest with myself, I felt a sense of emptiness. So I came often to sit on that embankment, alone in the dark, staring into the wide river. I contemplated, I prayed, I cried. Something was calling me away from the life I was just coming to know and the life I had just left behind. I couldn't make sense of the madness of war and of the hate and greed and hypocrisy that surrounded me. I couldn't understand the many atrocities committed in the name of God. So as I gazed at Big Ben's rippling reflection on the Thames's current, I wondered where the current of my own life was leading me.

Now, standing before my audience in the House of Commons, I thought, *Forty-one years have passed, and in that time I've been carried across the world and stripped of almost everything I once thought I was — and led into a destiny unimaginable to the teenager on that riverbank.*

I pulled my eyes from the river and began to share my story.

All the twists I have taken in life have led me to a simple, ageless truth, one that sparked an incredible transformation in how I view life: all our countless desires, our insatiable longings, our fleeting gratifications, and our inevitable frustrations arise from a single origin: we've forgotten the love that lies dormant within us. Discovering and reawakening that love is our greatest need. By its nature, this love offers both fulfillment and the empowerment to become an instrument of change for ourselves, the people around us, and our environment.

The path I have taken to rediscover that love has been what ancient India calls bhakti yoga, the yoga of love. We tend to think of yoga as a kind of practice, but the word itself means "a joining" or "union." Ultimately all yoga practice aims at helping us unite with the truth of who we are as pure spiritual beings.

I discovered bhakti yoga after an arduous hitchhiking journey overland from London to the Himalayas. I chronicled this adventure in my memoir, *The Journey Home: Autobiography of an American Swami.* After trekking through Europe, Turkey, Iran, Afghanistan, Pakistan, and the Himalayas, I was eventually led to Vrindavan, an idyllic village in northern India on the banks of the Yamuna River. In Vrindavan's forests and pastures, filled with parrots and peacocks, monkeys and cows, I realized I had found my home. I didn't understand what it was about Vrindavan that gave me that feeling; all I knew was that when I was living there, I felt in harmony with God and the world. I slept and meditated under the trees on the Yamuna's bank. I was homeless, but I had never felt so at home.

Vrindavan is an ancient place, home to thousands of temples dedicated to the one God who is called by many names in the world's many spiritual traditions. In Vrindavan he is known as Krishna, "the all-attractive," or Rama, "he who gives pleasure," or Hari, "thief of hearts." In the bhakti teachings, the feminine feature of God is inseparably interwoven. In Vrindavan, she is known as Radha, "the abode of love."

While wandering Vrindavan's forests in 1971, I met A.C. Bhaktivedanta Swami. Although he considered himself a humble servant of God and all other beings, his students called him Prabhupada, "beloved master." Prabhupada was a teacher of the tradition and philosophy of bhakti yoga as he had received it from a lineage of enlightened sages that stretches far into the past. I was especially sensitive to sectarianism at that time in my life, and I found that Prabhupada's presentation of bhakti harmonized the truths I had gathered from other paths. He put everything I admired about the world's many faiths into a fascinating perspective that seamlessly reconciled whatever differences appeared on their surface. From him I learned about the self's true nature and its longing for unconditional love. I also learned that that longing reaches its full realization only in the self's relationship with the Supreme Self, God. Once love between God and self is awakened, it flows naturally out into the world in the form of compassion for all beings, just as water is first absorbed by a tree's roots and then flows into every branch and leaf.

On my journey I came to value compassion as the essential expression of true spirituality. Prabhupada embodied that compassion. Through his simple analogies, he resolved the questions that had challenged me since childhood, and later that year, in that beautiful, holy place, I accepted him as my guru, resolving to follow his teachings and example for the rest of my life.

From 1971 until the mid-1980s, I practiced bhakti yoga in a variety of settings. I lived as a riverbank ascetic in Vrindavan, became a cave-dwelling yogi in the Himalayas, and, after my Indian visa expired, moved to an isolated mountaintop ashram in the Appalachians, where I farmed, cared for cows and goats, and tended an altar in a simple farmhouse temple. Later, I began traveling again, this time lecturing on the philosophy, sociology, and spiritual practices of bhakti yoga at American universities. I also taught the yoga of cooking! Sharing the joys of practicing bhakti has been my heart's calling, and I hope you will find my experiences meaningful and relevant.

In 1987 I returned to India, where I was entrusted with a small, dilapidated, one-room ashram in Mumbai. The ashramites were engulfed in bitterness and scandal, and the surrounding congregation seemed to be at war too. I reluctantly consented to take charge. As I waded into the existing complexities and uncertainties and dealt with my own shortcomings, I tried to establish a model of living that genuinely represented the sublime principles of bhakti.

By God's grace and the dedication of numerous souls, that Mumbai ashram is now a thriving spiritual community with dozens of branches, hundreds of ashramites, and tens of thousands of congregation members. People of all ages, social backgrounds, and vocations have discovered balance and harmony in expressing their own spirituality while living out the other aspects of their lives, and with their families they have learned to practice the culture of bhakti in peace. In just a few years, these people have cooperatively built spiritually based schools, temples, ecovillages, hospitals, hospices, an orphanage, a food distribution program for impoverished schools, and outreach programs to a number of Maharashtrian villages.

All of this service has come from people who have appreciated the power of the yoga of love. It's thrilling to see people united by a higher principle and working with a genuine appreciation of one another. It is this higher principle I share with you in this book. I hope to convey my own experience of how true spirituality opens the door to an extraordinary life, regardless of your vocation, religion, or spiritual path. All it takes is a willingness to journey within and explore this timeless way of transforming consciousness. Awakening our potential to love is a most ancient practice that is especially relevant today.

In the end, this inward journey will culminate in a reunion—a reunion with the Supreme Source of everything that exists. We usually call that source "God," although I understand that many thoughtful people struggle with that word. After all, we've seen deceit, hate, and egoism divide humanity in the name of God. Still, I ask you to open your mind to the notion of an infinitely loving and beautiful Supreme Being.

Who is God? He's our father and our mother, both a person you can meet and an all-pervading presence. In this book I often refer to our origin as "God" or "the Lord" or "the Supreme," or "he" or "him" because these are all terms familiar to the Western ear. But don't let my language limit this wondrous, omniscient Supreme Being, who is both feminine and masculine, who is more than you or I can imagine and cannot be confined by our limited conceptions or language.

I hope this book builds you a bridge to the universal teachings of bhakti as it has been practiced for thousands of years and continues to be practiced today. To help you gain a deeper insight into the teachings, I've included the timeless wisdom of gurus, saints, and sacred texts, along with contemporary anecdotes and stories of my own experiences.

*The Journey Within* is a call to adventure. It will ask you to reach beyond sectarian spirituality as well as the distractions, routines, or monotony you may have in your everyday life. I invite you to pursue your heart's deepest calling, to discover the beauty of your own true self and appreciate life's miracles at every moment.

PART I

*The Big Questions*

# What Is True Wealth?

*If you want to know how rich you are,*
*Try to find how many things you have*
*That money cannot buy.*

—PROVERB

To be truly wealthy is to have a fulfilled heart, and that means to love and be loved. The joy of love is the true wealth inherent in all of us, and learning to recognize it is what spiritual practice is all about. But in today's stressful times, we tend to forget our own spiritual potential and fail to recognize it in others. I share an encounter with you, one that humbled me and led me to recognize what we are so prone to forget.

## DOROTHY

It was a sweltering summer day in the Florida Panhandle. The morning sun glared through the expansive windows of the airport departure lounge, where I was waiting with other passengers. A young woman in a neat navy-blue uniform stepped up to the counter and announced a one-hour flight delay. Eager to escape the heat and embark on their journeys, the crowd heaved a collective sigh of disappointment.

Suddenly a middle-aged woman with coiffed, auburn hair stood up. Her dress and demeanor suggested she was a woman of wealth and stature. Her face flushed red in anger, and flinging her boarding pass on the floor, she shouted: "No! You can't do this to me!" Her outburst startled her fellow passengers. Everyone stared as she furiously made her way to the counter.

"I don't care what you have to do or how you have to do it, but you have to put me on that plane," she demanded. "Now!"

"Ma'am, there's nothing I can do," replied the airline attendant. "The plane's air-conditioning system is broken."

The woman's lips quivered in anger and her eyes burned. "I cannot, under any circumstances, be late. Understand? Don't argue with me, damn it, do something!"

"Ma'am, if you don't calm down, I will have to call security."

Exasperated, the woman scanned the lounge. Her scowl came to rest on me in my saffron-colored robes sitting alone in the quiet corner I had chosen. After an arduous week of lectures and meetings, I really wanted to be left alone, but the woman stormed over. Towering above me, her face distorted by rage, she asked, "Are you a monk?"

*Oh, God, why me?* I thought.

She persisted. "Are you a monk?"

"Something like that," I said finally, as the whole room looked on. I could almost hear their relief that she had chosen me instead of them.

"Then I demand an answer," she challenged. "Why is God doing this to me? Why is my flight late?"

"Please, sit down," I said. "Let's talk about it."

To my surprise, she sat on the chair next to me and suddenly seemed more confused than angry. I realized her anger was masked desperation.

I introduced myself and asked a question I've posed a thousand times: "Please tell me what is in your heart."

Her name was Dorothy, she said. She was fifty-seven years old and an upper-middle-class housewife from the East Coast. She had lived happily with her family until . . . and at this she began to cry.

"In a terrible tragedy I lost my husband of thirty years and all my children," she said. "Now I'm alone and I can't bear the pain."

Not wishing to exacerbate her misery, I didn't ask for details. She gripped the chair's armrest.

"Then, to make matters worse, I was cheated in a business deal. The bank put my house into foreclosure and kicked me out on the street. You see this carry-on suitcase? This is all I have left."

Dorothy went on to tell me that just a week earlier, her already difficult situation had become worse: she had been diagnosed with terminal cancer and given one month to live. In a fervent effort to save her life, she had discovered a cancer clinic in Mexico that claimed it might be able to cure her. But she had to be admitted that day. If she missed her connecting flight in Washington, D.C., she would not make it to Mexico in time.

In my services as a minister and in overseeing the hospital I helped to establish in Mumbai, I have had close encounters with victims of everything from terrorist attacks to massive earthquakes, tsunamis to rape, auto crashes to suicide attempts, violent crimes to terminal disease. Heartbreak is not new to me. But I cannot remember seeing more anguish on a human face than I saw that day on Dorothy's.

"And now," she cried, "this flight is late. I'm losing my last chance to live. I tried to be a good wife and mother. I went to church, I gave to charities, and I never purposely hurt anyone. But now no one cares whether I suffer or die. Why is God doing this to me?"

How easily I had judged Dorothy as I had watched her at the ticket counter. Now that I knew what was below the surface of her behavior, my heart filled with sympathy.

She looked me in the eyes while she told me her story, compelling me to listen. Now her voice softened. "Do *you* care?" she asked. "It seems that maybe you do."

"I do," I said, and I meant it. "You're a special soul, Dorothy."

"Special? Me?" she scoffed. "I've been thrown out like a worthless piece of trash. But thank you for saying so." She broke down sobbing and could hardly speak. "There's no one left for me, no one to even talk to."

As I looked into her despairing eyes, her misery was palpable to me, and I told her so. I gently asked if I might share with her a way of dealing with her crises from another perspective.

"Please," she replied.

"There may not be anything you can do about what's happened," I said, "but as difficult as it is, you still have the freedom to choose how to respond to it. How you respond now will determine your future in this life and beyond."

"What do you mean?"

"You have every right to lament about how cruelly this world has treated you, but you can also search for ways to turn your life's circumstances into positive opportunities for growth. As the Bible says, 'Seek, and ye shall find. Knock, and the door will be opened to you.' We can all choose to live and die depressed or with gratitude."

"But I'm afraid," she said. "I'm afraid of dying."

"I understand," I said, "but since we're not going anywhere for a while, may I take you on a brief journey within your self?"

Dorothy told me she had nothing to lose, so I asked her to close her eyes and take deep breaths, focusing her attention on exhaling her pain and sorrow and inhaling God's grace. As she did this I offered a silent prayer on her behalf, then said, "In order to understand death, we first need to understand life. Please ask yourself, 'Who am I'?"

"I already told you. I'm Dorothy," she said, opening her eyes. "I'm not sure what else you want me to say."

"When you were a baby," I replied, "before you were given the name Dorothy, were you the same person? At that time you yearned for your mother's milk. You have grown in countless ways since then, and naturally your desires have changed. But are you not the same person? Throughout your life, you have changed in many ways; you've maybe changed your name by taking your husband's. People can change their nationality and religion. Nowadays people can even change their sex. Who is that 'you' who has watched you change from childhood to adulthood?"

She nodded slowly, and seemed to understand, but I could see in her eyes that fear of the unknown, of death, possessed her.

"It's natural to fear death," I continued, "but if you want to overcome it, it's helpful to recognize what distinguishes a living body from a dead body. The difference between them is consciousness."

I explained that according to sages in various traditions, consciousness is a symptom of the presence of the spirit self, or soul. Since we're so often focused only on the physical, it's common to assume that when we die, we'll stop being conscious, and so we'll stop existing. But this thinking ignores a critical understanding of our actual identity and our relationship with the world.

Dorothy and I discussed this idea for a few minutes, and I asked her to consider some simple questions: Are you your eyes, or are you seeing *through* your eyes? Are you your ears, or are you hearing *through* your ears? Are you your nose, or are you smelling *through* your nose? Don't you touch *through* your skin, think *through* your brain, feel *through* your heart? Given this, what do you feel is the ultimate difference between a living body and a dead one?"

She paused for a moment, and then said, "When I really think about it, it seems that I live *in* my body but my body isn't me."

I nodded and explained that the body is like a car, and the self the driver. We should take care of the vehicle of the body as much as we're able, but we shouldn't neglect the driver's needs. The car needs oil and gas, but the driver needs something else. We are eager to nourish the needs and wants of the body and mind, but we've all but forgotten the needs of the soul, which means we miss out on the greatest opportunity of life and the real pleasure we're each seeking.

"What do you mean by 'pleasure'?" Dorothy asked.

I explained that almost every living being is pleasure seeking by nature. This is true of the ant crawling across a kitchen counter and the CEO of an international corporation. It's pursuit of pleasure that impels us to populate and shape the world. We struggle to fulfill our desires, and we battle against anything that interferes with our plans.

People spend their lives chasing one attraction after another but are never satisfied for long. The pleasures of wealth, power, fame, and sex are fleeting and don't stretch beyond the mind and senses. They don't touch the heart. True happiness is an experience of the heart—to love and be loved—and it originates in our innate love for the Supreme Being and our awareness of his love for us.

I told Dorothy the words Mother Teresa of Calcutta once spoke to me: "The greatest problem in this world is hunger—not hunger of the stomach but of the heart. All over the world, both the rich and the poor are suffering. They are lonely, starving for love." With a soft smile Mother Teresa concluded, "Only God's love can satisfy the hunger of the heart."

"But you're a Hindu and I'm a Christian," Dorothy said. "Which God are you talking about?"

"There is only one God," I replied, "the source of all that exists, the all-loving, all-beautiful father, mother, and dearest friend of all beings, the God who has many names in many languages."

I looked out the window and pointed to the blazing summer sun. "In America we call that the sun, in Mexico it is called *sol*, and in India *surya*. When the sun rises in America, is it an American sun? Or is it Mexican in Mexico or Indian in India? If we don't understand that the sun is universal, we can wind up in endless arguments about the sun's name and where it's from."

I then shared with Dorothy one of the prominent messages of the most loved and venerated scripture of India, the Bhagavad Gita. The Supreme Being has appeared on earth many times in different places to teach us how to revive awareness of our original nature. The path begins with a transformation of character—a transformation of arrogance into humility, greed into benevolence, envy into gratitude, vengeance into forgiveness, selfishness into an unselfish willingness to serve, complacency into compassion, doubt into faith, and lust into love. True religion helps us experience God's love and be an instrument of that love in every aspect of our lives.

"In church," she said, "they teach that the good go to heaven and the bad to hell. What do you believe happens after death?"

"Actually," I said, "our own minds can create a heaven or a hell for us, even right now." Then I again cited the Bhagavad Gita, which explains that while the body is temporary, the self is eternal. For the self, there is neither birth nor death; after death, the self moves on to another body, carrying with it its karma from its previous lifetimes, as well as whatever state of consciousness it has achieved in this one. This is transmigration of the soul, or what is commonly called reincarnation.

The underlying meaning common to both the Bible and the Gita is that we should take our spiritual development seriously and be morally responsible, knowing we'll be held accountable in this life and beyond for our actions. Humanity will benefit when we learn to appreciate each other for the values we share and respect our brotherhood and sisterhood despite our personal, social, or apparent philosophical differences.

"While you're talking about reconciling differences," she said, "you mentioned karma. Someone told me that my suffering was because I have bad karma. What is karma?"

I explained that karma refers to the actions that we perform and the corresponding reactions that they attract. Karma is a natural law, just like the law of gravity. As gravity pulls objects toward the earth whether or not we believe in gravity, so the law of karma acts. It's only natural that what goes up must come down. The Bible teaches the same thing when it says, "As ye sow, so shall ye reap." Newton's third law of motion tells us, "For every action, there is an equal and opposite reaction." If I cause others pain, I should expect to feel corresponding pain at some point. If I treat others with compassion, I should expect the same in return—if not immediately, then in due course.

The point of knowing this law is to appreciate that human beings have been entrusted with a priceless gift, one we can use to create profound benefit for ourselves and others—or horrible disasters. That gift is one of the most powerful things in all of creation: free will. But with the blessing of free will comes the responsibility of choice. While beings in other forms of life tend to act instinctively according to their particular species, humans can choose to be saints or criminals, or anything in between. The price of having the choice is that we're responsible for our actions; we have to face the reactions to both our good and bad deeds.

"Wait a minute," Dorothy interrupted. "Can't this philosophy be used to justify blaming people for their own suffering—the classic, 'You brought this on yourself' line? Are you blaming me? Is all this suffering *my* fault?"

It was a good question. Sadly, I had seen in myself and others the tendency to use the idea of karma insensitively. I explained my understanding, that the reason to learn about spiritual teachings such as karma is to urge us to improve the quality of our lives by taking responsibility for the choices we make. It's not enough to have a good life map; we have to know how to use it. All spiritual truth is meant to uplift and encourage us, to lead us into the joys of devotion to God and compassion for all beings. Proper understandings soften the heart; they shouldn't make us callous. A loving relative, like a good doctor, doesn't judge us in our misfortune but reaches out to help—and we are all related.

"In whatever situation we find ourselves," I said, "we have the opportunity to gain wisdom, adopt a spirit for positive action, and humble ourselves before the Divine. In today's stressful world, people are especially vulnerable to depression. Depression can impede our progress, but with appropriate help, we can stabilize the mind, foster positive thinking, and awaken to our higher nature. The soul is divine; you are forever a beloved child of the Supreme. Nothing can ever change that."

"But why should we believe in karma when we see good people suffering and bad people prospering?" she asked.

"Years ago," I said, "an old recluse in the Himalayas shared with me a story that addresses this often bewildering phenomenon. May I tell it to you?"

For the first time since we'd started talking, I noted a trace of a smile on Dorothy's lips. "Yes," she said quietly. "I'd like to hear it."

"Years ago, a farmer half-filled his silo with excellent grain. Eventually, though, he began to add grain of a lower quality. Because grain is poured into a silo from the top and removed from the bottom, the good grain came out first and the farmer was awash in money. Inevitably, though, the good grain was exhausted, and he began to sell bad grain. Over time, people stopped buying his grain, and he lost his prosperity.

"Another farmer in the past had filled *his* silo with poor grain and consequently found himself with few customers. Having learned that his practice wasn't sustainable, he added tons of excellent grain from the top. And just as inevitably, as his suffering from his past deposits dwindled, he began to move into a more prosperous future.

"We create our own destiny by the choices we make. But while we are free to make choices, once we have acted on them, we are bound to live with their consequences. That's karma. You may choose to get on a plane to Washington, D.C., but once the plane takes off, you can no longer choose a different destination; you'll have to disembark in D.C. Still, you can make new choices as to what to do while you're on the plane or after you arrive. The practical lesson in all of this is that no matter what challenges await us, how we choose to respond to them determines our destiny in this life and in the next."

"Why did God give us free will," she asked, "when it causes so much suffering?"

"Free will facilitates the most perfect love. If we were programmed like a computer to love, or forced to love by a superior power, our love would be incomplete and not truly satisfying to either lover or beloved. Along with the freedom to love our Supreme Beloved, we have the choice to turn away from that and seek happiness elsewhere. But at any moment, every immortal soul can still choose to return to that love."

The airline attendant's voice suddenly boomed across the room, announcing another hour's delay. Dorothy groaned. What was an ordinary delay for the rest of us was a traumatic life-and-death struggle for her. I pondered how each person interprets and responds to situations according to his or her unique state of mind.

I waited for the announcement to end and then described how the Gita tells us that our thoughts, words, and actions, when performed in a spirit of devotion and service to the Supreme Being and with compassion for other souls, are beyond the laws of karma. "In fact," I said, "even a *little* devotional service can free us from lifetimes of karma. Devotional service sows and nourishes the seed of love of God in the heart. Such love in its pure state is unconditional, free from selfishness, and filled with happiness. As the Bible says, the kingdom of God is within."

Dorothy suddenly began to cough. Her whole body shook, and I saw a flash of desperation in her eyes as her face reddened.

"Water!" she gasped.

I rushed to a nearby shop and bought her a bottle of water. Her hands were trembling so much she could barely hold the bottle to her mouth. Finally, she regained her composure, but slumped forward in her chair and said, "I think you're saying that in my condition, I should feel the need for God like I feel the need for this water. Still, I need time to process all of this. Does meditation help? Can you teach me?"

I told her that of the many types of meditation, I had chosen to practice mantra meditation. The word *mantra* in the Sanskrit language refers to a sound vibration that frees the mind from anxiety.

"How does it work?" she asked.

"Think of a mirror," I said. "A mirror is meant to perfectly reflect your image when you look into it. But if it's covered with dust, the image will be clouded or distorted, or you might not be able to see yourself at all. The mind is like a mirror. Over the years, we've allowed it to become covered in the dust of misconceptions, desires, and fear. All these are born of a false sense of who we are, or false ego. When we look into that inner mirror, we mainly see dust. Worse, we think the dust-distorted image is a true reflection of ourselves.

"Meditation on the mantra helps clean the mental mirror so we can see something truer about ourselves—the pure soul we really are, the special part of the eternal Supreme Soul, full of knowledge and bliss. As the mind clears, the fog of misperception fades, and the natural qualities of the soul emerge. We begin to feel the love that's inherent in us, and we recognize that all beings are our sisters and brothers because, like us, they are related to our Beloved."

The speaker system crackled, and everyone in the room perked up and looked at the airline attendant hopefully.

"I'm sorry," she said, "we're still working to resolve the issue. At this point, we're anticipating about another hour's delay. We apologize for the inconvenience and appreciate your continued patience."

Dorothy put a hand to her forehead and exclaimed, "Please, teach me the mantra."

I paused for a second to think of how for thousands of years priests and sages, royalty and commoners, have recited the *maha-mantra*, or "great chant for deliverance." This mantra has the power to significantly change one's life for the better, to take us from distress to peace of mind, and from peace of mind to spiritual freedom. I asked Dorothy to focus her mind and repeat each word of the mantra after me:

*Hare Krishna, Hare Krishna*
*Krishna Krishna, Hare Hare*
*Hare Rama, Hare Rama*
*Rama Rama, Hare Hare*

She repeated after me, then reached into her purse and pulled out a slip of paper and a pen. "Please write it down," she said, "but I also want to know what it means."

I explained that the mantra consisted of names of God. *Krishna* means "the all-attractive one," and *Rama* "the reservoir of all pleasure." *Hare* is a name of the feminine, compassionate aspect of God.

Dorothy took a few minutes to try chanting. She recited it over and over again, her eyes glued to the slip of paper. In the meantime, I asked to borrow her cell phone and stepped away for a minute to call a friend with news of the delay.

When I returned, Dorothy was still quietly studying the words. To my surprise, she looked up at me and smiled. "I don't know what lies in store for me, but I do think I realized something today," she said. "This delay has been my good fortune, because it allowed me to learn something from you."

I felt humbled by her words. I knew that I too was fortunate because I had been given the opportunity to share with her, in her time of need, the teachings I had received from my mentors.

Six hours passed before we finally heard the announcement we were waiting for: the plane was ready to board—sort of. Once we were on board we learned that in addition to the air-conditioning not working, the lights and toilets were also malfunctioning. The fifty-seat commuter jet was dark and muggy as it soared into the sky with us aboard.

When we finally landed, I trudged down the plane's steps with the rest of the passengers and was delighted to see Dorothy again at the airport's entrance. She smiled and waved me over. She told me she had spent the entire flight meditating on the mantra. "No matter what happens," she said, "I know that God is with me and I can feel his love for me. I think I have found my real wealth, and I am grateful."

With a prayer and a tear, I said goodbye. I was amazed at how much this relatively brief encounter had affected us both. As I watched, the airport staff offered Dorothy a wheelchair and then wheeled her to her connecting flight to Mexico. I wondered what her future held. *Perhaps*, I thought, *she is embarking on her journey home.*

# Who Am I?

*Never was a time when I did not exist, nor you, nor*
*all these kings; nor in the future shall any of us cease to be.*
—Bhagavad Gita 2.12

In our demanding world, it's easy to be distracted from the things that matter most in our quest for happiness. True happiness can be realized when we harmonize the needs of our body and mind with our true self, the soul.

But we are prone to divert our attention from the search for spiritual love to more immediate physical and mental demands. Think of a child whose parents give her adequate clothing but inadequate love. The child looks lovely but lives in misery. Similarly, preoccupied by worldly pursuits, people too often neglect the calling of their own hearts. Simple stories can help to remind us. Here is one I heard while visiting a holy place in India.

In South India there is a mystical island in the Kaveri River that has been frequented by pilgrims for over a thousand years. The island is called Sri Rangam, and it is home to the largest temple complex in India, covering more than 150 acres. Throngs of pilgrims visit Sri Rangam daily and participate in the continuous ceremonial music, mantra chanting, and elaborate rituals.

During the twelfth century, the great bhakti saint and scholar Ramanuja lived in Sri Rangam. To this day he is a beacon of wisdom for his tens of millions of followers. Ramanuja's immediate successor was Parashara. When Parashara was still a boy, the all-India champion of debate came to visit Sri Rangam. Arriving on an elaborate palanquin and carried in procession by his followers, the man ignored the custom of offering respect to the temple priests. In fact, he showed no respect for anyone, but instead boasted that there was no question he could not answer.

Five-year-old Parashara ran up to the scholar and exclaimed in his little-boy voice, "I have a question for you!"

The scholar looked at him with disdain. "Silly child, your mother's breast milk is still on your lips. Get away from me."

"Sir, if you really see the true self in all beings, why should my age matter? Can you answer any question or not?"

Frowning down from his palanquin, the scholar retorted, "I have challenged and defeated every scholar in the land. There is no question I cannot answer."

Little Parashara reached down, scooped up a handful of sand, and asked, "How many grains of sand do I have in my hand?"

The scholar was speechless. This was not the kind of question he meant.

Parashara continued, "Sir, forgive me, but you are so blinded by arrogance that you can't see the good qualities in others. A tree with good fruits bends down, and a person with good qualities bows low to others' virtues. All of your knowledge is as worthless as sand if it doesn't help you develop good character and devotion to God."

Those words, spoken without malice by a child, pierced the scholar's heart. He climbed down from his palanquin, bowed before the boy in defeat, and begged to learn from him as his disciple.

Years later, another disciple approached Parashara and asked, "What qualities do I need before I'm able to realize who I am?"

"Only a self-realized person can give you a thorough answer," Parashara replied, humbly. "The saint Ananta lives in the town of holy Tirupati. Go to him. He will answer your question."

Tirupati is more than four hundred miles from Sri Rangam, and there were no cars in those days, so the disciple set out on the long journey by foot. He had to cross rivers, pass through snake- and tiger-infested forests, and climb seven mountains before he finally reached the sage Ananta's mountain hermitage. Ananta greeted him warmly, served his guest dinner, and then showed him to a simple but comfortable room.

The next day, the disciple approached the sage. "My guru, Parashara, told me to come here and ask you a question: What qualities do I need before I'm able to realize who I am?"

Ananta took a moment and then said, "Let me think about it. I'll answer you later."

Six months passed without Ananta's addressing the question, but the disciple waited patiently and busied himself with menial service in the hermitage, meditation, and attending classes.

One day a festival was held near Ananta's hermitage. Thousands of people attended. The disciple volunteered to help serve a feast to the many pilgrims. At some point, he took a break and sat down with his own plate, but Ananta said, "Don't eat just yet. First, please serve the next group of pilgrims." The disciple followed Ananta's instruction. Later, he again sat down to his own plate. But again Ananta stopped him. "You can eat later," he said. "There's another group arriving."

So the disciple served the third group—and the fourth and fifth. Late that night, after it was clear everyone else had eaten and the festival field was empty, Parashara's disciple finally sat down to eat.

Ananta approached him. "I believe," he said, "you have a question for me."

Brimming with eagerness the disciple jumped up and asked, "What qualities should I develop so I can realize who I am?"

Gently smiling, Ananta replied, "One should be like salt, like a chicken, like a crane, and like you. I have nothing else to say." And he walked away.

The disciple was bewildered. "I waited six months for *this*?" Confused, he offered his respects to Ananta, packed his belongings, and set out on the long trek back to Sri Rangam. Seven mountains and four hundred miles later, he arrived home.

"So," Parashara said, "did you get an answer to your question?"

"Yes," his disciple said, "but I didn't understand it."

"Tell me."

The disciple explained the various trials he had gone through during his time in the hermitage and concluded with the cryptic answer to his question. On hearing Ananta's response, Parashara clapped his hands with delight. "What a perfectly comprehensive, realized answer," he said.

"What?" cried the disciple. "What do salt, chickens, and cranes have to do with anything?"

"Listen carefully," Parashara said, "and I will explain Ananta's fathomless wisdom. The amount of salt in a dish must be just right. If there's too much or too little, the dish will not be satisfying. Like salt, one on the spiritual path must find balance. The Bhagavad Gita teaches that those who aspire to a holy life should not eat too much or too little or sleep too much or too little. They should give proper time to work, recreation, and their spiritual practices. It is especially important that they are balanced when dealing with challenges or complicated issues, avoiding extremes, just as one needs just the right amount of salt in a dish for it to taste good.

"You asked Ananta what qualities you need to realize yourself. Another quality of salt is that it remains hidden even though it adds flavor to a dish. People praise a dish by appreciating the quality of its grains or vegetables or spices, but no one says, 'The salt in this dish was fabulous!' Like salt, true yogis serve without wanting recognition or praise. They are happy to give credit to others and interested simply in doing their best to give pleasure to the Divine and benefit others.

"Yet another quality of salt is that it relinquishes its sense of separateness and melds with the other ingredients. Like salt, we aspire to relinquish whatever egoism separates us from a loving relationship with the Supreme and others. By becoming absorbed in our identity as soul, we can integrate ourselves fully as eternal loving servants of the Supreme.

"A chicken," Parashara continued, "will select nourishing seeds from a pile of trash and leave the worthless items behind. Like the chicken, a true yogi will find the good in others and disregard the rest. We should be eager to see others' good qualities and not dwell on their faults. If we're compelled by circumstances to address someone's faults, we should do it only to benefit that person or others who may be affected by them. If we fill our mind with the apparent shortcomings of those around us, we'll become polluted. Focusing on their good qualities, however, is enriching.

"Through this analogy we also learn to seek constructive opportunities in every situation and not complain about the problems. If you look for reasons to complain, you'll see them everywhere. Similarly, if you search for opportunities to do good, you'll see them in abundance. Like the chicken, we should seek the essence of our spirituality and its practices and focus on their true goal, leaving aside the unnecessary distractions of sectarianism. In this way we can appreciate the essence not only of our own path but of other paths as well.

"The crane," Parashara said, "stands patiently on one leg and looks into the water. It lets small fish pass while it waits for a big fish. When a big fish comes, the crane feasts. This teaches us the values of patience and remaining focused on what matters. It takes patience and a willingness to let small stuff pass if we want to reach our goals. It's easy to get lost in the superficial, but yogis go deeper. Like the crane, they focus on bigger issues and release smaller ones. Their reward? They can feast on the truth and don't take the world's gossip and propaganda seriously.

"As for Ananta's inclusion of you, a true seeker of the self is like you. In your eagerness for truth, you endured much difficulty. That enthusiasm is essential for spiritual progress. You waited for six months without complaint before Ananta answered your question. You selflessly served thousands of pilgrims before you served yourself, without objecting. Your willingness to endure difficulties in service to others is the nature of a true seeker.

"Ananta is so kind," Parashara said, shaking his head in appreciation. "He could have explained all these things to you the day you arrived. I'll tell you why he didn't. The heart is like a field, and wisdom like a seed. A seed will grow only in a field that has been properly tilled and fertilized. We till the field of the heart through humility, gratitude, and service to others, remaining eager to learn despite obstacles. And love grows alongside wisdom when we cultivate these qualities.

"Spiritual knowledge is the most valuable gift," Parashara said. "It's not cheap. So we should wholeheartedly persevere in our pursuit of it, while having the patience to wait as long as it takes to achieve it."

The teacher and disciple sat in silence while the wind rustled the leaves of the coconut palms. Then Parashara smiled. "Ananta could have explained all this to you instead of giving you a cryptic answer," he said, "but he is an old friend of mine, and I think he wanted to share these priceless lessons with me as well. When our eyes are opened by the words of the wise, we see lessons in even the most common of things—chickens and salt!"

## SO, WHO AM I?

For most people, the question of who they are may not come up. When we are engrossed in physical and mental identities, we simply have no time or need to ponder our true nature. The question really becomes relevant only when we feel a call to find deeper meaning in our life. Then we are ready to inquire into what lies beyond this short lifetime and how to find lasting fulfillment.

The great spiritual texts of India, the Bhagavad Gita and the Upanishads, begin with a thorough analysis of our identity in all its layers. These texts are written in Sanskrit, and in Sanskrit the self is referred to as *atma*, the ever-existing, indestructible, conscious essence, the nature of which is blissful awareness. Since the atma experiences time and the physical world through the body, understanding who and what we are begins by understanding who and what we are not.

We are not the body we inhabit.

We are not the mind either.

We live *in* a body and mind.

Let's return to the analogy of the body as a car and the self as its driver. No matter how impressive the car, it cannot function without its driver, but the driver can always function without the car. There's a difference between the material body we inhabit and the atma.

There are tangible elements—the physical body and its senses—that we can identify with, considering them to be our selves, and there are more subtle elements—the mind, intelligence, and ego—that we can identify with. These temporary elements are invaluable because they allow us to engage with the world around us. But if we are not careful, these temporary selves can also cover our understanding of our real identity.

We identify with the body and mind because of the direct experiences they provide and our attachment to those sensations. In fact, we spend so much time seeking out those sensations through our physical and mental bodies that we feel as if we are practically one with those bodies.

But that is an illusion. The atma is not one with the body; the atma is the observer living inside it—the "I" who is experiencing. Matter, the gross and subtle elements that make up our body and mind, has no power to act unless the atma moves it. Perception and the other life symptoms stop when the atma leaves the body, a phenomenon we call death.

To live with wisdom means to live in such a way that one's physical, emotional, and spiritual faculties are nourished and one's thoughts, words, and deeds are attuned to the self within the body. When we forget we are something other than the physical body and mind, we suffer all the vulnerabilities inherent in that body and mind.

It may not be a popular word, but suffering is a universal experience. We all suffer physically and emotionally. But as we develop a deeper self-awareness, we learn to acknowledge suffering without identifying with it. Eventually we even transcend it. I know someone who has done this.

When my teacher, Prabhupada, was in the final days within his physical form, his body was so emaciated that it was nothing more than skin and bones. Yet until his last breath, he continued to give of himself to others and translate Sanskrit wisdom texts for future generations. When one of his students, a scientist, came to meet him, the student was distressed to see his beloved teacher in such a condition. Prabhupada smiled. "You are a scientist, and your method requires proof. I have been teaching all my life that you are not the body, and now I am proving it. My body is practically gone, but I am still the same." The student was reminded that a great teacher brings his words to life through his example.

How can *we* transcend like that? Begin by transforming your perceptions and attitudes. To paraphrase Albert Einstein, "We cannot solve our problems with the same thinking we used to create them." The Gita aids us in our transformation process by teaching us the hierarchy in the layers of matter that cover the self:

> *Higher than dull matter are the senses.*
> *Higher than the senses is the mind.*
> *Higher than the mind is the intelligence.*
> *Higher than the intelligence is the immortal self.*
> —BHAGAVAD GITA 6.6

This hierarchy can be explained through an analogy. The atma is a passenger seated on a chariot pulled by five horses. The chariot is the body, and the five horses are the senses. The reins are the mind and are held by the intelligence, the charioteer. All of these are directed by the atma. Ideally, it is the atma that disciplines the intelligence to control the mind, which in turn controls the senses. When enlightenment, or self-awareness, is absent, the passenger is not in charge. Rather, the atma forgets it has the power to direct the intelligence, so the intelligence is easily pulled this way and that by a restless mind and uncontrolled senses.

Transformation begins when we use our intelligence to take control of the reins of what might be called the sixth sense, the mind.

# THE MIND

*For those who have conquered the mind,*
*it is the best of friends.*
*But for those who have failed to do so,*
*the mind remains the greatest of enemies.*
—BHAGAVAD GITA 6.6

For the atma to process the information it receives through the senses, it uses the faculty of the mind. The eyes may see a red flower. From the optic nerve, electrical impulses travel to the brain and make the image available to the "seer." It is the mind that responds to the flower, the mind that recognizes it, calls it "red" and "flower," and perhaps responds with an emotion. The brain is the physical organ in the physical body that links the physical body to the intangible mind.

Historically, thinkers have wrestled with whether the mind, with its responses to sensory stimuli, determines who we are. Five hundred years ago, Western philosopher-mathematician René Descartes proposed that it's by the actions of the mind that we know we exist: *cogito ergo sum*, "I think, therefore I am."

The Bhagavad Gita turns this idea on its head. "I am," the Gita teaches, "and therefore I think." Without the presence of the atma, the mind cannot think.

The Gita informs us that as the brain is part of the physical body, the mind is part of a "subtle body." But physical or subtle, both bodies are material. The mind is responsible for thinking, feeling, and intention. These faculties are generally informed by the stimuli we receive from the senses. Like a computer's hard drive, the mind is a repository of facts and memories. It doesn't necessarily understand the significance of the information it processes, but it places sensation into two broad categories, pleasure and pain, and responds accordingly. How sensations are categorized is largely based on past associations with similar sensations.

Just as the height of an ocean's wave is influenced by the weather, so the mind, according to how it has been influenced by the sensory experiences we've had, responds to new sensory input with either desire or repulsion, elation or depression, courage or fear, celebration or lamentation. Every sense experience, whether it comes from the eyes, ears, nose, tongue, or skin, leaves an impression on the mind. The software of the mind is constantly updated through daily experience.

Here's an example: You see a car coming toward you. Depending on how fast the car is moving and your previous experience with cars moving at that speed, the mind will produce an instinctive response. If you associate cars with accidents and death, you may feel fear. If you associate cars with prestige and glamor—and if it's the right kind of car—you may feel avarice. Phobias are heightened responses to past sensory input that has left a strong, negative impression on the mind.

Is the mind ever neutral? Not for long. The mind changes constantly based on our ever-shifting experiences. As children, we may be afraid when we look over a cliff; by the time we are experienced adults, that same view may seem exhilarating. Even things that invoke little emotion in us can become objects of passion within a moment. If we identify with the mind, we subject ourselves to all these shifting emotional states.

Every morning I sit down to meditate on the divine sound of my mantra. Anyone who meditates knows what comes next: my mind races through whatever I struggled with yesterday (or will grapple with today) or, if not my problems, then the problems of my loved ones, or it chews on an old argument, or gets lost in memory (the joy of the first Chevrolet I ever owned, or the shame of striking out and losing the championship game for my Little League baseball team, for example). If someone is baking in the next room, I can switch in an instant from meditation on my mantra to meditation on cookies. At some point, I'll become aware of the wandering mind and ask myself, "What happened to the mantra?"

This reveals something important: we are separate from our thoughts. If we weren't, how could we direct the mind away from them?

The mind is an amazing instrument. Objectively, it's an absolutely brilliant creation. Subjectively, it can make life unbearable. As John Milton put it in *Paradise Lost*, "The mind is its own place, and in itself can make a heaven of hell, a hell of heaven."

## THE MONKEY'S LESSON

In 1989, my parents came to visit me in India. I took them to the popular Elephanta Caves, on an island near Mumbai. After disembarking from the ferry, we walked along a dirt footpath through a forest. Suddenly a large monkey leaped from a tree and grabbed at my mother's purse. This was culture shock for a Chicago suburbanite, and my mother screamed. But she didn't lose hold of her bag. A tug of war ensued. The monkey snarled and bared its fangs, then jumped at my mother with a screech, finally ripping the purse from her grasp. It then darted up a peepal tree.

The attack was distressing not only because of its suddenness but because the purse contained my parents' passports, airline tickets, credit cards, and all their cash.

"Everything is lost," my father sighed once the shock had worn off. "Now what?"

My mother turned to me. "You brought us here! What are you going to do about this?"

I closed my eyes and said a prayer. Anyone who's spent as much time in India as I have knows how hard it is to "talk" monkeys into returning stolen goods.

But about fifty yards away, I saw a vendor pushing a small hand-cart piled high with fruit. I hurried over and pleaded for a banana. He demanded payment. I had no money and couldn't pay, and now neither did my parents. With a hurried apology I grabbed a banana from his cart and ran. He let out a yelp and chased after me with a stick. As soon as he turned his back on his cart, though, a different monkey invaded it, and the agitated vendor rushed back to protect his goods from this second thief.

When I reached the peepal tree, I saw our monkey thief on a high branch. My mother's purse was open, and the monkey was enthusiastically chewing on her American Express credit card. Aiming carefully, I threw the banana at the monkey. Fortunately, I wasn't a good shot and the monkey had to leap to catch it, dropping the purse in the process. As the monkey happily peeled and ate the banana, I returned the purse to my mother.

My mother handed me ten rupees for the fruit vendor (I didn't think of that myself), and by the end, the vendor was happy, my parents and I were happy, and the monkey, relishing its fresh banana, also seemed happy. It was a win-win situation.

The mind functions very much like that trouble-making monkey, making it hard for us to concentrate on any one thing. What is important to us at one moment is dropped as soon as something else comes along. That thing doesn't even have to be better. But like the monkey with the banana, when we give the mind a more fulfilling and beneficial focus, we can easily overcome its distractions.

When I began to experiment with yoga and meditation, I sought an enlightened, peaceful mind. The teachings of bhakti yoga added critical insight to my understanding. I learned that because keeping the monkey-like mind quiet is extremely difficult, it's effective to give the mind a higher engagement. When the mind is engaged in more meaningful and satisfying thought patterns through how we think, what we say, and what we do, inclinations harmful to our well-being such as envy, selfish passion, and anger are forgotten and gradually disappear. Bhakti yoga teaches us that a dynamic life of devotional service, mantra meditation, and association with uplifting people creates a foundation for our spirituality that keeps the mind steady. Time and again in my spiritual counseling work I hear how these three components of a spiritual life have provided people the means to break bad habits and overcome addictions.

Spiritual practice begins with healthy engagement of the mind. One of the definitions of yoga given in Patanjali's *Yoga Sutra* is *citta vritti nirodhaha*: "Yoga is the stilling of the mind's fluctuations." By taking practitioners through a series of "seats," or postures (*asanas*), controlled breathing (*pranayama*), and meditation (*dhyana*), yoga helps them withdraw the mind from superficial distractions and focus it within. When the mind's fluctuations have been stilled, according to the *Yoga Sutra*, the self becomes "situated in its own true nature."

So the mind is something to be used by the self, not the other way around. Understanding this truth brings us closer to who we are inside, and nearer to fulfillment.

What is that fulfillment?

It is love. Love is the most satisfying way to control the mind. Love is the complete expression of the soul. When we're in love, our thoughts are focused and our energies directed toward the beloved. We become "single-minded." Bhakti makes us single-minded when it awakens our innate spirit of love.

So we start by cleaning the mirror of the mind, so we can see who we really are. With the help of a well-grounded intelligence, our mind can become our dearest friend.

## THE INTELLIGENCE

*Gradually, step-by-step, one should become*
*situated in trance by means of intelligence*
*sustained by full conviction, and thus the*
*mind should be fixed on the Self alone.*
—BHAGAVAD GITA 6.25

The power of discrimination—to be able to decide the value of what we want (or don't want) and whether we should strive to achieve it—is beyond the mind's scope. Rather, this is the function of the intelligence.

Intelligence (*buddhi* in Sanskrit) holds the reins of the body-chariot. In other words, it is the faculty that guides the mind, distinguishing right from wrong, moral from immoral, truth from illusion, and pro from con.

If I walk past a bakery and smell something tempting, my mind likely interprets the aroma as pleasurable and decides, "I want it." But if I have diabetes, my intelligence, I hope, will stop me from actually eating whatever it is I smell. If the intelligence is not properly trained, however, it will give in to the mind's demand and I may find myself suffering the consequences.

## Two Fighting Dogs

A Native American wisdom story tells of two dogs that live in every human heart: a bad dog and a good dog. The bad dog represents the lower tendencies of envy, anger, lust, greed, arrogance, and illusion. The good dog represents the higher tendencies of compassion, integrity, generosity, humility, and wisdom. These two dogs battle one another. Which dog will win? The one we choose to feed!

We "feed" the dogs through the choices we make. Using the intelligence for spiritual pursuits, to express compassion, and to live with integrity nourishes the good dog and keeps the bad dog at bay. Sometimes that's easier said than done. For many of us, the bad dog has become so entrenched in us that its deafening howls drive our actions. Meanwhile, the good dog, weak and undernourished, is only a whimper in the corner of our conscience.

Practicing yoga strengthens the intelligence and empowers us to neglect our bad-dog qualities, however loudly they may howl. Then we're free to feed the good dog, or our more divine nature. At each moment, life hands us the choice to be cruel or kind, duplicitous or honest, arrogant or humble, greedy or charitable, vengeful or forgiving. We can choose between selfish passion and selfless devotion. There are many things in this world that are beyond our control, but how we choose to act isn't one of them. So we're free to elevate our consciousness—feed the good dog— or degrade it.

Surprisingly, we may struggle with this choice more than we'd like to admit. This is because we've conditioned the mind to swing one way or the other with every past choice we've made. These choices have shaped our current proclivities, desires, and perceptions, and the choices we now make will affect every choice we'll make in the future. People trapped in addictive behavior have fed a desire again and again until in time it became a habit. Studies show that addictive behavior usually begins in childhood, where, for whatever reason, the mind-set for it is formed. These habit patterns are also called *samskaras* in the yoga tradition. By definition, addictions take such a hold that we feel almost powerless to resist them. Still, we retain the freedom to create new impressions, change negative samskaras for good ones, leave the bad dog to starve while we give attention to the good dog. By developing a strong intelligence and steering the mind in a new direction with the help of spiritual practice and a good support system, we can break free even of addiction.

## THREE TYPES OF INTELLIGENCE—AND BEYOND

The bhakti tradition describes four types of intelligence. The first is the ability to learn simply by hearing or observing, or to absorb information and then draw conclusions. For example, if a man with this type of intelligence is told it's illegal to steal and that stealing sends the thief to prison, he won't steal, even if the opportunity presents itself.

The second type of intelligence is the ability to learn through experience. Those with this type of intelligence hear that stealing is illegal, but overwhelmed by temptation they do it anyway. The consequences of their actions lead to regret, which in turn leads to wiser choices in the future. Although those with this kind of intelligence learn from their mistakes, there is danger in relying on trial and error rather than exercising discernment before making mistakes in the first place. As Benjamin Franklin said, "Experience keeps a dear school, but fools will learn in no other." Or as a Roman proverb says, "Only the foolish learn from experience—the wise learn from the experience of others."

The third type of intelligence could be called misdirected intelligence—one in which we chronically act contrary to our own well-being, refusing to learn despite experience. Those with this kind of intelligence hear that stealing is wrong, are caught and punished, but steal again and again, either because they believe they can beat the system, or that what they're stealing is worth the possible consequences, or that they have no other choice. We usually think of intelligence as proper discernment. This type of intelligence calculates based on a misunderstanding of one's real self-interest and can cloud one's ability to make good choices and avoid bad ones.

Yet there is a state of intelligence that is above and beyond the three types I have described. We find it within us when we tune the intelligence to the soul. The guidance of sacred texts and enlightened people helps us make this attunement. Despite the dreadful news we encounter every day—war, terrorism, murder—self-realized men and women understand that deep in each person's heart lies the capacity for a healthy life rooted in unselfish love. They try to live their understanding, so they naturally refrain from harming or stealing from others. The capacity to love is innate in all beings and is the purest expression of intelligence.

## THE EGO

Once, a sage was sitting on the bank of a river. Gazing into the sweeping current, he saw a scorpion struggling fruitlessly to save itself from drowning. His heart softened, and he reached down and gently scooped the scorpion out of the water. The scorpion swung its tail and stung his hand. Distracted by the pain, he dropped the scorpion back into the water. Realizing that it was again drowning, he again lifted it up, only to be stung again. Pain jolted through his body a second time, and for a second time he dropped the scorpion back into the river. As the sage reached into the water a third time, an onlooker asked, "Why are you trying to save a creature that keeps hurting you?"

The sage whisked up the scorpion and was stung again. This time he managed to toss it onto the riverbank and save its life. As the scorpion crawled away, the sage smiled at the passerby and said, "We all live according to our natures. Just as it's the nature of a scorpion to sting, so it's the nature of one who loves the Supreme to be compassionate."

This seems like an extreme example of compassion, and perhaps it is, but it gives us a glimpse into the nature of one particular enlightened person. If our intelligence becomes purified through spiritual practice like this sage's, we too can tune into our own spiritual nature or, as the Gita puts it, turn false ego into true ego.

*A person who has given up cravings*
*and all sense of proprietorship, who is*
*devoid of false ego—he alone attains peace.*
—BHAGAVAD GITA 2.71

When you are asked, "Who are you?" you'll probably give your name. If pushed for more information, you might say where you were born or list your nationality, occupation, or social roles or positions. "I am Sarah, from Minnesota, a mother who works as a secretary." If you're asked to go deeper, you might say something more personal — perhaps state your religious or political affiliations or your tastes in music, art, or fashion. That's because we feel these designations define and distinguish us from others.

But do they?

From a yogic perspective, all these self-conceptions are actually expressions of the ego. The ego is self-identity. The dictionary defines *ego* as a "conscious thinking subject," or "the part of the mind that gives us a sense of personal identity." In social interactions, ego may refer to our "sense of self-esteem," and someone who expresses his or her self-esteem at the expense of others is called "egotistical."

Various schools of thought have explained the ego in different ways. For example, the German philosopher Immanuel Kant wrote, "The transcendental ego is the thinker of our thoughts, the subject of our experiences, the willer of our actions, and the agent of the various activities of synthesis that help to constitute the world we experience."

The Vedic texts define the true ego (distinguishing it from the false ego) in a similar way, as the eternal self, the atma, the conscious living force within us. The pure self, or the pure ego, has a natural, innate identity in relation to the Supreme Being. When we deny or negate that relationship, we are left with only superficial designations; we become American or Chinese, male or female. That ego is false, and to maintain it requires that we forget our spiritual identity and identify instead with all the secondary, material aspects of ourselves that don't extend beyond this life in this body. It leaves us thinking in terms of "I am this body, and everything in relation to this body is mine."

Because we have to live in this world, it's easy to pin our identity on social labels — man, woman, young, old, Indian, American, black, white, Muslim, Jew — or to base it on what we have, know, or feel. But excessive identification with these external labels is the root of suffering.

Beyond the suffering we ourselves may endure as a result of these misconceptions, people acting under the false ego profoundly affect the people around them. External labels by definition set us apart from others. They divide us into groups and species. Worse, they allow some of us to assume that we are more important than the rest of us. The false ego is powerful. It leads to selfishness, arrogance, and the desire to dominate and exploit others, and it can find reasons to justify almost anything. The more we give in to these tendencies and the more we allow ourselves to be driven by our differences, the further apart we are pulled from one another.

But the most troubling effect of the false ego is the toll it takes on the atma. If we allow our material ego to take charge, the atma will enter a dreamlike state. Ignorant of our divine nature, we'll spend all our time between birth and death suffering and enjoying what we can, but we'll never find peace.

If the real ego, or self, awakens to its full potential, like the passenger in the chariot, it will direct body, mind, and intelligence to help us live an enlightened life.

## A LESSON FROM A COCONUT

Yoga aims at reviving our spiritual nature while living within the body and mind. Think of a coconut. As the inner pulp dries, it separates from the shell. If you shake a dry coconut, you'll hear the hardened pulp bounce against the inside shell, free from its attachment to the shell wall. Shake an immature coconut, and you won't hear anything because the pulp is stuck to the inner shell.

The outer shell represents the body, the inner shell the mind, and the pulp the self (atma). The false ego makes the pulp stick tightly to the inner shell. But when we grow out of our false identifications and allow the true ego to mature into itself, we are free to detach ourselves from unwanted bonds. This leaves us free to be happy. We'll still honor our humanness, but we'll also realize our spiritual essence. As Jesus suggested, we can live in the world without being of it.

Those who are forgetful of their true self are like fish out of water struggling to breathe in an alien world. No amount of money, sex, or prestige can satisfy them. The fish simply needs to return to the water. Living and loving in harmony with the Supreme is our natural state. Therefore, it's also the path to fulfillment. It frees us from all the misconceptions that stunt our growth and connects us to our eternal nature. In the end, our success is not determined by what we achieve but by our integrity. Integrity is a state of undivided wholeness, of being true to our real selves and acting accordingly.

The bhakti path teaches us that both the goal and the means to attain it are the same. The goal is to love. The means to attain it is to serve the Supreme and others with love. Even a simple practice of devotional service will let us see the equality of all beings because, like us, everyone has a relationship with the Supreme Self. Dr. Martin Luther King Jr. gave us a glimpse into this understanding when he said, "Everybody can be great, because everybody can serve. You don't have to have a college degree to serve. You don't have to make your subject and verb agree in order to serve. . . . You only need a heart full of grace. A soul generated by love."

# Who Is God?

*It is not possible to describe the devotional path completely. The ocean of loving relations with the Supreme is so big that no one can estimate its length and breadth. However, just to help you taste it, I am describing but one drop.*

—Sri Chaitanya, *Chaitanya Charitamrita: Madhya-lila* 19.136-7

A thens is a small town in southeastern Ohio surrounded by fertile farmland and rolling hills. In the early 1980s, the majority of its shops were family owned, made of wood and brick. At the town's heart is Ohio University, founded in 1870. In the 1980s, it had about fifteen thousand students.

I remember a day on the campus green when autumn leaves of bright yellows, oranges, and reds adorned the trees and carpeted the lawns. It was a crisp day, warmed only slightly by the sun. Clouds like puffs of cotton floated through the sky on a cool breeze.

As I sat on the grass near a wide oak, a young student was sharing his thoughts with me. But my attention was drawn away by something that was happening across the lawn. A rowdy crowd of about a hundred students was heckling a soapbox preacher.

"Fornication!" the preacher boomed, as he shouted to a couple holding hands. "Repent or choose hell."

"You defile God! Repent or burn!" he yelled at a smoker. To a young man carrying a beer can he roared, "Sinner! Satan awaits you!"

His conviction blazed intense and unperturbed, even in the face of the students' jeers. Fifty yards away, I watched. Then a student pointed at me and yelled, "What about him? He's a Hindu. Where's *he* going?"

The circle around the preacher opened. He stared at me and shouted, "He will suffer eternally in the flames of hell!"

"Why don't you tell him?"

Challenged, the preacher stomped over, the crowd trailing behind. I could hear the autumn leaves crunch under his shoes. Seconds later I was sitting in the center of a ring of students, with the preacher standing over me. The crowd seemed to have doubled in size. The preacher was in his late twenties. He wore a dress shirt and tie and was well built. His eyes and face reddened as he shouted down at me, "Pagan! You are condemned to hell!"

The crowd held its breath. It was clear there'd be a showdown between a swami and a fire-and-brimstone Christian preacher, like two rival football teams. They awaited my reaction.

After a moment of silence, I said, "Sir, if I'm going to hell, where are you going?"

The only sound was the birds.

"I'm going to heaven," he finally thundered.

I looked up into his narrowed, condescending eyes and said, "If you're going to heaven, I think I'd be happier in hell. I would find it unbearable to live for an eternity with a fanatic like you."

I hadn't planned to say that; it just came out. The students burst into a deafening cheer of approval as the preacher looked at me in shock.

Then I asked, "*Why* am I going to hell?"

"Because you worship a false god."

"How do you know?"

"Because you worship Krishna."

"Do you know what 'Krishna' means?"

"Krishna," he yelled indignantly, "is a false god!"

The crowd stirred.

"Can I ask you something? Do you believe God is the embodiment of all beauty and the source of everything beautiful?"

"Of course," he replied.

"Does he possess unparalleled strength, knowledge, wealth, and fame?"

"Of course," he replied again.

"Possessing these excellences makes God all-attractive. Do you find God all-attractive?"

"Of course."

"Well, the name *Krishna* simply means 'the all-attractive one' in the Sanskrit language. Why do you oppose such a wonderful name for your heavenly father?"

Knitting his eyebrows the preacher proclaimed, "Jesus said, 'I am the way, the truth, and the life. No one comes to the Father except through me.' Accepting the blood of Jesus is the only way to attain heaven. Hell awaits everyone else."

"I believe deeply in Jesus," I said. "He echoed the words of the Old Testament, 'Love the Lord with all your heart and with all your soul and with all your mind' and 'Love your neighbor as yourself.' These teachings are at the heart of all theistic religions. I may have a long way to go in my spiritual development, but I'm trying to dedicate my life to following those two commandments. I searched for God for years. I believe he has inspired me to follow the path I'm on. It's a timeless path from India."

He continued to frown down at me, but I could tell he was listening.

"I respect your faith," I said, "but please understand that on my spiritual quest, I left my home and traveled the world. In the Middle East, I found beautiful Islamic lovers of God, but I was also confronted with hardliners who preached that anyone who doesn't embrace Islam as the one true religion, Mohammed as the seal of all prophets, and the Holy Koran as the final revelation are condemned to suffer perpetually in hell. According to them, you, being a Protestant, will burn in hell.

"In Jerusalem, I met Jews who melted my heart with their love for the Lord, but I met others who preached that Jews were the chosen people and everyone else was inferior in God's eyes. In Nepal, I met loving, peaceful Buddhists, but among them were those who hammered me with the doctrine that unless I accepted the Buddha's path, I would remain trapped on the wheel of birth and death. In India, I met devout Hindus who inspired me immensely, but I also met Hindu priests who claimed anyone not born Hindu is unclean, outcast, and unfit for self-realization.

"Each of these hardliners had scriptural evidence and logic to support their views. Each was totally convinced that their religion had a monopoly on salvation. I'm sorry I spoke to you the way I did, but I'm sick of fanaticism. It breeds hate, not love. The Bhagavad Gita explains that God appears in many places throughout history to guide humanity to the love each of us yearns for and to grant us entrance into the spiritual world. Sometimes God descends personally, and at other times he empowers others to perform his will. I've seen that the fruit of following any genuine spiritual path under the guidance of realized teachers is that one develops compassion, self-control, humility, forgiveness, and love. Jesus taught us that we would know false idols by their fruits. I have seen good and bad fruits on all the paths I've explored. Didn't Jesus also say, 'Judge not lest ye be judged'?"

The preacher nodded, musing. The fire in his eyes had abated a little.

"I have a problem with some of what you said," he said slowly, "but maybe we'll talk another time." With those words he left, and the crowd dissipated into the slowly disappearing afternoon.

I had been invited to teach a regular class on campus, so every Wednesday evening during the following weeks, I spoke to about two hundred students who piled into a room in a dorm basement. Most of them stayed for the vegetarian dinner I had prepared for them.

One evening I arrived to find the door locked and the students standing in the hall. A notice, signed by the dean, was taped to the door: class canceled. The students circulated a petition, and the next day they met with the dean in his office. He told them the class had been canceled because that same preacher had bitterly complained about it. But hearing that so many students ardently supported the class, the dean promised to allow it to continue. We started up again the next week.

After that, the preacher showed up at my class every week without fail, contempt written across his face. He was on a mission to prove his case. Armed with a tape recorder, camera, and notepad, he searched for evidence to support his claims that I was teaching a dangerous theology, but he never said a word aloud. At dinner, I greeted the students and also greeted him, but he ignored all my attempts to be friendly.

Curiously, it seemed that each week he was becoming a little less antagonistic, and although he continued to avoid any direct interaction with me, he was making acquaintances among the students. He even started eating the meal.

Then about four weeks later, during dinner, he got up from his chair and walked over to me. Everybody turned to watch.

"I have a question for you," he said.

I braced myself.

"How do you make this?" and he pointed with his spoon to the *halavah* (a popular Indian dessert) on his plate. "It's fantastic. I want to make it for my church meetings."

I happily wrote down the recipe for him. He took it with a smile, the first I'd received from him, and shook my hand.

The next week, while dozens of students, professors, and townspeople were gathering, I stopped to ask him how his congregation had liked the halavah. "They loved it," he beamed. "I think God—or may I say Krishna?—was pleased."

We embraced, and I joked, "I've changed my mind. I'd be happy to be in heaven with you."

"Me too," he said.

## THE IDEA OF GOD

Whenever we look at a beautiful painting, listen to music, or marvel at a work of engineering, it's natural to ask who made it. Similarly, when we look at the wonders and precision of this universe—planets in space, huge mountain ranges garlanded by clouds, rivers that flow thousands of miles for thousands of years, a butterfly's precision flight across continents, the DNA in each organism—it's just as natural to ask who created it and why.

Like other theistic traditions, bhakti yoga accepts that there is a divine intelligence behind the universe. But while many people spend their time, as the preacher once had, fighting over "which God is better," it's important to remember that the quality of a person's faith isn't measured by the apparent shortcomings in another's. What matters is whether a particular expression of faith inspires and guides us in our evolution toward unconditional love of God. Sadly, the Supreme Being, whom most faiths exalt as the greatest, is often imagined to be petty and partial to one group to the exclusion of all others. This misunderstanding of God's nature can manifest in every spiritual tradition, including my own.

I've met teachers from various faith schools whose conceptions of the Supreme contradict another's. At times I was torn by these opposing doctrines. I couldn't accept the common argument that these views were ultimately one when their conclusions were so clearly different. Eventually I discovered in the bhakti texts an understanding of God that helped me unravel and then reconcile these contradictions.

The bhakti texts explain that God can be perceived and understood in a variety of ways. They also teach that while throughout history God comes to this world with various names and forms, he reveals himself eternally in three distinct features: as an all-pervading presence; as the inner guide in every being's heart; and, in his fullest expression, as the all-loving, all-attractive Supreme Person. That these three features are all aspects of the same Absolute Truth is explained in a seminal verse of the *Bhagavata Purana*. This verse encapsulates a vision of God that clarifies and harmonizes the apparent contradictions.

> *Learned transcendentalists who know the*
> *Absolute Truth call this nondual substance*
> *Brahman, Paramatma, or Bhagavan.*
> —BHAGAVATA PURANA 1.2.11

Simply put, the Supreme has three divine aspects: the all-pervading oneness, the localized guardian in the heart, and the personal reciprocator of love.

A comparison can be given to a train approaching a station at night. At first it appears as a brilliant light illuminating all directions. As it gradually pulls into the station, we begin to see that the train is more than a bright light; it is made up of individual cars with a single engine pulling them. But when the train has pulled in fully, we can board it, meet the conductor, and see the cars up close.

## BRAHMAN, THE ALL-PERVADING LIGHT

*I worship Govinda, the Supreme Being, whose effulgence is the source of the nondifferentiated Brahman mentioned in the Upanishads and who appears as the indivisible, infinite, limitless truth.*

—*SRI BRAHMA SAMHITA* 5.40

The Vedic texts describe the Absolute reality as nondual (*advaita*): the one unchanging truth within and beyond everything that exists and the source and sum total of all energy. This omniscient, omnipresent truth is referred to as Brahman and is described as being impersonal, formless, and changeless—what many people call "the white light."

Within the Vedas is a body of literature called the Upanishads, which are known for their lofty philosophical explanations of Brahman. The *Mundaka Upanishad* states:

> In the spiritual realm, beyond the material covering, is the Brahman effulgence, which is free from material contamination. That effulgent light is understood by transcendentalists to be the light of all lights. In that realm there is no need of sunshine, moonshine, fire, or electricity for illumination. Indeed, whatever illumination appears in the material world is

only a reflection of that supreme illumination. That Brahman
is in the front and in the back, in the north, south, east, and
west, and also overhead and below. In other words, that supreme Brahman spreads throughout both the material and
spiritual skies. (2.2.9-11)

Think of Brahman as the divine energy that permeates everything.
It is present in the atom and the space between the atoms. The Upanishads tells us that Brahman is "as bright as millions of suns rising
simultaneously." One who looks into it sees only light and nothing
else. It contains no dualities—no "this but not that"—and is never
affected by the kinds of imperfections we find in matter. Brahman is
the ever-pure, spiritual substance that underlies all space and time.

Realizing we are spiritual by nature, transcendental to pleasure,
pain, birth, and death, and that we are one with Brahman, brings
total peace. Realizing oneself as nondifferent from Brahman, a state
attained through meditation (dhyana) and the cultivation of spiritual knowledge (the jnana yoga path), leaves us understanding that
we are intrinsically blissful and not vulnerable to suffering—not
vulnerable because we're not made of the matter of this world.

In yoga circles you may hear this understanding referred to by
the Sanskrit phrase *aham brahmasmi*, "I am Brahman." You may also
hear terms like *moksha*, *mukti*, and *nirvana*, which are all used to
describe the attainment of this transcendental state.

## The Paramatma, the Inner Guide

*As the one sun appears reflected in countless jewels,*
*so the Supreme Being manifests Himself in the*
*hearts of all living beings.*

—Sri Chaitanya, *Chaitanya Charitamrita: Adi-lila* 2.19

A number of spiritual traditions speak of an aspect of God that is found in all beings. The Vedic texts call this feature "the inner guide" or "the witness." In Sanskrit, the individual soul is called the atma, whereas God as the inner guide is called the *paramatma*, or the "Supersoul."

Out of love for all beings, God, who is already present everywhere, presides in every being's heart and takes a personal interest in each being's welfare. When we calm the mind and senses through yoga, prayer, or some other contemplative practice, we can feel his presence and, if the mind is very quiet, hear his guidance.

The *Katha Upanishad* compares the individual soul and the Supreme Soul to two birds sitting on a tree. The individual soul spends its time tasting both the sweet and bitter fruits of the tree, while the Supersoul, ever-satisfied, remains as friend and witness. The Supersoul never abandons any soul, because he loves each of them, but neither does he interfere with any of the soul's choices. Rather, he's eager to bestow his grace and offer direction to those who turn to him. This is why the Lord in the heart is sometimes called "the inner guardian," a fitting description of the safety and protection this close friend provides. Patanjali's *Yoga Sutra* declares that meditation on this divine inner guide, this "guru of all teachers," leads to *samadhi*, a state of unshakable peace.

Most of us have a number of mental voices that influence us. Most of us are dominated by the voice of the ego-affected mind—the voice that compels us to act out against those we envy or urges us to gratify our physical or mental passions. There are also the voices of our parents and teachers, of popular media—even the advertising jingles we heard as children. Paramatma, however, is not just another voice. His voice is the prime voice, the voice that reminds us how to act in the best interests of the true self.

The Gita tells us how to find him:

*Those who conquer the mind realize paramatma and know tranquility. To such souls, happiness and distress, heat and cold, honor and dishonor are all the same.*

—BHAGAVAD GITA 6.7

Paramatma could be described as the source of our higher intuition and the insights that surpass our ordinary intellectual or creative conscience. Ralph Waldo Emerson, a leader of the nineteenth-century transcendentalist movement, wrote in his essay, "The Oversoul," "Within man is the soul of the whole; the wise silence; the universal beauty, to which every part and parcel is equally related; the eternal One."

Many Christians refer to the Supersoul as the Holy Spirit.

*Do not worry about what to say or how to say it. At that time you will be given what to say, for it will not be you speaking, but the Spirit of your Father speaking through you.*

—MATTHEW 10:20

Paramatma chooses not to interfere with our free will, but he is always present in our hearts, lovingly waiting for us to turn to him. Paramatma guides us, but the amount of guidance he gives is reciprocal with how much we want to receive it. If you want to hear paramatma's direction over all other voices in your head, it requires to lead a clean, healthy life and follow genuine spiritual practices. Without these lifestyle changes, we may mistake our ego-affected imagination for paramatma's voice.

We can find guidelines for living such a life by hearing from enlightened teachers and reading revealed scriptures, both of which are said to be the "external voice" of paramatma.

# BHAGAVAN, OR THE SUPREME IN HIS FULLEST EXPRESSION

The Vedas teach that the Supreme has a purely spiritual, beautiful form. That form is not composed of matter, so it is not part of the material creation. In the language of yoga it's *sat-chit-ananda*, eternal and full of knowledge and bliss.

The word *bhagavan* means "the source of excellences," and the Vedas list those excellences as beauty, strength, knowledge, wealth, fame, and independence. The Supreme Person possesses these excellences to an infinite degree. Imagine what it would be like to see infinite beauty or truly unlimited wealth. Imagine what God knows if he knows everything. What does "everything" actually mean? With our limited minds, we have no way to understand God's personality and qualities.

Our deepest, most fundamental need is to love and be loved. Bhagavan is the beautiful, personal, loving, and lovable aspect of the Supreme Being. Bhagavan is God when he is fully himself. And what is he doing in that fullest expression of himself? He's offering his love to each of us so intimately and completely that we feel that we are his most beloved.

Love is something we understand because we share it with one another. The love we feel now toward others can help us begin to understand the personal relationship we have with the Supreme, because the propensity to love has its origin and finds its ultimate fulfillment in God's love.

We can learn about how God shares love with us in many scriptures, and in particular texts like the *Bhagavata Purana* and *Ramayana* there are detailed descriptions of his personal loving exchanges with others. To help us become lovers of God, these books also describe, for our contemplation, his beautiful form, wonderful qualities, and activities in this world and the spiritual realm. It's hard to love someone you've never met, so revealed scriptures the world over try to make God accessible to us.

Unlike those seeking oneness with God's impersonal energy, bhakti yogis aspire to love God eternally and with all their heart and soul, and to let the light of that love shine forth in their love for others.

The bhakti tradition offers the inclusive philosophy of unity in diversity. The one Supreme Being reveals himself according to the aspirations of a spiritual seeker—the one who moves toward him as Brahman, the limitless light and oneness of all that exists; the one who seeks him out as paramatma, the inner guide; and the one who wants a relationship with Bhagavan, the Supreme Lover and Beloved. The Bhagavad Gita (4.11) states, "As souls approach Me, I reciprocate accordingly."

## ONE GOD APPEARS IN VARIOUS TRADITIONS

Let's briefly explore how the Supreme has appeared through the ages in various traditions. In the Bible, God is the all-powerful, loving father. He appeared as a burning bush to enlighten Moses, as a pillar of fire to save the Israelites from pharaoh's army, as a thunderous voice to proclaim the Ten Commandments, and, allegorically, as a youthful lover in the Old Testament book, Song of Songs. In the New Testament he appears through Jesus Christ, who through his teachings and sacrifice showered infinite grace on the world. In the Holy Koran he is Allah, the Supremely Great and Merciful One who manifested his message of truth through the Prophet Muhammad.

In the Vedas, written in Sanskrit, he is called Vishnu, or Krishna, the transcendent, all-knowing Lord of all beings, who by infinite kindness incarnates into the material world again and again. Each descent of the one God is called an *avatar* (meaning "one who descends"). These same ancient scriptures foresaw the descent of the Buddha; Buddha is considered an avatar of the Supreme Being come specifically to personify compassion toward all beings.

In the epic *Ramayana* the descent of Rama, teacher of the highest human ideals, is described. Rama displayed both limitless power and a limitless sweetness. In the Bhagavad Gita, he is Krishna, spiritual master and friend to all, who reveals the universal knowledge quintessential to the Vedas. In the *Bhagavata Purana* Krishna further reveals himself as an ever-youthful cowherd boy, who possesses all the qualities of all the avatars but whose beauty and sweetness overshadow his majestic power to facilitate intimate loving reciprocation.

The essence and goal of all true scriptures is to connect us to an all-loving, forgiving God and to teach us how to live as instruments of that love and forgiveness. Yet religious scriptures have, in places, descriptions of harsh punishments, bloody histories, or teachings that appear to be polarizing. These accounts, and the lessons they teach, need to be balanced and understood in the light of the essence and goal: to love the Supreme, to see the innate divinity within ourselves and in all beings, and to be infused with compassion.

# SHAKTI: GOD'S FEMININE SIDE

*O Radha, You are a flowing river of incomparable compassion. Please allow me to serve You.*

—ARCHANA PADDHATI: THE PROCESS OF DEITY WORSHIP

Once, when I was delivering a talk in Mumbai, a young man said, "It is said that behind every successful man, there is a woman. Does this statement hold true for a celibate like you?"

Yes, it does. The spiritual gifts I seek are possible to attain only by grace, and divine grace originates in *Shakti*, the motherly, feminine quality of the Supreme. Behind a monk like me is the Supreme Goddess, whom in my tradition we call Radha. She is Krishna's feminine counterpart.

The Vedic literature informs us that the one Infinite Being is both male and female. The one becomes two to exchange love, and their love is the origin of all other love, all beauty, all ecstasy, and all compassion. They are called by many names, such as Krishna and Radha, or *Shaktiman* (the source of power, which is the masculine principle) and *Shakti* (the feminine, divine activating energy). It's easier to think of these two through an analogy. Shaktiman, or the power source, is the sun, and Shakti, the sun's energy, is the sunshine. The two can never be separated. There is no meaning to one without the other.

This concept of masculine and feminine divinity is found in other spiritual traditions as well. Think of the yang and yin of the Taoist tradition, the Logos-Sophia of the Christian tradition, and the Yahweh-Shekinah of the Hebraic tradition. The word *shekinah* means "dwelling place," and in classical Judaism, it is thought that when the Shekinah is near Yahweh, she makes it easier to see him.

In each of these traditions, grace is personified by this feminine dimension of God. Forgiveness, compassion, and the nourishment of suffering souls with wisdom and love are all elements of grace. Grace is all powerful, yet reveals herself in the sweetest and gentlest of forms. Grace descends from the divine realm into this world by the Supreme's own will. As with other devotional paths, bhakti yoga practices aim at reconnecting us to that current of grace.

The notion of divine grace is an intriguing concept. In a world where the powers of illusion are oceanic and our insatiable desire for self-gain daunting to overcome, grace intercedes and forgives our transgressions, compensates for our shortcomings, and awakens our spiritual potential. Divine, motherly grace blesses us with gifts that would otherwise be far beyond our reach. It can inspire inexhaustible hope and irrepressible determination, and it can awaken in us an irresistible desire to receive it.

As pure water flows downward, so grace flows down to the humblest and most grateful. I have seen grace do amazing things in people's lives. Grace is the mother, the soft, compassionate nature of the Supreme, and devotion to Radha, the fountainhead of grace, is the key to the realm of love and forgiveness, happiness and freedom.

It's puzzling why under the banner of religion, this nourishing, compassionate side of God is so frequently neglected in favor of the pursuit of power and control. Even in God's name, people too often feel the need to conquer, plunder, and manipulate. The bhakti school teaches us to balance our lives with devotion to both the masculine and feminine aspects of God as a way to honor humanity, life, and nature. As Father Thomas Schipflinger explores in *Sophia-Maria: A Holistic Vision of Creation*:

> The Chaitanya school of bhakti devotion understands the divine couple Radha-Krishna as two and yet one, the archetype of all existence and the most intimate, divine, and primordial form at the center of all existence. . . . The texts about Radha and Krishna . . . recall the Old Testament passages which depict Sophia as Yahweh's Amon, the Beloved who dances and plays before Him, sharing God's life, knowing God's plans, and choosing from among them.

Mother Nature is a manifestation of the Divine feminine in this world. As our divine mother, nature nourishes and sustains us body and soul with food and water and air and beauty. Like infants, we are dependent on her for every breath. That's why bhakti yogis respect the environment. Caring for Mother Earth and protecting her resources and all her children thus becomes an integral part of our expression of love for the Supreme.

As the soothing light of the full moon induces the petals of a blue lotus flower to open, so grace, the feminine divine, induces our spiritual love to awaken, blossom, and spread its fragrance into the world.

## THE DOG'S WISDOM

Years ago, I lived in a small ashram on the bank of the Ganges in the Indian state of Bihar. Every day I met with an eighty-year-old man named Narayan Prasad, a Hindu, and his close friend, Mohammed, a Muslim. One day I asked Narayan Prasad, "How is it that you are so affectionate with someone from another religion in a country where there is so much conflict between Hindus and Muslims?"

Narayan told me something I've never forgotten: "A dog will recognize his master in whatever dress he wears. The master may dress in robes or a suit and tie or stand naked, but the dog will always know him. If we cannot recognize God, our beloved master, when he appears in a different dress in other religions, then we have much to learn from a dog."

Narayan Prasad's simple but sobering analogy stays with me. Today, more than ever before, we need to understand unity in diversity. We are each being called on to have the courage to resist pettiness, selfishness, and hypocrisy and know that we are all children of the same Supreme Truth, the ultimate lover and beloved.

# What Is Yoga?

*Perform your duty equipoised, O Arjuna,*
*abandoning all attachment to success or failure.*
*Such equanimity is called yoga.*
— Bhagavad Gita 2.48

## DHRUVA'S ATTAINMENT

The *Bhagavata Purana* tells the story of a child named Dhruva who, at age five, attained samadhi, the perfection of yoga practice. Dhruva was a prince, but fortune had not smiled on him. His father had married a second, younger queen, who had given the king another son. To please his younger wife, Dhruva's father tended to neglect Dhruva and favor the younger queen's son. One day Dhruva attempted to climb on the throne along with his younger brother and sit on his father's lap, but Dhruva's stepmother rebuked him: "You, who were born of an inferior woman, have no right to sit on the throne with your father. Better you pray to God that he allows you to take your next birth from my womb."

Although the king knew that Dhruva was his first-born and the heir to his throne, he thought it prudent to say nothing. But Dhruva's heart was crushed—as much by his father's betrayal as his stepmother's words. In tears, he ran to his mother, Suniti. Poor Suniti shriveled in the face of Dhruva's anguish like a leaf burning in a forest fire. Her tears turned Dhruva's humiliation into fury, and he now craved justice. In his childish way, he vowed to attain a kingdom greater even than his father's.

Suniti tried to temper her son. "Don't wish for anything unfavorable toward others," she said. "Anyone who inflicts pain on others will himself suffer that same pain. Child, I don't think anyone can soothe your distress but the Supreme himself."

When Dhruva asked where the Supreme could be found, Suniti told him that the forest sages would know.

To his mother's surprise, young Dhruva left immediately and headed into the dense forest. It's said that God will send us a guru to show us the way when we sincerely desire to find him, and so God sent Dhruva the renowned sage Narada. Narada was impressed with the child's determination, so he taught Dhruva to practice yoga asanas and meditation, and to chant the mantra *om namo bhagavate vasudevaya*, "I meditate on Vasudeva (Vishnu), the Infinite Being who lives everywhere."

Under Narada's guidance, Dhruva journeyed farther into the jungle, arriving, finally, at Madhuban, on the bank of the Yamuna River. There he practiced what Narada had taught him with a mature persistence that belied his years. Months passed, during which Dhruva survived on roots and fruits from the forest, or, later, on only water. He spent each day chanting the sacred mantra he had been given and performing his asanas.

After a time, he was able to decrease his physical needs. He fasted for weeks at a time and stood on one foot, like a pillar, as he meditated on the limitless beauty of the Supreme in the heart. After about six months, he achieved samadhi, and his natural feelings of divine love awakened.

Suddenly the beautiful form of the Lord in his heart, whom he had been observing, disappeared. Alarmed, the boy opened his eyes. There standing before him was that same Supreme Being, Vishnu, his divine guide. Vishnu's complexion was a beautiful bluish color, and every one of his limbs was graceful and soothing to the eyes. He smiled at Dhruva, whose uncommon devotion had commanded his attention.

Vishnu said, "Ask me for anything you desire."

Dhruva had begun his yoga practice craving wealth, power, and revenge, but meditating on the Supreme Beloved had lifted these burdensome feelings from his heart. He felt foolish for ever thinking they were important. "My Lord," he said, "the only boon I now ask is that I am always able to remember you and serve your servants."

"What about the kingdom you wanted—the one that was better than your father's?" Vishnu asked.

Dhruva replied, "I was looking for pieces of broken glass, but by your grace I have discovered the rarest of jewels in your love."

The sixth chapter of the Gita describes this love as the perfection of yoga. The chapter concludes with this verse:

> *Of all yogis, those who abide always in Me with great*
> *faith, who think of Me within themselves, and who offer*
> *Me loving service—they are intimately united with Me*
> *in yoga and are the highest of all.*
> —BHAGAVAD GITA 6.47

My teacher would tell us that God accepts not only what we offer; even more, he accepts the sincere intent and humility with which we make our offering. Yoga practice is about purifying our intention and cultivating self-realization, or seeing ourselves as we truly are. Pure love is possible only when we're honest with both ourselves and our beloved Lord. So self-realization and humility are inseparable. The perfection of yoga for a person on the bhakti path is absorption in *prema*, pure love.

## THE PATH OF YOGA

Dhruva is an example of someone who began practicing yoga for one reason and, through the course of his practice, purified his heart and transformed his purpose. What he first saw as a path to material prosperity later opened him up to his spiritual potential. Each of us can experience this transformation.

The root of the word *yoga*, *yuj*, means "to unite." The Latin root of the word *religion*, *religio*, means something similar: "to bind back." Yoga and religion actually refer to the same thing: They are each paths that unite us with our spiritual essence. Since coming west from India, yoga has been appropriated for less transcendental purposes, such as stress relief and physical fitness—valuable goals, but goals that fall short of its original, full purpose.

Although yoga is practiced in many forms, there are four major, widely practiced traditions. Each is discussed in the Bhagavad Gita: jnana yoga, the path of knowledge; karma yoga, the path of knowledge in action; ashtanga or raja yoga, "the path with eight limbs," which includes asana practice, breath control, and meditation; and bhakti yoga, the path of divine love. There are many good books on the various aspects of yoga. This book focuses on bhakti, so we will leave you with only this brief description of yoga's other branches.

# Yoga's Principles of Freedom: Help Along the Path

Yoga is the science of cleansing the heart and experiencing the joy of living in spiritual harmony with God, nature, and others. It begins with cultivating good character: the willingness to make personal sacrifices for a higher cause, to make the right choices even in the face of temptation or fear, and to put concern for the well-being of others before selfish interests.

All the schools of yoga include regulative principles to ground our spiritual practice in ethical behavior, which is necessary for genuine progress. These regulative principles, or observances, relate to both behavior and attitude and are known in the ashtanga yoga system as *yamas* (ethical disciplines) and *niyamas* (disciplined practices). I am often asked how these principles are viewed from the perspective of bhakti yoga, so what follows is a brief exploration of that topic.

The first regulative principle, *ahimsa*, is nonviolence, to cause no harm to any living being through our actions, words, and, as far as humanly possible, our thoughts. This will protect us from accruing negative karma, which only further covers the self. The biblical equivalent to ahimsa is, "Do unto others as you would have them do unto you." Logically, the Bible's positive injunction embraces it's opposite: "Do *not* do unto others as you would *not* want done unto you."

The practice of ahimsa involves being respectful, patient, and forgiving—nonviolent. The Bhagavad Gita teaches that a yogi sees the Divine in the heart of all beings and therefore wishes all beings well. We advance in yoga to the degree that we consider the suffering of others as our own suffering and the happiness of others as our own happiness. In this spirit, compassion is the basis of ahimsa.

Ahimsa is the primary reason that bhakti yogis choose to be vegetarian: their aim is to minimize the suffering they cause other creatures. Animals feel pain just as humans do. Animals express emotions and may love their offspring and those close to them not so differently from the way we do.

My dear friends Sharon and David once told me a moving story that illustrates this. While in the ancient city of Varanasi, India, they noticed a female dog with only three legs struggling to find food. Dogs in the West are generally kept as pets, but in India, dogs usually live in the street, where the competition for food is fierce. Sharon and David, feeling sympathy, walked some distance to a shop to purchase bread to feed the local dogs. Within moments, a crowd of homeless, hungry dogs surrounded them. The dogs fought one another, snapping for the bread and immediately devouring whatever they could snatch.

My friends took note of one dog, who stood patiently to the side, meekly waiting his turn. After all the other dogs were fed, this dog approached them with his head lowered. His eyes seemed to gloss with gratitude as he gently accepted a piece of bread from Sharon's hand. Interestingly, he didn't eat it; rather, he held it carefully in his mouth and trotted away.

Intrigued, Sharon and David followed the dog to see what he'd do next. After about a block, the dog crawled beneath a large-wheeled cart. There, Sharon and David saw the same three-legged dog they had seen earlier. She was lying on her side with a puppy snuggled up to her belly. The male dog still hadn't taken a bite from the bread. He tenderly placed the bread in the puppy's mouth. As the puppy ate it with enthusiasm, his parents, who were obviously hungry themselves, looked on with a parental affection that touched the hearts of the two human onlookers.

There are many such stories, and yet we eat animals as if they are soulless creatures. Sadhu Vaswani, a well-known yogi from the early twentieth century, says,

> All killing is a denial of love, for to kill, or eat what another has killed, is to rejoice in cruelty. And cruelty hardens our hearts and blinds our vision and we see not that they whom we kill are our brothers and sisters in the One Brotherhood of Life.

The more we expand our spirit of compassion to honor the sanctity of life, the more deeply we connect with our own spiritual nature.

The second principle, *satyam*, or truthfulness, teaches simplicity: it tells us that with a simple heart, we should refrain from lying and instead speak what is true. Lying easily becomes habitual. Lying doesn't refer only to untruths but to rationalizations as well. Lies, rationalizations, justifications, hypocrisy: All of them accustom us to duplicity, or falsity, and over time, we may even come to think of lying as a stepping-stone to freedom. But that itself is not true.

There are several reasons that people choose not to speak the truth. One is selfishness, but another is fear. Even well-intentioned people may lie when they are afraid of how others may react to something or may perceive them. Often these repercussions are exaggerated by the mind.

Although it may seem that lying is a way out of unwanted complications, telling lies taints relationships and one's own heart. Freedom is supported by honesty, and spiritual life has to be built on truth. "The truth shall set you free," John tells us in the Bible. Meaningful relationships require trust. To be worthy of receiving trust, we have to be trustworthy, and trustworthiness means being truthful.

Satyam should be based on the goodness of one's character. In very sensitive cases, ahimsa may be a higher truth than speaking factually. For instance, during the World War II, some people lied to the Nazi Gestapo to protect innocent families from being killed; they are honored for their courage and compassion.

On a deeper level, truthfulness includes accepting that we are not proprietors but caretakers of whatever we have. Both our possessions and our talents are divine property entrusted to us, and we are truthful when we recognize that and use them with humility and gratitude. This is why bhakti yogis choose to refrain from gambling, as it tends to generate greed, obsession, and a lack of respect for the wealth that has been entrusted to us.

*Asteya* is the "avoidance of stealing," and it means we should overcome the tendency to take what belongs to others. Our lust for things can never be satisfied, and when we don't understand that, greed intoxicates the ego and blinds us to our true self-interest. Yogis aim to become free of the effects of obsession for more and more things, something that stealing perpetuates.

In addition to not stealing from others, we should not steal from ourselves. We have been given the capacity to awaken our natural, liberated state of consciousness and be instruments of goodness for the world, but we can squander this gift as well. One of the most common ways to do so is to indulge in mind-altering substances like drugs and alcohol. These potentially addictive things cloud the consciousness and steal our potential. That is why serious bhakti yogis avoid intoxicating substances. Narcotic drugs and alcohol in particular may leave us feeling free for the moment, but over time they may enslave us. Our spiritual practice can help us reach states of awareness far beyond what any intoxicant can offer. In yoga, fulfillment is found in a sober, healthy life, a life of integrity.

*Brahmacharya* means to act in ways that lead us to Brahman or spiritual unity. It generally refers to sexual regulation or, in some cases, abstinence. Spiritual traditions have always honored seekers who are able to properly regulate their sexual energy and transform it into an aid for enlightenment.

Most of us have probably known someone who has focused in an unhealthy way or even been misguided by his or her sexual impulses. The Bhagavad Gita compares lust, *kama*, to a blazing fire. The more we feed it, the hotter it blazes. Giving in to unbridled sexual impulses can cause all kinds of problems, from embarrassment to the devastation of families to the spread of disease to all types of abuse and violence. At the very least, it's a serious mental distraction. Therefore bhakti yogis (and the followers of most other schools of yoga) refrain from indulging in unhealthy, obsessive, or unethical sex.

Some traditions have their celibates — their monks and nuns who completely abstain from sexual relationships in order to focus their lives on their spiritual goals. Those who are working in society and raising a family with spiritual values can achieve the same spiritual focus. Such householders are taught to use their sexual energy for something higher than just physical and emotional pleasure. Krishna says in the Bhagavad Gita, "I am sex that is not contrary to spiritual principles." The blessing of spiritually oriented sex is especially relevant when two people, united through a lifetime of mutual care, choose, in the service of God, to bring a child into the world.

The sexual drive is a powerful force. Sexual repression without channeling that powerful energy toward a higher, more fulfilling reality could degenerate into excessive frustration, mental instability, or, in extreme cases, abuse. Brahmacharya, in either monastic or family life, becomes an experience of freedom and joy when practiced in a responsible, thoughtful, and honest way, with moral and spiritual guidance.

*Aparigraha* means not to fall prey to the obsession of over accu-mulating material possessions. "Simple living and high thinking" is a motto for the yogic way of life. People lose the chance for true happiness by choosing quantity of objects obtained over quality of life, and unsurprisingly so; we are surrounded by a consumer-ori-ented culture that pounds its propaganda into us at every turn. One's wealth is too often calculated by bank balance and prestige rather than character and contentment. We can live fulfilled without many things, but we cannot live well without healthy relationships or peace of mind. Often we find that those who excel only in pursu-ing money and power become lonely prisoners of their own success.

Success should liberate and inspire us, not lead us to become its slaves. Too often success brings the danger of becoming over-whelmed by addiction to popularity, wealth, or power. When we're carried away by our own affluence, we may flaunt our superiority or suspect that even our friends and loved ones are out to exploit us, leaving us feeling ever more isolated.

Yoga practice adds balance to acquiring and holding on to mate-rial things. Bhakti yoga especially encourages a mood of gratitude, which allows us to focus on the true measure of success: spiritual fulfillment. As William Blake wrote, "Gratitude is heaven itself."

Simple living doesn't necessarily mean living impoverished. Kings and queens have become saints, as have many wealthy people, even millionaires and billionaires. Whether you live in a cave or a palace, the secret to simple living is a simple, well-wishing heart. In an evolved spiritual culture, we love people and use things. Unfortunately, in today's world, people are prone to love things and use people.

The next principle is *shaucham*, physical and mental cleanliness. An awareness that we are a soul and not the body is no excuse for neglecting or abusing our body. Birth in the human form is a rare blessing. Of the millions of species, humans are especially capable of self-realization and giving care and protection to all others. To help this process, we are advised to keep ourselves in optimum physical and mental condition. Internal and external cleanliness is a starting point; bathing daily and wearing clean clothes helps reinforce mental purity. My teacher, Prabhupada, reminded his disciples that our body, home, and property are sacred items entrusted to our care. "Cleanliness is not only next to godliness," he said, "but if it's practiced with devotion, it *is* godliness."

*Santosh* means contentment. Being peaceful despite the uncertainties of life requires a positive attitude. External circumstances change constantly, often in ways beyond our control. But we do have control over how we respond to them. So while we try our best to improve life, we need to learn to be satisfied with the sincerity of our efforts, however things turn out. Even our greatest achievements are hollow unless we've achieved a measure of inner satisfaction.

Happiness is a state of mind. Dualities of all kinds—honor and dishonor, success and failure, pleasure and pain—come and go "like the winter and summer seasons" (Bhagavad Gita 2.14). Contentment lives only in the hearts of those who are grateful. When we're grateful for the opportunities and gifts we've been given in both good times and bad, we can attract grace.

A story about a farmer and his neighbor illustrates contentment. One day, the farmer's only horse breaks out of the barn and runs away. Seeing this, the neighbor cries out, "Bad luck! You lost your only horse."

The farmer shrugs. "Bad luck, good luck. Let's see."

A few days later, the horse returns to the barn with a wild mare it met in the mountains. The neighbor is nonplussed.

"Huh. I guess it was good luck after all that your horse ran away. Now you have two."

The farmer shrugs. "Good luck, bad luck. Let's see."

The next day, the farmer's son tries to tame the wild mare. She throws him and he breaks his leg.

"Bad luck," his neighbor laments. "Your only son broke his leg. Now you have no one to help you with your work."

The farmer shrugs. "Bad luck, good luck. Let's see."

Soon the country goes to war, and all the young men are sent off to fight. All are killed — except the farmer's son, who was not drafted into the army because of his broken leg.

By this time the neighbor knows better than to judge the situation. Instead, he asks the farmer, "Is this good luck or bad luck?"

Looking up at the clouds, the farmer rubs his chin and replies, "Over the years I have discovered that we can't always judge a thing at face value. The sun lies behind both white clouds and black ones. If we're grateful, patient, and faithful during bright periods and dark, the light of grace will shine upon us."

Yoga helps us to learn tolerance, like that of the grateful farmer. Is the glass of water half full or half empty? Yogis generally vote for half full and see the sun shining behind even the darkest cloud. Behind life's dualities is the hand of grace, and when we're touched by it, we realize that the universe is benign and life worth living fully. The Gita teaches:

> *One whose happiness is within, who is active and rejoices within and whose aim is within, is actually a perfect mystic. Such a person ultimately attains the Supreme.*
>
> —BHAGAVAD GITA 5.24

*Tapas* means to accept what is favorable for spiritual progress and avoid what is unfavorable, even if doing so is difficult. Whether something is easy or difficult is not of primary importance. The more relevant question is, "Is this the right thing to do?" To live true to the answer to such a question requires discipline. There's very little in life we can accomplish without discipline. It's discipline and determination that allow one to pursue goals and overcome obstacles.

This is especially true for those on a spiritual path. Laziness, cowardliness, and egotism are obstacles to spiritual progress, and overcoming them takes strength of character. The Bhagavad Gita (2.41) states, "Those who are on this path are resolute in purpose, and their aim is one. The intelligence of the irresolute is many-branched." Everyone has the capacity to act with dignity. What people lack is the will to do so.

Some people think that austerity means enduring self-imposed, sometimes even extreme, hardships. But such austerities can exacerbate false ego. I knew a yogi who lived in the hollow of a tree in the Himalayan forest. He had no possessions, wore only a loincloth, and woke early every morning to perform severe yogic exercises. He ate practically nothing and hardly slept. But he used to boast of his own greatness and ridicule others. His stomach fasted from food, but his ego feasted on other people's apparent faults. Although he went practically naked, he was clothed in garments of pride. He may have woken his body early every morning, but day and night, he was asleep to the needs of his soul.

Therefore the heart of tapas is cultivation of humility, not severe physical practices. Like gratitude, humility gives us access to the grace required to overcome obstacles, especially the most difficult one, the ego. We don't have to kill the ego to become humble; we have to realize our real ego, or self, by liberating it from the false ego and be true to ourselves. It's a profound paradox: the more we expand our consciousness, the smaller we feel, because when we see ourselves in truth, the actual definition of humility, we realize we're

just a small, loving part of God, interconnected with the whole creation, and the servant of all beings. Connection with the unlimited
plane makes us feel proportionately tiny. Humility is the true measure of an authentic spiritual person, and it transcends all material
and spiritual designations.

*Svadhyaya* means "self-study," or introspection. In the bhakti tradition, there are two important sources of knowledge: the sacred texts
and the persons who exemplify them. Regular study of sacred texts
and association with sincere practitioners nourish us and provide a
perspective that allows us to contemplate the nature of the self and
view every aspect of our lives through the lens of timeless wisdom.

And finally there is *ishvara pranidhana,* or "surrender to the
Supreme." This means to dedicate one's actions, words, and
thoughts and ultimately, one's *prana* or essence, to the will of the
Divine. On the bhakti path, surrender is the art of dedicating our
abilities, resources, family—whatever we have—with love, to the
Supreme Being, for his pleasure.

Krishna describes this state of consciousness in the Gita:

> *For those who see Me everywhere and everything in Me, I am never*
> *lost, nor are they ever lost to Me. . . . Such a yogi, who engages in My*
> *loving service, remains always with Me in all circumstances. . . .*
> *Perfect yogis are they who, by comparison to their own self, see the*
> *true equality of all beings, in both their happiness and their distress.*
> —BHAGAVAD GITA 6.30–32

From the perspective of bhakti yoga, all forms of yoga culminate
in ishvara pranidhana. Surrender to the will of the Supreme is the
ultimate victory. In this liberated state, one offers one's whole being
as an instrument of the highest power: unconditional love. As the

sage Patanjali states, "*Samadhi siddhi isvara pranidhanat* [the perfection of samadhi is to surrender to the Supreme]." Graham Schweig, an esteemed professor and scholar of Sanskrit, translated ishvara pranidhana as follows: *isa*, the divine center; *vara*, of all reality; *pra*, that is discovered by moving; *ni*, deeply; *dhana*, within the core of ones being or heart. By sincerely and honestly offering one's heart to the Supreme Beloved, the ultimate goal of all religions, all yoga processes, and all life — is received.

# What Is Bhakti?

*I have no way to repay your love. I can only give you myself.*
—RAMAYANA (RAMA TO HANUMAN AS THEY EMBRACE)

Each of us, beyond the plethora of life's distractions, is a unique vessel of God's love, with the potential to recognize, give, and receive this love through our daily interactions. This truth is at the core of the bhakti teachings. Long ago, when I was still wandering the world starving for an experience of truth and beauty that was beyond my acquired prejudices, I learned this lesson from an unlikely but unforgettable teacher.

On a chilly day in 1971, as winter was finally coming to an end, I was walking alone along a jungle path, heading north into a vast Himalayan wilderness. Absorbed in my contemplations, I stepped out of the dense forest into a clearing, then froze, unable to bear the chilling sight before me: a crowd of homeless, starving people, some naked, others in filthy rags. Their faces were deformed, their noses melted away, and their hands and feet mangled, bloody stumps without fingers or toes. I had stumbled into a leper colony. I'd heard of such places, but nothing could have prepared me for the devastation I saw. As I stepped amid them, a mob of lepers encircled me, pushing in so tightly that I felt smothered. "Alms!" they cried, and they tugged and pushed one another in a desperate attempt to grab whatever they could take off me. A long twenty minutes later, they realized I had nothing to give, and they dispersed.

On the ground to one side lay an old, ragged woman, a hole of decaying flesh where her nose had once been. Our eyes met, and she smiled in what I thought seemed a sad way. I could see she understood the shock I had just received, and in that moment, surprisingly, she conveyed to me wordlessly the tender, sympathetic love of a mother. Her look assured me she wanted nothing from me. Rather, she pitied me, seeing how devastated I was by my encounter with her people. She held her fingerless hands together in a gesture of respect and then extended one hand to bless me. Moved, I approached her and sank to my knees. She placed her palm on the top of my head and whispered, "May God bless you, my child. May God bless you."

I looked up. Her face was lit with joy. She was beautiful! I felt that God had sent me to her so she could do the one thing any mother, rich or poor, healthy or sick, has the right to do: bless a child. I wept, overcome by the pricelessness of the blessing. Then, with a last exchange of smiles, I walked on.

Not far from the colony I found a spot to rest by the Ganges. I gazed down into the rushing current. I tried to glimpse something beneath the swirling waves, but I could see nothing of the river's depths. That poor leper woman was plagued with an appalling disease, but like the river, she had depths invisible to the eye. She was a beautiful soul who seemed to want only to love and be loved.

Both the woman and the river overwhelmed my natural tendency to judge others by their appearance. If we look beneath the surface, no matter how imperfect that surface may seem, we may discover that every soul is pure. The physical and mental suffering we each experience may have remote causes, causes we no longer remember, but they play themselves out in different ways. Still, by its nature, the soul is always pure. Flowing even deeper than the inconceivable laws of karma is the current of grace. It didn't seem to me that the leper woman blamed God for her suffering; rather, she seemed to emanate a deep joy and sense of contentment while offering God's blessing to another.

Thirty-six years later, I returned to that leper colony. Public funding had moved it to a more accessible location and created housing and food programs. These residents of the colony were living in conditions vastly better than what I had encountered as a young man. I didn't expect to find the woman who blessed me and, of course, I didn't, but I remembered her. And I remembered how, before public funding and housing and food programs, before any evidence existed that anyone in the world cared about her, this woman had cared for me. Her blessing had penetrated to the core of my heart, a reminder that beyond the differences that divide us—nationality, religion, gender, race, appearance, health, or illness—lies the common essential quality we all share: the soul's inherent ability to love.

## Defining Bhakti

*Love is not a matter of getting what you want. Quite the contrary.*
*The insistence on always being satisfied, on always being fulfilled,*
*makes love impossible. To love you have to climb out of the cradle,*
*where everything is "getting," and grow up to the maturity of giving,*
*without concern for getting anything special in return.*
—Thomas Merton, *Love and Living*

The word *bhakti* means "unconditional love for the Supreme Being and deep compassion for others." This love is so complete that it inspires love not only for God but for everyone and everything connected to him. In other words, bhakti is expressed in a dynamic, practical way by our loving God, showing kindness to others, and caring for the environment, knowing that it's God's sacred energy, essential to the well-being of all life. Bhakti is also the name of a path of yoga dedicated to awakening this love within us. It is not a practice exclusive to any particular religion or creed; it is the essence of all religions and creeds because it's the natural condition of the soul.

## THE HISTORY OF BHAKTI IN INDIA

Bhakti is central to India's spiritual culture, and its teachings date back to the Vedic period. But over the course of India's history, a misconceived system that discriminated against people labeled as lower caste, along with materialistic rituals, became prominent. Both the bhakti tradition, which focuses on personal devotion, and the ascetic school, which emphasizes God's aspect as Brahman, have challenged these misconceptions.

Beginning around the sixth century C.E., a bhakti revivalist movement developed around the writings of mystics who were extracting the essence of the Vedas and deemphasizing the formalities of ritual and caste. These mystics were mostly in South India, and they expressed their intimate love and longing for God through philosophy, song, and poetry. Their devotional revelations were gradually expanded on by their disciples and organized into schools of devotional yoga by scholars and saints like Ramanuja (1017–1137), Madhva (1238–1317), Nimbarka (circa eleventh century), Vallabha (1479–1531), and Chaitanya (1486–1533).

Focusing on sincerity of intent and development of character over formal ritual, these revered teachers ushered in a movement that is still growing. In the 1960s, the bhakti movement finally left India in the hands of my teacher, A.C. Bhaktivedanta Swami Prabhupada, and arrived on the shores of countries all over the world.

Still, while history provides an interesting context for the development of the bhakti movement, bhakti itself is timeless. Love for the Supreme is the eternal nature of all souls, and all religions or philosophies that strive to help their adherents awaken that love are essentially practicing bhakti.

## The Path of Love

*The most beautiful things in life cannot be seen or touched,*
*but can be felt by the heart.*
—Helen Keller

Mistaking lust for love is a serious problem for most people. In our search for love, we perceive the mirage of temporary pleasures as love's oasis. Many of us have had the experience of coming across a feeling that feels like love, but in time the thrill of it fades, and with it the feeling of love, until we're left unsatisfied, lonely, and sometimes heartbroken. Too often we try to alleviate our pain by indulging in other kinds of pleasure, burying deeper the silent plea of our heart. Just as only food can satisfy the hunger of the stomach, so only love, both giving it and accepting it, can satisfy the hunger of the heart.

Bhakti teaches us that giving and receiving love is the purpose of life. That's why every being seeks it out so relentlessly. But where does the yearning to love and be loved come from? The bhakti tradition explains that we are eternal spiritual beings with an inherent capacity for love, which originates in our personal relationship with the Supreme. In our purely spiritual existence, God is the object of our affection, and we are the objects of his. But somewhere along the way, we were cast into the drama of material experience. Weighed down by the demands, desires, and expectations that come with a material body, the soul's propensity to love is transformed into selfishness and gets derailed from its natural course.

Consider the Himalayan musk deer. The male is born with a gland that, when mature, releases one of the most treasured fragrances in the world: musk. The deer, having smelled this alluring aroma produced by its own body, roams the forest seeking its source. In this fruitless quest, the deer never realizes that what it's looking for is actually within itself. We are very much like that deer.

## THE PSYCHOLOGY OF BHAKTI

The bhakti tradition teaches that at the core of our being lies our full potential—that each of us is a perfect part of God. When we integrate this truth into our worldview, we realize that our strengths and weaknesses are of no significance when held up to the power of God's love. The power of grace is always greater than the power of illusion. The mercy of the Supreme is infinitely stronger than our egos, insecurities, and self-destructive tendencies, so it's neither helpful nor healthy to unduly castigate ourselves for our shortcomings. Rather, when we see our failings, bhakti teaches us to turn to the source of grace and then be inspired to make positive change while clearing the mind-set that is hindering spiritual awareness.

In bhakti we're invited to redefine ourselves as divine beings. Each of us has been blessed with the potential to make an invaluable contribution to God's compassionate mission. Whether our contribution is big or small in the eyes of the rest of the world has little spiritual relevance. Our unique potential lies in the sincerity of our intent to harmonize our thoughts, words, and actions with our inner selves.

Becoming aware of the self's divine nature allows us to move past the harmful habits that arise from fear, depression, and self-doubt. We rise above these propensities as we reconnect with our own miraculous potential. As they say, "Everybody is a genius. But if you judge a fish by its ability to climb a tree, it will live its whole life believing that it's stupid." We all have our special God-given talents and the capacity to be well-wishers, to love, and to be happy.

Becoming self-aware also allows us to feel compassion for others, because we come to understand that they too are souls struggling to recall their higher nature. This awareness is central to the psychology of bhakti. When we embrace it, we learn that every moment in life is perfect and sacred, and that a divine power has engineered it in some imperceptible way and woven it into the intricate tapestry of our life for our spiritual progress. We learn to trust God with humility, patience, and courage.

## A HUMBLE HEART

A humble heart is one that gives no resistance to the natural flow of grace. When we open ourselves to receiving divine grace, humility becomes effortless. This is similar to how small we feel in relation to the expanse of the ocean or when we stand before an enormous mountain. I learned this lesson from a dear friend who was in an apparently hopeless condition.

One night, feeling helpless and sad, I lay down, but sleep evaded me. Four days earlier, my good friend Shruta Kirti had called me from London to tell me that his wife, Amekhala, would likely die in the next five days. She had asked if I could be at her bedside.

I was in Mumbai at the time, and on the day I was scheduled to fly out, Iceland's volcano, Eyjafjallajökull, erupted, releasing immense amounts of ash into the sky. All the airports in Europe and North Africa were closed and all flights canceled. It was a strong reminder of the power of nature and how even a tiny island country can affect the whole world.

Several days passed, and Amekhala had only about a day to live. That night I was unable to sleep. Then a friend stopped in for a visit. Unexpectedly, he invited me to travel with him to Central Africa by private jet. When I told him of my predicament, he assured me he would do everything possible to fly me to London afterward. Despite the enormous detour, we made it to London in time. I spent a day with Amekhala and her family, and then early the next morning, she departed into the arms of her beloved Lord.

Amekhala was the mother of five children and a dynamic person who loved to serve others. In the last stages of her life, crippled and emaciated by her cancer, she graciously accepted her fate as God's will. She expressed an understanding of what looked like her diminishment in the face of what she had once been, and then with a smile, added, "But still, I have infinite relevance. Why? Because Krishna loves me. Nothing can take that away. Actually we all have infinite importance, because God loves each of us."

These simple words perfectly capture the essence of volumes of scriptures. God loves each of us. Whoever we are or are not, whatever we've done or not done, nothing can change this one eternal truth: the Supreme loves us unconditionally and eternally. To access that love, we need only be grateful for and reciprocate with his love by living in harmony with his will. Amekhala lived this truth with dignity, and through her words she demonstrated how others could practice it too.

It is natural for people to ask, "If God loves someone, why is that person subject to terrible disease or immense pain?" I address this question later in this book, but in essence, material suffering can take place only on the outer layers of the body and mind; it cannot touch the soul. The body and mind are vulnerable to the ever-changing nature of the world and the laws by which it operates. The Lord may intervene with the physical challenges of a devotee who turns to him. However, as Amekhala teaches us, even if pain or struggle persists, it can be an impetus to readjust our values, seek shelter of a higher power, and reconnect us to the joys of the soul, where true love awaits.

## FINDING HOPE: THE TREE OF LIFE

In 2013, I went to Bahrain to speak at a meeting of the Young Presidents' Organization. My hosts, Ahmed and Lamis, took me to see a national landmark called the Tree of Life, one of the seven natural wonders of the modern world. The tree stands on a hill in the Arabian Desert surrounded by miles of sand. There is not another tree as far as the eye can see; there's actually no life at all in that vast, arid desert. The average temperature in the region is 105° Fahrenheit, often soaring to 120°, and bone-stripping sandstorms are common. How does the tree survive?

No one is certain. Scientists have speculated that the nearest possible source of water is an underground stream about two miles away and that the tree is somehow drawing water from that stream. Others say the tree has learned to extract moisture from breezes blowing in from the Persian Gulf or squeeze moisture from grains of sand. Others claim that the tree is standing in what was once the Garden of Eden, and so has a more mystical source of water.

Whatever the reason, the Tree of Life is more than four hundred years old, thirty-two feet high, and abundantly covered in green leaves. As I sat in its shade against its wide trunk, I meditated on how this tree represents our willpower. If we can tap into our willpower, we'll be inspired to thrive even in apparently impossible situations. The Tree of Life represents hope—a hope beyond logic. Hope can nourish, sustain, and inspire us to grow even in challenging circumstances. From a devotional perspective, the Tree of Life represents faith in a power beyond this world—the power of the Supreme's love for us.

The Tree of Life stands alone. Somehow, against all odds, it finds water in the desert and has been doing so for centuries. And the tree's growth is not stunted. It reaches into the heavens and offers its shade to any who sit beneath it.

## MAKING FRIENDS WITH THE THORNS: MOTHER OF THE ORPHANS

In Mumbai in 2012, the International Women's Day event was a significant occasion considering the recent horrific rape cases in India and the mass public demonstrations against such abuse. The keynote speaker was Sindhutai Sapkal, a sixty-three-year-old woman. She was dressed simply, in a traditional village sari. Her story brought the assembly to tears.

Sindhutai had been raised in poverty in the state of Maharashtra. At age six, she had longed to go to school, but her parents needed her to care for their small herd of water buffaloes. Every day she would herd the large animals with a stick, eventually taking them to cool off in a nearby pond. The buffaloes would submerge themselves up to the neck, and Sindhutai would escape for a few hours of schooling. Because she always arrived late, her teacher beat her. While she was at school, the water buffaloes often wandered onto others' property, and those farmers would also beat her. Still, she said, these were the best years of her childhood.

Her childhood was over when she was ten years old and was forced to marry a thirty-year-old man. By twenty, she had three sons and was pregnant with a fourth child. Over time, she learned that a local member of the mafia was exploiting villagers, especially women, by forcing them to work as slaves. Sindhutai reported this to the district collector. Furious, the criminal told Sindhutai's husband a lie: Sindhutai was cheating on him. He claimed she was even having a secret affair with *himself*. In fact, he said, the child she was carrying was not her husband's but his. Infuriated, Sindhutai's husband kicked his wife in the stomach over and over again until she lost consciousness. Thinking she was dead, he dragged her into a cowshed so the neighbors would assume she had been trampled to death.

But one of the cows took pity on her and stood over her to protect her from danger. The cowshed was overcrowded, but this cow didn't allow either animals or humans near Sindhutai, and under that cow, Sindhutai gave birth to a daughter. She cut the umbilical cord with a sharp-edged rock. The selfless compassion of the cow had saved her life. Sindhutai embraced the cow and promised she would dedicate her life to helping the helpless.

Sindhutai decided to return to her parents' home with her baby, but according to village tradition, a daughter cannot return home after moving into her husband's home at marriage. Her parents rejected her. Afraid to be alone and vulnerable to rape and other types of abuse, Sindhutai spent her nights at a riverside cremato-rium, where corpses were burned under an open sky. Because peo-ple thought the place haunted, no one bothered her there. At times, desperate with hunger, she gathered what little wheat flour she had, mixed it with water, and cooked it on top of burning human corpses.

Sindhutai contemplated suicide regularly. Late one night she resolved to throw herself and her baby in front of a moving train. As she prepared to do the unthinkable, she heard an agonized groan. She followed the noise and found a dying man begging for food and water. At that moment, she said, she heard through that man's cry the voice of God calling her to help the helpless as she had promised. She realized that instead of killing herself, she could infuse her life with meaning.

But broken as she was, what could she do? Sindhutai sat under a tree in a field to think about this. When she looked up, she saw a branch that had been brutally chopped by a woodsman hanging from the trunk by a splinter. She realized that despite the harm that had been done to the tree's body, the branch was shading her and her baby from the scorching sun. It was then that she discovered her calling: she would become a mother to homeless, orphaned children. She began to collect them around her. To feed them, she sang and begged for money on railway platforms. She protected them while they slept in whatever place they could find that was relatively safe.

In time, as the number of children grew, pious people arranged to build her a simple structure where she could keep the children safer. She became known as "mother of the orphans." She strove to give them love, care, and an education, all things she'd been denied. Over the years, she mothered over a thousand orphans. Many of them now lead successful lives as doctors, lawyers, teachers, farmers, and engineers.

As people came to know of her work, her biological sons left their father and came to live with her. Today, two of them have earned doctorates, and Sindhutai has received more than 270 awards and been invited to speak in fifteen countries.

Overcome with emotion at the International Women's Day event, Sindhutai told the captivated audience about her most meaningful accomplishment. Decades after she had been beaten and abandoned, a homeless, sickly, eighty-year-old man asked her for help. She recognized him: her merciless husband. He asked her forgiveness and she forgave him. She also gave him shelter in the orphanage, not as his wife but as a mother. She told her many children to "give him your love; he needs it the most." When visitors come, she now introduces him as her eldest son and sometimes adds, "He's a very naughty son, indeed."

Much like the Tree of Life, Sindhutai's life reminds us never to lose hope even in the darkest times. "When difficulties come," she says, "we should stand and rise above them so they look small. Don't be afraid to go ahead and fight."

"This was my life," she concludes. "My path was full of thorns, so I made friends with those thorns, and my life became simple and beautiful."

I first met Sindhutai in 2013, about a year after I had heard her story. We joyfully shared our realizations. She told me she had discovered the magic in her life when, like her own helpless baby, she had cried for God's grace. Just as I got up to leave at the conclusion of our conversation, Sindhutai turned my attention to the beaming, energetic young woman sitting quietly beside her. "This is one of my daughters," she said. "She's become a medical doctor and now oversees one of the orphanages." With a teary smile, Sindhutai added, "She was the one born that day under the cow."

# SELFLESS LOVE

Whether we hear about acts of self-sacrifice in real-life accounts like Sindhutai's or in the lives of fictional characters, these stories touch us at the deepest level. They show us that people are inherently decent and beautiful, and they inspire us to become better people ourselves. In the words of Dr. Martin Luther King Jr., "Darkness cannot drive out darkness; only light can do that. Hate cannot drive out hate; only love can do that." The practice of bhakti yoga can help you uncover the light.

Love is selfless when it's given simply to please another without any expectation of return. In selfless love we consider our own risk, loss, or inconvenience secondary, if we consider them at all. Selfless love is offered in a spirit of gratitude, enthusiasm, and courage. It gives one the kind of inner satisfaction that makes all selfish pleasures pale by comparison.

In bhakti, the goal is to connect with the origin of selfless love, the love between the Supreme Soul and the individual soul. Once we've made that connection, the love extends naturally outward toward other souls. The bhakti path has countless examples of this expanded expression of love. One is the story of Hladini (Linda Jury).

# BEAUTY WITHIN TRAGEDY

Linda Jury was born in 1949 to middle-class parents of European descent and brought up in the suburbs of Detroit. In 1969 she found her calling in the practice of bhakti yoga and accepted the name Hladini Dasi ("servant of God's compassionate energy"). In the early 1970s, she moved to an old, isolated farmhouse in a small community in the Appalachian Mountains, where she gave her full heart to serving the Supreme by making offerings on a simple altar. This made her incredibly focused and happy, and her bliss was contagious. People who knew her then say that she always had a radiant smile that seemed to beam out from the beauty of her soul. Despite the austere conditions of that farmhouse, she never complained and never seemed to find time to criticize others. Envy and sectarianism seemed foreign to her awareness.

Everyone around her saw that her relationship with God was deeply personal. She loved and served Krishna with the intimacy of a mother for her child. Each day, she cut wood, drew water from a well, and cooked meals over a wood fire. She offered the food on her altar and then to everyone who came. However busy she was, she always found time to help anyone who needed her. Through all this, she spent hours every day absorbed in meditation on God's names, studying scriptures, and singing Krishna's praises.

I first met Hladini in 1972. We had accepted the same guru, Prabhupada, and she and I were doing the same types of services, she in her farmhouse and me in an ashram for monks on another remote mountain. Through occasional letters, she shared with me her many inspirations.

In 1979 I left my mountaintop ashram and began lecturing at American universities and colleges, gradually helping to form devotional communities in Ohio and western Pennsylvania. Meanwhile, like an erupting volcano, Hladini could no longer contain the love and joy that filled her life; she longed to share it with others, so she too left her mountain and we often served together. She was magical. Her enthusiasm and gentle compassion conquered the hearts of the people with whom she connected. She loved Krishna in such a sweet, simple way that even people who had no idea who Krishna was or what bhakti was about never wanted to leave her side. I saw many times that when she saw someone connect to the joy of God's grace, she would, from a little distance, beam a radiant smile and cry tears of happiness.

Hladini took her first pilgrimage to the holy places in India in the late 1980s. At that time I was living in India. We traveled together with a few friends to Vrindavan, a holy site for devotees of Krishna. At each sacred place we visited, she seemed to be in trance. After almost twenty years of devotional service, she was thrilled to finally see the places she had been meditating on every day. She rarely spoke on that pilgrimage, but a number of times, struggling to contain her emotions, she said, simply, "I am so grateful."

Back in the United States she heard from our spiritual brother, Bhakti Tirtha Swami, about the suffering of the people in West Africa. To many people's surprise, she decided to go there to help. Soon after her arrival, she was being interviewed by television stations and on the radio and meeting heads of state. But she spent much of her time in the tribal villages, serving the people, teaching them, and inspiring them to chant God's names. She was especially fond of dancing with the village children. In a photo she sent me of herself with a crowd of these people, I saw the same spontaneous smiles on the villagers' faces as I used to see on the American students and families she had touched.

A saint once said that where there is the greatest necessity, there is the greatest opportunity to serve. Hladini chose to live in Liberia just when the country was being torn apart by a bloody civil war. Bloodshed and death were everywhere, and eventually over 200,000 civilians were killed. In Monrovia, the capital, where Hladini lived, a third of the people were homeless, and there was mass starvation. Hladini cooked and served meals to the people and helped them find happiness in God's love even in the midst of such disaster. The desperate people loved her as a mother and saint. Even the savage warlords honored her.

When the U.S. Marines ordered all American citizens to evacuate Liberia and sent a fleet of ships to remove them from the war-zone, Hladini chose to stay. She later wrote to me that she was not afraid of dying; she only feared offending those who love God.

One naive devotee from another place sent Prince Johnson, the leader of the violent coup, a letter asking him to stop the needless killing. Insanely furious, Johnson and his military stormed Hladini's residence late at night and at gunpoint rounded up Hladini and her African students. The group was driven to the bank of a nearby river and lined up to be shot. But then Johnson released Hladini and another woman, saying he would kill only the men. The women were free to go. Johnson was surrounded by aides holding machine guns.

As he raised his pistol to murder the five men one by one, Hladini knew she could not bear to see her students massacred. She ran over to Johnson and grabbed the arm that held his gun, crying, "Do not kill these innocent devotees!" She knew she didn't have a chance, but she chose to die rather than do nothing while others were harmed. Bullets filled the body of that gentle, loving woman while she struggled with him to make him stop. She lay on the ground with the names of her beloved Lord on her lips and departed for her eternal home.

The young woman who was released with Hladini saw everything and later told one of my friends what had happened. Hladini knew that as an eternal soul, she was beyond the frailties of her body, and she was willing to give up her life to serve those who needed her. She was not given any medals or celebrated as a hero — not in Africa and not in the United States. And she wouldn't have wanted that. She wanted only to be able to serve. I can still almost hear her saying, "I am so grateful."

Few of us will experience the kinds of cruelty persons like Sindhutai and Hladini did. Their lives are extreme examples of people who faced the crucible of compassion. We may never be put to such tests, but we can still learn from their examples.

Hladini lay down her physical life not only for five African students but for all humanity. She embraced her ideals and lived a life of compassion rather than a life centered on personal concerns. And she felt intimately connected with God when she did. God's ways are mysterious indeed. We often do not see the larger picture and are baffled by apparent injustice.

Hladini was naturally blissful. She loved her life in this world and the world she was already beginning to live in beyond this one. What she did at those last moments of her life was natural for her, and I think if she were faced with the same choice today, she would do it again, because she truly did love God with all her heart, soul, strength, and mind and her neighbors as her self.

No one is suggesting that we imitate people like Hladini. But in our own lives, at home, in the workplace, and in our social and spiritual circles, we can practice bhakti, or pure love, as our highest ideal and live that ideal as honestly as we can. Hladini would consider it the glory of her life if even one of us were to do so.

## Love Conquers the Beloved

Bhakti yoga culminates in loving service to God unmotivated by desires for personal enjoyment or the miraculous powers some types of yoga promise, or even freedom from suffering. Rather, true bhakti is motivated by the desire to please the Supreme Beloved through loving service. All other material and spiritual goals are contained within the pure love of God, just as the desire to have a hundred dollars or even a thousand is satisfied when one has a million.

The Vedas are filled with examples of people from all walks of life who have realized this love. For example, Hanuman was a powerful warrior who leaped over oceans and single-handedly conquered the capital of the empire of an evil tyrant, all in the service of the one God, who appeared as Rama. Indebted, Lord Rama, the proprietor of all that exists, confessed, "I have no way to repay your love. I can only give you myself." With these words he embraced Hanuman.

Similarly, the cowherd girls (*gopis*) of Vrindavan were simple village girls who loved Krishna. They cooked, cared for their families, wove flower garlands, milked their cows, and sang and danced, all in a deep, unwavering meditation on giving Krishna pleasure. Like Rama, Lord Krishna confessed that he could not repay them for such dedicated love. He said, "I can only ask you to be satisfied with the love itself, because there is nothing else that can compare to it."

Although Hanuman was a hero in Rama's army and the gopis were village girls, they all were absorbed in remembering their beloved Lord, singing his glories, and personally offering whatever they did for his pleasure.

As you may enjoy being swept away by the one you truly love, the bhakti texts tell us that the Supreme enjoys being overwhelmed by the love of each of his pure-hearted devotees. This love is within all of us. Bhakti teaches us how to interact with the world through the strength of this love. When our love for the Divine begins to awaken, it illumines every aspect of our lives: the roles we play in family and society, our routines, our responsibilities, and our relationships.

PART II

*Living
Spiritually in
a Material
World*

# Distinguishing Reality from Illusion

*The manifestation of the world is not accepted as false; it is accepted as
real but temporary. This material manifestation takes place at a certain
interval, stays for a while, and then disappears.*

—PRABHUPADA, *BHAGAVAD-GITA AS IT IS*

In 1966, some of Prabhupada's followers took him for a walk
around New York City. They got lost and unintentionally led
him into a filthy slum in the Bowery, where rats scampered and the
streets were strewn with trash. When one of his companions, feeling remorseful, apologized, Prabhupada replied, "Don't be sorry.
Can't you see? Beyond this temporary appearance, it is the spiritual
world, but you don't have the eyes to see it yet." Embedded within
Prabhupada's words of encouragement to a student is a timeless
philosophical truth.

Learning to look at the world with spiritualized eyes is something
most spiritual paths teach. Like anything else, there are different
levels to spiritual vision. Bhakti yogis focus on a spiritual vision that
is infused with love of God. Later in this book, we explore some

specific practices that can help foster such vision, but first I elaborate on the spiritual qualities inherent in the material world.

## DISTINGUISHING THE DREAM FROM REALITY

Some schools of philosophy propose that the world does not exist—that it's an illusion, a dream we'll one day wake up from. But the bhakti school has another perspective: it considers both the soul and the world around it, both real and divine—the created energy of the Supreme. Because the world is temporary, we might call our experience of it dream*like*. Actually, the dream is just that we, the eternal soul, think we are matter when we live only in matter. We also don't realize that while we're in this temporary world, we have the opportunity to free ourselves from suffering and instead live lives of peace and love.

When the sun of the truth rises in our consciousness, there's no place for darkness and no fear. When it's dark, we can't see where we're walking; in the light of day, however, we can clearly see the path.

Why does this matter? Because recklessly applied, the world-is-an-illusion philosophy can make us irresponsible toward our home on earth. Why take care of the environment if the world isn't real? Although bhakti yogis hope to transcend the material world altogether one day, they also feel the sacredness of the earth and a sense of stewardship for what the Supreme has entrusted to them. So bhakti yoga encourages people to have a responsible social conscience.

Let's take a closer look at the "dream" philosophy from the bhakti perspective. Say you're dreaming that you're running from a tiger. You freeze for a moment, and then no matter how hard you try to pump your legs, you can't move them fast enough. It's as if you're wading through mud. The tiger closes in. The dream feels so real that you begin to sweat as you toss in your bed and your heart races.

And then you wake up. It was only a dream. Was it real?

Yes and no. It was real in the sense that it happened: you experienced it. Still, it was also an illusion. The illusion lies in the fact that you identified with the person in the dream, but it wasn't you. It was a person created by your mind. In dreams, you usually forget who you are and identify with a dream self.

Bhakti yogis think even temporary reality deserves attention because it reflects a permanent reality somewhere else. Putting the dream aside for a moment, it's true that you exist and so do tigers. Like the dream, the material world is real. But when we forget our real spiritual identity, we fall into an illusory perception of it. Self-realization includes understanding our relationship with this ever-changing temporary world.

One of my students, an airline pilot, explained to me how pilots in training use flight simulators—machines so sophisticated that they immerse the trainee in the sights, sounds, and physical movements of a real airplane. A successful performance in this virtual realty machine helps the student gain the status of a pilot. This is similar to how the soul lives in the material world. Although the soul is distinct from matter, while living within the "virtual reality" of this world, we have the experience of being matter, and so we try to navigate ways to be happy and avoid pain. Yet in this material world, we have the opportunity to apply enlightened principles to all aspects of our lives and thus prepare ourselves for the ultimate enlightened state.

When we live our lives with devotion, this world becomes a virtual reality version of the spiritual world. To the bhakti yogi, the world is sacred, and service to the Supreme in this world is no different from service to the Supreme in the enlightened realm: it is service offered with love that matters, not where that service is performed. A successful performance here earns us enlightenment.

The Gita helps us further understand the soul's predicament in the material world:

*It is said that there is an imperishable banyan tree that has its roots upward and its branches down. The real form of this tree cannot be perceived in this world—but with determination one must cut down this strongly rooted tree with the weapon of detachment and then seek that place from which one never returns.*
—BHAGAVAD GITA 15.1, 3–4

Where can we see an upside-down tree, with its roots up and branches down? When a tree is by the side of a lake, its reflection appears upside-down. The reflection is not the tree, but it couldn't exist without it. The Gita uses this example to show how material pleasure is a mere reflection of spiritual fulfillment. The Gita tells us that everything in this world has its original, perfect counterpart in spiritual existence.

From another perspective, the banyan is an amazing tree: immense, with roots and branches so intertwined that it's difficult to say where one part ends and another begins. Our situation in the material world is like that too: complex, difficult to untangle, with up looking like down and down like up. We wander all over this tree of the world, from one branch to another, birth after birth, without end.

Still, despite its seemingly chaotic and entangling nature, the world around us operates according to laws that can be understood.

Understanding these laws enables us to live undisturbed under their jurisdiction and achieve the clarity of mind needed to view every situation as an opportunity to progress toward self-realization.

## WHAT'S THE PURPOSE OF THIS WORLD?

*Because of indifference to the Supreme Being,*
*the living entity becomes covered by illusion in the form*
*of the conception that he too is the Supreme Master.*
— BHAKTIVINODE THAKUR, *SRI AMNAYA SUTRA*

The atma, or soul, shares the Supreme Being's qualities in minute quantity. One of those qualities is independence. The soul yearns for love—ultimately for a loving relationship between itself and its source. But for love to be a perfect offering, one has to have the freedom *not* to love. That's true in our relationships with one another as well as with God. Some souls choose to turn away from the Supreme, the reservoir of infinite love, and experiment with a life independent of him. This material world accommodates that choice.

And here again is the "illusion" part of this world. To carry out this experiment, the soul has to forget it's true self, which is naturally in a loving service relationship with the Supreme Person; it has to assume another identity.

In this dreamlike state the soul forgets that there is only one Supreme Beloved who is the center of every soul's existence. All souls by nature orbit around him, some from near and others from far away. The material world allows us the pretense of stepping out of our natural orbit and making ourselves the center. When we try to take the Supreme Beloved's place, though—when we try to become the proprietor, enjoyer, and controller of material resources—we find ourselves clashing with others who want to see themselves in the same way. Conflict and unhappiness inevitably follow.

Of course, none of this unnatural role-playing is sustainable. The world then fulfills another function: through the laws of cause and effect (karma) and under time's influence, we are pushed to ask ourselves why we are unhappy and how we can rise above the fleeting pleasures and pains of material life. Such questions inspire us to seek knowledge. Those among us who have followed knowledge to its source are those we call "enlightened."

The enlightened appear to do the same things others do, but their focus is different. They are back in orbit, so to speak, so are naturally filled with love for the Supreme and his children. They are no longer working in the shadow of illusion but see the spirit in everything, including this world.

## THE PARADOX OF PLEASURE

In our quest for fulfillment, we generally want the world to operate according to our desires, but the world doesn't always move that way. This is nature's way of nudging us back to our natural state. Here is a simple story to illustrate how the world rarely follows our dictates, for our pleasure.

One summer I visited Venice, Italy, with a few hundred students and friends. The region was suffering a record-breaking heat wave that had destroyed crops in rural areas and even killed several people.

Early one evening, after giving an outdoor lecture and then having congregational chanting in the Piazza San Marco, we took a ferry to a nearby island to cool off in the sea. By that time, the oppressive heat had beaten us down. After we got off the boat and walked almost an hour in the heat, we finally reached what looked like a lifesaving oasis: a long, wide stretch of fine sand with an invigorating breeze and moonbeams dancing enticingly on the sea's gentle waves. We could hardly wait to jump in. And it was worth it. The water was refreshingly cool, the perfect temperature for washing away our fatigue.

Then suddenly there was a scream, and then another and another. Within seconds almost everyone was screaming. I heard, "Medusa! Medusa!" I didn't understand the word until a burning sting translated it for me. The area was infested with jellyfish. Some of us splashed quickly to shore, while others decided to brave the stings so they could stay in the cooling waters.

I wasn't one of those who remained in the water. I returned to the oppressive heat of the beach having learned a valuable lesson: material joy may seem thrilling at times, the perfect relief to the struggles and worries of daily life, but we often fail to see what lies beneath the surface. In the sea of material nature, just below the surface of apparent pleasure, swim all sorts of jellyfish with stinging tentacles.

## SEEING THE WORLD WITH SPIRITUAL VISION

While living in the material world, it's not that having spiritual vision will save you from the physical strains of hunger or thirst or financial need or the heat and cold of changing seasons. Practicing bhakti doesn't eliminate the jellyfish. But bhakti practice helps develop a different perspective on those jellyfish. It's natural to want to seek the cool waters and avoid the jellyfish stings, but as much as we try to avoid it, we still get stung sometimes. When you practice bhakti, however, you begin to learn to see those jellyfish stings for what they are: catalysts for growth.

Whatever happiness we may know in this world, it is never complete and it never lasts. This is a universal truth. Even the happiest life is interrupted by death. When unhappiness drives someone to introspection and to doubt the value of his or her imperfect happiness, the question arises: Is there something more than this?

The material world is inherently sacred because it is part of the energy of the Supreme Person. It is also sacred because it's filled with limitless opportunities for liberation or, if we choose, for distraction. According to the Bhagavad Gita, it's a crucial element of knowledge to be conscious of the material truths of birth, old age, disease, and death. Yet along with this apparently gloomy warning comes a bright promise:

*When the embodied beings are able to transcend these three modes [tamas, rajas, and sattva] associated with the material body, they can become free from birth, death, old age, and their distresses and can enjoy nectar even in this life.*
—BHAGAVAD GITA 14.20

# Practicing the Dharma of Bhakti

*For one who sees me everywhere and sees everything in me,*
*I am never lost, nor is he ever lost to me.*
—BHAGAVAD GITA 6.30

*D*harma comes from the Sanskrit root *ðhri*, meaning "to hold, maintain, or keep," and by extension, in its noun form, "that which cannot be taken away [because it is firmly part of something]." Think of dharma as a thing's inherent quality—that part of something that cannot be separated from it: the heat in fire or the sweetness in sugar, for example. If we want to follow knowledge to its source and pursue spiritual enlightenment, understanding the meaning and practice of dharma is invaluable.

Bhakti yoga teaches that the dharma of every living being is *ðeva*, or loving service. This means that loving service is the essential nature of the soul. Practicing bhakti yoga is about honoring the soul's dharma and focusing on transforming material actions into spiritual ones. Imagine two people studying or cooking or paying bills or painting. One person is acting in harmony with the true self, trying to please God, and the other for some selfish, material purpose. From the outside, the results may appear to be the same, but these two sets of actions are actually generating different outcomes. One person is becoming progressively free from the pull of matter on the path to liberation, and the other is sowing the karmic seeds of his or her bondage to temporary pleasures and pains.

What determines whether an action is spiritual or material? The consciousness, or intention, behind it. For example, a knife is good in the hands of a surgeon and bad in the hands of a murderer. Morphine is good in the hands of a hospice nurse and bad in the hands of a drug dealer. Everything in the material nature can be used for good or bad or, in a higher sense, for spiritual growth or material entanglement, and we choose how to use things based on what we want to gain from life.

Bhakti yogis try to see the world through a spiritual lens and to perceive even material objects in ways that relate to the Supreme, and then they try to use those material things according to that relationship.

Once a student asked my teacher, "How can we see God in material things?"

Prabhupada replied, "When you see my eyeglasses on the table, what do you see?"

"Well," the student said, "these are my guru's glasses, so seeing them makes me remember how much I love you."

Prabhupada smiled. "As you develop love for God, you will gradually come to see everything as his property, and in being reminded of him you will feel great love for him."

Odd as it may seem, our freedom from this world begins with our developing the eyes to see this world as it really is. By learning to love and serve God while living in this world, we transcend illusion. Through our love for God, we will celebrate the joy of that love and naturally serve with compassion those who are suffering. Beyond material existence is our original home, the spiritual world, where in the light of infinite love, the darkness of suffering and illusion cannot exist.

## SEE THE WORLD WITH COMPASSION, THE HIGHEST EXPRESSION OF DHARMA

*It is said that great personalities almost always accept voluntary inconvenience because of the suffering of people in general. This is considered the highest method of worshiping the Supreme Soul, who is present in everyone's heart.*
— BHAGAVATA PURANA 8.7.44

Our spiritual progress is directly connected to how we help others make progress. In an age when it seems impossible to disconnect from matter, many holy people strive to detach themselves from their role playing (called, in Sanskrit, *ahankara*, or false ego) simply to be better able to give themselves to help others.

The *Yoga Sutras* of Patanjali call this ahimsa, "nonviolence," which means more than just not harming other beings; it also means to act positively: to be kind, to love others, to want their spiritual and material well-being, to be compassionate. If we can sacrifice even a part of our comforts to show compassion to others, we enrich our lives.

The most essential form of service to others is to enlighten them with the joy of realizing their true self. My spiritual teacher touched many people's hearts in this way by his personal example. In 1965, at the age of sixty-nine, Prabhupada left India to bring the teachings of bhakti to the West. He was given a free ticket on a weather-beaten cargo ship that sailed for thirty-eight days from Calcutta to New York. While crossing the Arabian Sea he suffered severe seasickness and two heart attacks. There were no doctors or medical facilities onboard. When he arrived on U.S. shores, he thanked the Lord for seeing him through the journey and wrote in a prayer, "As your puppet, my Lord, make me dance as you want me to dance."

When he arrived in New York, he was penniless and alone. He lived in the Bowery, in New York City, which at that time was occupied by homeless people beaten down into lives of alcoholism, drug addiction, and crime. While there, he was robbed, evicted, and physically threatened. Why did a scholarly saint from India leave his home in a beautiful holy place for this? It's because even from India, he felt our suffering. He endured these hardships so he could share the gift of spiritual love with us. Such compassion, according to the *Bhagavata Purana* and almost all other scriptures, is the highest expression of dharma. This is especially true when compassion extends, according to one's ability, beyond service to humanity and includes all living beings, who may love life just as we do.

## A SIMPLE FORM OF AHIMSA

Mahatma Gandhi said, "The greatness of a nation and its moral progress can be judged by the way its animals are treated." According to the Vedas, nonviolence should extend beyond our relationships with other human beings to include all living creatures. There is a Sanskrit phrase, *para duhkha duhkhi*, which means "empathy": to feel pain when others suffer and joy when they're happy. Empathy is a quality of any evolved human being, but interestingly, it's not absent in animals. Once when I was in Udupi, South India, I was deeply affected by the empathy in a dog.

Udupi is lush with coconut trees that sway at even the touch of the ocean breeze. Green agricultural fields reach out to the horizon in every direction. You can see teams of black, curve-horned water buffalo and pure white oxen bound together with wooden yokes. The steel plows they pull are gripped from behind by wiry, barefoot farmers with cotton *lungis* wrapped around their waists.

The one-story homes are made from the red stone blocks local to the area and black-stained logs. The roofs are tiled orange or thatched with straw. Beside each home is a small, man-made *pukkur* (pond), where families bathe and do laundry and pull water for cleaning their homes. In each pond, water buffalo often wade up to their necks, seeking relief from the heat.

Each cluster of families shares a community well, and the well is invariably the gathering place of the village women in their colorful red, blue, and yellow saris. They draw water with wooden buckets and then pour it into clay pots, which they carry with perfect grace on their heads.

The seaside is a paradise, with its miles of soft sand. The beach rolls down hundreds of yards to the shore, where high waves break and create a symphony of sound. Under the blazing sun, fishermen in simple wooden rowboats spend the day casting nets into the Arabian Sea.

Not far from here, I spent a month at an Ayurvedic health clinic. Part of my treatment was to take a long daily walk through the countryside. I lived in one of the few two-story houses in the area. It was on a dirt road, not far from the railway track. On that same road lived a mother dog and her four puppies. My neighbor told me that two of the puppies had been crushed under the tires of moving cars in the past week. No one had bothered to stop for a puppy in the road. Both times the woman living next door had buried the dead puppy — only a mother can fully understand the loss of another mother. The woman told me she had tried again and again to take the family of dogs in, but almost all dogs in India are street dogs, and the mother kept returning to her roadside existence.

This mother dog, a mutt with beige fur, clearly grieved the deaths of her children. Day and night she guarded her two surviving puppies as they romped in the nearby fields or slept near her side.

One of the puppies, a furry ball of energy, became obsessed with digging himself a hole on the side of the road. It took him two weeks, scratching away, to create a hole that satisfied him. Every once in a while his mother would clean him with gentle licks or nurse him and his brother with her milk. When the hole was finally complete, the puppy curled up inside it and went to sleep. Whenever he wasn't playing, I could see him curled up in that hole.

One morning as I was returning from a walk along the railway track, about twenty yards ahead I saw an SUV turn onto the dirt road where I was living. Someone had parked a motorbike in the center of the road. To avoid it, the SUV veered off to the side. Its right front tire sank into what appeared to be a pothole, but even from where I was, I heard the piteous cry. It was the puppy. A moment later the rear tire sank into the same hole. This time there was silence. And then the SUV was gone. The mother dog began to howl in her anguish, and I hastened to the site.

The mother dog was frantically licking her baby, whimpering in what I could only understand as the language of her heart. The crushed puppy flapped his front legs a little, and blood flowed from his nostrils and mouth.

I sat in the dirt beside him and chanted the names of Krishna to him in hopes that he would receive a last blessing. There was nothing else I could do. The Bhagavad Gita states that one who remembers the Supreme Lord at the moment of death will attain the spiritual abode. The name of the Supreme Being is endowed with his divine presence, so it is considered the greatest act of love one can offer to a dying being to let that soul hear the holy name.

I think the mother dog understood that I cared about her puppy, and she sat silently while I chanted. For those few minutes, her puppy remained still, twitching weakly. Ten minutes later, the puppy moved his paws for the last time and was gone.

His mother breathed a soft, piteous whimper. I will never forget the sound of her broken heart. She gazed into my eyes helplessly. I patted her as she cried tears without sound.

Then I walked away so that she could take care of her puppy's body. She stood over the little hole and licked him again and again. It was as though she was trying to lick life back into his corpse. Her sole surviving puppy stood to the side of the hole and howled in anguish. Six hours later, she was still licking and crying. I sent a message to the neighbor asking her to bury the dead puppy, and eventually the woman was able to take him away from his mother. The hole the puppy had dug remained, and neither the puppy's mother nor his brother seemed able to leave it. It was well past midnight before there was silence. When I looked down at the street from my balcony, I saw both dogs still sniffing the hole. Every now and then, the mother would walk away and then run back to it.

That mother dog may not have had human intelligence, but it was clear she had both feelings and affection and that she suffered in ways similar to how we humans suffer. Why were her piteous cries so personal? I believe it is because she was a life-loving person.

I saw this same emotion when I took care of cows and goats at my mountain monastery in the United States. I often watched the tender affection shared between a mother and her calf. I also saw joy in the cows, bulls, and goats when, after a long winter, they would frolic in the fresh spring grass. I heard them express pain when they were wounded by thorns or feeling ill. Why are there laws against cruelty to pets, yet we are willing to send millions of cows, goats, lambs, pigs, chickens, ducks, and other animals to be tortured and slaughtered every day without a thought? Perhaps we have much to learn from the puppy and his mother's love.

## COMPASSIONATE EATING

Wherever there is life, the soul is present, and the soul is a part of the Supreme Soul. Species other than humans may not share the same type of intellect as humans, but all sentient beings feel; that is, after all, what it means to be sentient. In their own ways and according to whatever body they inhabit, they enjoy and they suffer as we do. They also cherish their lives and in the case of many species, especially the ones we tend to eat, the lives of their offspring too.

As the most developed of all forms of life, humans are meant to be caretakers of the environment and the world's other living beings. Understanding and practicing this principle is ahimsa—not just nonviolence but empathy and compassion—and it is a basic tenet in Patanjali's *Yoga Sutras*, sacred to the Bodhisattva dharma of Buddhism, and inherent within the Golden Rule of the Judeo-Christian faiths. It is also prominent in bhakti teachings. To be genuinely compassionate, to feel another's suffering as your own, to make the serious, lifelong attempt, as far as possible, not to inflict pain on any living being, directly or indirectly, through our actions, words, or thoughts, is ahimsa.

The principle of ahimsa underscores the importance of a compassionate diet. The unnecessary suffering caused by killing animals for food is not only heartbreaking but creates serious negative karma for those associated with the killing, and on a collective scale, it affects almost everyone in the world due to its widespread effects. So in the spirit of compassion, bhakti practice encourages a vegetarian diet. As our consciousness expands, it's natural that we become more sensitive to how we honor our relationships with other life-loving beings. The higher our ideals are and the more we're willing to live by them, the more meaningful and fulfilling our lives become.

## THE DHARMA OF EATING

One may ask, "Since plants also feel pain when we eat them, how is consuming vegetarian food less violent than nonvegetarian food?"

The spirit of ahimsa is to consciously minimize pain to others. An animal, bird, or fish will fight for its life and feel fear and pain much the way we do because it has a central nervous system similar to our own. The psychological and physiological makeup of species on the lower level of the food chain, such as plants, is such that they have extremely undeveloped senses and nervous systems and therefore a minimal awareness of pain. Ahimsa means to avoid causing even those beings pain as far as realistic. But by the law of nature, we have to eat to survive. Our diet should be as compassionate as possible.

Instinctively, we know the difference between harvesting plants and killing animals. Just compare the natural, invigorating scene of harvesting a wheat field or vegetable garden to the screams of horror, the morbid stench, and the pooling blood at a slaughterhouse. Still, it's true that killing plants is also an act of violence.

What can we do? The world is made in such a way that it's not possible to be 100 percent nonviolent. So the Vedas tell us that when we offer to the Supreme, with devotion, foods low on the food chain such as grains, vegetables, and fruits, the souls in those plants are propelled forward in their spiritual evolution because they become infused with the devotional intent of the offering and the blessings of the Supreme Person who receives them. Vegetarian foods are in the mode of goodness, and when they are prepared and offered with love, they are freed of all karmic reactions. They nourish us physically and spiritually.

Most children naturally love animals. Perhaps they relate better to animals than to complicated adults. When I was small, my friends and I were in love with cartoon animals like Donald Duck and Mickey Mouse, and we loved our pets too. My younger brother, Larry, had a turtle named Lucky. When Lucky died, my brother cried for days.

I wonder what would happen if we showed our children the horrors of the slaughterhouse. I also wonder whether afterward, many of them would still choose to eat meat. We program our children to eat meat as if it grows on supermarket shelves. By the time they are old enough to make the connection between live animals and what's on their plates, they're so culturally habituated to their diet that they rarely question its acceptability. Most people are good at heart, but from birth, they are inundated by advertisements to think of animals as food. They never learn to consider the suffering of those animals.

In my memoir, *The Journey Home*, I tell of the first time I made the connection between meat and the life-loving animals that die so we can eat them. It was on my first day in India, and I was sitting at a sidewalk café, watching the affection between a cow and her frisky calf. Cows wander the streets freely in India, so I was able to watch them for a while. The mother's large, shiny black eyes glazed with affection as she adored her calf's every move. As they lay on the roadside, she licked his furry body, and he nestled into her side. I remember walking over and petting the calf, who reciprocated by licking my hand again and again as his mother gazed at me and mooed tenderly. I thought, *These animals love life and each other just as I do.*

Then my dinner arrived, and I went back to my café table. I didn't recognize many of the preparations. One item, I was told by my host, was made with meat. The word *meat* suddenly sounded dissonant, and for the first time in my life, I felt the emotional connection between what was on my plate and the animals before me.

More recently I learned that today's dairy and slaughter industries are often connected. When calves are born, dairies keep the females and usually kill the bulls for meat. The cows are often kept in inhumane conditions until their milk production drops off and it is no longer lucrative to keep them alive. Then they are likely to be crammed into trucks and shipped to a slaughterhouse.

Aware of this, many thoughtful people are becoming vegans, avoiding all animal products. In most Indian spiritual traditions, however, including my own, people are encouraged to take milk products from places where cows and bulls are loved and protected throughout their natural lives. Unfortunately, these places are rare.

People inspired by the Vedic culture see cows in particular as sacred not only because of the gifts they provide but because they represent all the life forms that depend on human compassion. Cows eat grass and transform it into milk for their calves. The milk is an expression of the cow's love for her calf; in Vedic thought it is considered "liquid love." According to this Vedic way of thinking, when cows produce more milk than a calf can drink and the calf is fully satisfied, the surplus can be accepted to nourish human society.

The cow's gifts are numerous and precious. A cow's dung is a useful fertilizer, for example, and is commonly used as a fuel, and cow urine is used as a component of a number of natural medicines. Traditionally the bull too has been sensitively engaged to till the fields and enrich the earth with its dung. In several rural places around Maharashtra, India, we have been developing communities that include cruelty-free dairies where the cows and bulls are cared for throughout their natural lives. It's no small undertaking, but we've found that if we are attentive to the larger economic, ecological, moral, and spiritual issues, it's not only possible to run such a place but advantageous in every way.

Timeless codes for maintaining a balance in the environment have been recorded in the Vedas. Among these is a vegetarian diet. In a world spinning out of balance, both environmentalists and a growing number of scientists agree that a significant number of ecological problems stem from our society's massive animal production for human consumption, including tens of thousands of acres of precious rain forest cleared each year to grow food to feed cattle for meat production — not to mention the estimated 3,000 gallons of water it takes to produce only 1 kilogram of meat.

## FOOD AS BLESSING: THE ACT OF OFFERING FOOD

Food is a blessing central to health and enjoyment. As mentioned previously bhakti yogis offer their food to the Supreme Being and thus eat a sanctified vegetarian diet that adds spiritual well-being to the other blessings food brings.

This sanctified food is called *prasada*, or "divine mercy." In India, millions of people keep altars in their homes. They cook with the thought that they are preparing food for the Supreme as an act of love, and then place what they've cooked on a plate kept separate for the offering and ask God to accept it. Their prayerful offering, accepted by the Beloved, transforms the food into prasada, which they then share with their families. As the bhakti culture has spread all over the world, people worldwide now follow this timeless tradition. Even when traveling, one can offer food with a quiet prayer before eating it. The transformative element is love of God: we are offering not only food but also our gratitude and devotion.

Bhakti reorients our relationship with food by turning cooking and eating into spiritual practices. On the most fundamental level, food is sacred because it comes from nature and sustains us. Without it we die. On a deeper level, what we eat affects our consciousness and therefore our spiritual development. Preparing, serving, and eating food can be a powerful meditation, and while performing these functions bhakti yogis remember that the food itself has come from the gifts the Supreme has given the earth, including sunshine, rain, seeds, and the intelligence to know what to gather for our health.

## THE SUBTLE VALUE OF PRASADA

When we examine the thinking behind these devotional practices, we find that they make sense not only spiritually but also in terms of our stewardship of the earth. For example, as much as possible, the bhakti cuisine is prepared from pure, local, and organic ingredients. The less processed our food is, the healthier it is. Whenever possible, we choose natural foods, for they retain more of their inherent nutrients and are healthier for the planet as well.

Preparing meals is itself a meditation. Conscious intent informs each stage of preparation: growing or purchasing the ingredients, cleaning the kitchen and ourselves before cooking, cutting, kneading, spicing, cooking, and finally making the offering. Of course, the Supreme Beloved does not need our food. Mothers and fathers provide for their children. If the children take the ingredients provided by the parents and cook a meal for the parents, it's natural that the parents will be pleased. Similarly, the Supreme is pleased by our devotion when we cook for him and make our heartfelt offerings.

In early 2013, I was invited to a Slow Food Expo in Stuttgart, Germany, an elaborate event attended by thousands of people. The idea was to help us reevaluate how today's fast-food trends are affecting our physical health, our mental well-being, and the culture of love and care within our families. When food is prepared only to earn money or with an otherwise unclean mind, that energy will, on a subtle level, permeate the food and affect our consciousness as we eat it. When, instead, love and care go into food preparation, *that* energy infuses the meal and uplifts the consciousness.

A yogi is trained to not just eat but also to perceive the Divine presence in the sight, fragrance, touch, and taste of every meal, so eating too is an act of meditation. As they perceive the Divine, bhakti yogis also, of course, feel gratitude for what they are receiving. Here's a simple prayer of gratitude said before a meal:

*My dear Lord, we thank you for blessing us with this sanctified food. Please empower us to use the energy obtained from this prasada to serve you with love and to be an instrument of your grace.*

How much more satisfied does a person feel when he or she honors a meal with such thoughts? The many festivals celebrated by followers of Vedic culture culminate in joyfully distributing prasada to as many people as possible. Dining on prasada together is a blissful way of sharing our lives in a family atmosphere centered on gratitude and affection. Giving sanctified food to family, friends, and guests or distributing sanctified food on a large or small scale to the needy is a sacred form of charity.

Embedded in a simple concept, "You are what you eat," is a profound message for the health of the world. As individuals and as a global community, we all have the opportunity to move toward more conscious, compassionate living by changing our diet.

## NONVIOLENCE INCLUDES COMPASSION FOR THE ENVIRONMENT

As we try to appreciate a broader perspective of a compassionate lifestyle, we cannot help but feel concerned about how we treat the earth, considered by many to be one of our mothers. How we treat Mother Earth affects the well-being of everyone. I share with you an encounter that provoked me to ponder deeply on the idea of ahimsa toward the environment.

It was winter in New Delhi, when the days are mild and the nights bitingly cold. New Delhi's roads are wide and lined with massive government buildings, the older ones with carved stone pillars, ornate statues, and vast lawns built by the British more than a century ago. Others, built after India's independence in 1947, are more Indian in design, with classic Indian arches, columns, and domes. We were driving to the airport. Monkeys popped in and out of our view as they scampered along the tops of boundary walls.

We drove around circular islands of grass and trees with memorials to the country's freedom fighters. The streets were congested, and cars, trucks, and motorcycle rickshaws were spewing trails of exhaust fumes. Overhead, a murky cloud of yellow smog hung heavy in the air and reduced the sun to a gray lump. The fumes were thick and the roadside smells toxic, and they sat on our tongues like sour lozenges. I saw an elderly man squatting at the edge of the road, his back erect, performing yogic breathing exercises. I could see his chest heaving as he vigorously inhaled and exhaled. Given all the toxic fumes, I wondered if his exercises were doing him more harm than good.

As we crossed the bridge over the Yamuna River, I looked down into the waters and remembered how thirty years earlier, when I was visiting India for the first time, a pristine Yamuna had streamed under this same bridge. Now the river looked crippled, its water thick and blackish, with a head of foam floating on the surface and a current so weak it seemed to seep more than flow.

I was eager to get to the airport. I had just come from Vrindavan, where I had taken about five thousand people on pilgrimage. I was looking forward to a little quiet time while I waited for my flight. But a woman at my gate informed me that sitting across the way was Maneka Gandhi, the National Minister for the Environment and Forests and daughter-in-law of former prime minister Indira Gandhi. She wanted to talk to me, the woman said. I obliged.

Seeing me agree, Mrs. Gandhi walked over and greeted me with a "Namaste, Swamiji." After a short but pleasant exchange, her tone sharpened.

"What are you spiritual leaders doing to protect the environment?" she asked. I could feel her passion; it was clear this was not a rhetorical question. "Every second the air is being polluted with a cancerous smog," she said. "Tons of raw sewage and toxic waste are dumped hourly into rivers where millions of people bathe and drink. The earth is being stripped of its forests and has become a dumping ground for deadly waste. The world is on the brink of ecological disaster while you spiritualists spend your time meditating and praying. What is all your devotion doing to save the ecology?"

What *was* I doing? I had to agree with her: the environment is everyone's responsibility, including mine.

# KARUNA: ACTIVE, INTELLIGENT, DIRECTED COMPASSION

*Karuna* is a Sanskrit word that means compassion, which itself literally means "to feel with others." The dictionary defines *compassion* as "sympathetic pity or concern for the sufferings or misfortunes of others." But karuna goes beyond sentiment. Karuna is active, intelligent, and directed. It's something you act on, not just something you feel. As with ahimsa, karuna is essential to spiritual practice.

Mrs. Gandhi was right to ask me where my active compassion (karuna) was for the earth. But karuna isn't just action; it's thoughtful and committed action. The Bible teaches that the first and greatest commandment is to "love God with all one's heart, mind, and soul," and the natural effect of such love is "to love your neighbors as yourself." The earth is also our neighbor. More than that, she is our mother. She sustains us. She's alive. People have largely forgotten that. To practice karuna toward the earth requires that we think about the problem, diagnose it, and then see how to help. Being committed to this level of compassion may require that we stretch ourselves, acquire new information and skills, and become more adept at compassionate care. The Supreme has empowered each of us in different ways, and when we agree on what the problem is, we can each contribute our part of the solution.

The first thing we can do is look at the problem from a deeper perspective. I told Mrs. Gandhi that it's not that spiritual leaders are doing nothing when they pray and meditate. Yes, it's vitally important to pass strong laws to protect the environment, but we also need to address the root cause of the problem. If a person is covered with boils, a doctor will treat the symptoms, but if he or she doesn't address the underlying cause, inevitably they will recur or the body will develop some other disease. The root cause of environmental pollution is pollution within the ecology of the human heart. Even if we manage to clean the air, rivers, and oceans, people will pollute them again unless they reform their internal ecology.

A toxic greed has contaminated people's minds. What's happening to the environment is an external manifestation of the ecology of the mind. Greed is an obsession, an addiction. It can never be satisfied: the more you get, the more you want. Greed hardens the heart and allows us to rationalize cruelty and justify crime. Greed inspires envy, divides families, provokes wars, and blinds us to our real self-interest. The world is ravaged by greed—greed for money, power, fame, sex. It's an exercise in futility to try to clean up the environment when corrupt politicians accept bribes from industrialists who pollute the rivers to maximize their profits and scientists put aside ethics for funding. The Bhagavad Gita calls greed a symptom of ignorance, which covers the natural virtues of the soul.

So when spiritual practitioners are praying and meditating, they're also teaching by example how to purify the inner ecology. Spiritual life is the science of cleansing the heart and exploring the joy of living in harmony with the Supreme Being, each other, and nature. Reducing carbon emissions is important, but it's shortsighted when not coupled with reducing the toxic emissions from the heart, and that's something spiritual leaders are supposed to teach and something all thinking people should work toward.

Let's honor Mother Earth and be grateful for her gifts. The earth nourishes us, and we are all part of her ecosystem. It's our service to live in balance with her, seeing the larger picture—the effects of our actions—and exercising moderation. We're already witnessing the consequences of plundering resources.

We have made monumental progress in technology, medicine, science, academics, and globalization, but if we do not use them with compassion, what will be our fate? We have to take responsibility as caretakers of the planet and live as dedicated instruments of divine love. From a spiritual perspective, the crisis is not an environmental one. It is actually a crisis of the human spirit.

It is impossible to make a sustainable change in society without a corresponding change in people's behavior, values, and philosophy. Life must be viewed as a whole so that outward change and inward change go together. With this conviction Mahatma Gandhi said, "Be the change you wish to see in the world."

## KARUNA IN ACTION

*I am the original fragrance of the earth; I am the heat in fire and the life in all living things. Know Me to be the seed of all creation, original and eternal.*

— BHAGAVAD GITA 7.9

Those who see the world as a sacred creation have access to a uniquely powerful tool of inner and outer transformation. People and nature have always been interdependent, but in past generations, people were much more tied to the land through agriculture than we are today. How things have changed! The role of dharma is unfolding in new and exciting ways, based on the same understanding that has been in the Vedas since the dawn of time: that this world is part of the spiritual world. But what's happening to it?

The competition around technology is spinning frenetically. Technology has amazing benefits, but it's imperative to our future that we take a step back to reflect on where we're going and what's happening to our quality of life. Conditioned by high-tech special effects flashing on a screen, many people no longer experience the joy of watching a sunset or hearing birdsong in their own backyard.

How long can humanity keep up this frenzied pace? There's a frightening rise in cancer, heart disease, allergies, depression, and other illnesses linked to stress and toxins. Our scientific, technological, and economic pursuits have many good intentions behind them, but in our passion for material progress, we shouldn't lose sight of the possible reactions we could face or of what is favorable for our overall well-being.

As I will discuss later, the three modes of nature—goodness, passion, and ignorance—influence everything. Goodness relates to preservation, passion to creation, and ignorance to destruction. Sustainability is about directing the passion of creation to a point of balance and preservation, including self-preservation. Because there can be no self-preservation if we don't conserve the earth, it is crucial to our well-being that we recognize a simple truth: if we do not balance our creative passion with the sustaining quality of goodness, it will by default degrade to the debilitating influence of ignorance. The model we have now is passion leading to ignorance, creation leading to destruction.

Today, many people are seriously interested in living green; they want to play a role in positive change. But how?

First, recognize that you are nourished and sustained by nature, which is nourished and sustained by the Divine. Feel yourself part of a whole. You have a relationship with everything and everyone. A personal commitment to the health of the environment matures when we learn to be kind to *all* beings—from other people to insects to trees to the fish that swim in the oceans and rivers. And be kind to your own self.

A good way to cultivate kindness and interconnectedness with the natural world is to explore ways to consume less. The influence that the advertising industry has over us, especially through TV and the Internet, is daunting. It's just too easy to use some effective graphics and disguise sales techniques as vital information or to induce people to think they need or want things they neither want nor need. It's easy to convince people that consumerism in one form or another is good for their health and good for the world. But most of that consumption is not healthy for people or for the environment. And it is unsustainable.

The compassionate activism that is karuna is part of a cycle. Here's why it's important for your spiritual life. Awareness of our interdependence with the world and our ultimate dependence on the Source of this world has a strong and immediate effect: freedom from fear. Without fear, you can feel deeper compassion for those who suffer and then do something to alleviate the pain. To love the Supreme includes loving what is his: this earth, all living beings, and ourselves. We wash our heart clean of the idea that our small needs and demands have any serious weight in the greater scheme of things, and then we look to who's around us and try to help. In bhakti, we take that directed action and offer it with devotion in service to the Supreme.

## SMALL STEPS WITH BROAD CONSCIOUSNESS

My teacher, Prabhupada, stressed the need to see the earth's resources as God's property that should not be wasted. Once, early in the morning, he was walking the grounds of an expansive ashram in West Bengal with some of his disciples from around the world. He was being given a tour of the impressive developments in construction and landscaping since his last visit. Suddenly he pointed his cane toward something out in an almost empty field and exclaimed, "Why can't you see?" Everyone looked in the direction he was pointing, but no one knew what they were supposed to see.

"Why can't you see?" he repeated. "Are you blind?" He hurried across the field, bent down, and firmly closed the handle of a leaking water faucet.

When he returned to his students, he explained that everything is God's energy and should be cared for. "To be conscious of this at every moment," he said, "is Krishna consciousness."

Don't waste, he said. Because everything is God's property, we must take care of it even more carefully than if it were our own. If we do so, we can live in peace.

We may wonder what one person can do. Prabhupada's gesture was a small one, but he didn't let that stop him. No gesture is too small. Don't be discouraged from making your own small gestures.

## A SIMPLE ATTEMPT AT KARUNA: GOVARDHAN ECOVILLAGE

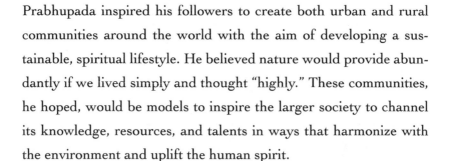

Prabhupada inspired his followers to create both urban and rural communities around the world with the aim of developing a sustainable, spiritual lifestyle. He believed nature would provide abundantly if we lived simply and thought "highly." These communities, he hoped, would be models to inspire the larger society to channel its knowledge, resources, and talents in ways that harmonize with the environment and uplift the human spirit.

Inspired by my teacher, I helped create the Govardhan Ecovillage, which is still in the development stage. The area, in the Indian state of Maharashtra, usually faces eight months of drought each year, so we developed several methods for harvesting and conserving water. The result has been that our fifty acres of crops and all of our residences have had plenty of water throughout the year.

We also developed a natural sewage refining system: the raw sewage flushed down toilets and the gray water washed down drains is filtered through a system of soil, roots, stones, and herbs and restored to purity.

To preserve the topsoil, as well as the nutrients in our food; all of our grains, vegetables, herbs, fruits, and flowers are organically grown with heirloom seeds. We use various types of wholesome, nonchemical fertilizers and nontoxic insect repellants. The fields are tilled with enriching plowing techniques, and a sizable area is dedicated to develop composting techniques. For building our homes and communal structures, we use various natural technologies to produce materials, such as sun-dried compressed-soil bricks, made from our own soil. Our electricity is primarily solar powered, and we cook for hundreds of people daily with methane gas produced from the dung of our cows, bulls, and other animals—and from our own organic waste.

Interestingly, most of these ecofriendly methods have been researched, discovered, and developed by a team of engineers who have graduated from world-renowned universities. They live in our ecovillage, with their families or as monks, along with our many indigenous families who have come from the surrounding villages. Considering their diverse backgrounds, I feel that the respect, cooperation, and affection the residents share with each other are vital assets of the community.

We are maintaining a sanctuary for the loving care and protection of cows and a variety of other animals and birds throughout their natural lives. We're also developing cottage industries such as handicrafts and traditional arts. And the ecovillage has an orphanage, a school, an ashram, and housing for families.

Whatever knowledge and resources we have been given, we are trying to share with the hundreds of struggling villages in our area whose economic, social, and spiritual conditions have since vastly improved. An important part of our outreach is in promoting the culture of giving honor to and empowering the village women.

Inspired by the principle of karuna, we at the Govardhan Eco village are trying, in our own small way, to live in harmony with God and nature while embracing the dharma of compassion.

# Awakening Divine Love

*As the infinite charm of the Beautiful One awakens in the heart, the mind is irresistably drawn to His form, pastimes, teachings, and love.*
— RUPA GOSWAMI

## THE COMPONENTS OF BHAKTI YOGA PRACTICE

The soul's ultimate potential is to taste divine love. That experience is realized when we are so absorbed in loving service to the Supreme and compassion for others that we transcend our own desire to be happy. In such a state, we are truly lost in love, and we realize the inner truth of the phrase "in giving we receive." This ecstatic love is dormant within each of us.

Bhakti yoga has five potent, timeless practices that help the practitioner to awaken this love:

1. Living in sacred space (and tuning into grace)

2. Spiritual relationships, spiritual community

3. Chanting the holy names of God

4. Hearing from sacred literature

5. Worshiping the Lord, however you know him, with faith and veneration

## ⊱— PRACTICE I —⊰

### LIVING IN SACRED SPACE
#### (AND TUNING INTO GRACE)

*When one is illumined with the wisdom by which ignorance
is destroyed, then this knowledge lights up all things,
just as the sun reveals the world at dawn.*

—BHAGAVAD GITA 5.16

While we progress on our journey within, it's helpful to be aware
of the influences that surround us. There is spiritual energy everywhere, even though it's invisible to the material eye. We are surrounded by other energies too—electromagnetic fields, for example.
All of these subtle material energies have always been there, even
though we can't see, feel, or hear them. In fact, it's taken centuries
for humans to discover and harness their power.

Tuning into the spiritual energy is not so different conceptually
from tuning in to some form of invisible material energy. If you push
a button on your remote to tune into a TV channel, you are choosing
a particular frequency—perhaps a football game from Texas or the
news from Baghdad. In the broader context, the buttons on the remote
that let us choose between material and spiritual frequencies are your
life choices and state of mind. Both are driven by your desires.

We humans have the power to receive and transmit "consciousness waves" according to our free will. The waves that ripple out
from us travel far and affect others in the world. We learn from
classic yogic texts that consciousness is one of the most powerful

energies in creation. Whatever we think, feel, want, speak, or do affects the environment and the living beings around us. In the same way, we are affected by other people's energies. Some people emit positive waves and some emit negative waves. If we're careful to absorb positive energy—kindness and compassion, for example—then we can relay it to others and contribute to the healthy energy in the world. If we give in to negativity, we will also relay that into the world. When people share the same frequencies, whether elevated or arrogant, selfless, or selfish, that collective consciousness has a powerful influence on the world.

We can elevate our energy to the spiritual through sincere prayer, meditation, meaningful ritual, and the chanting of sacred mantras. Different transcendentalists focus on different energies of the Supreme. Bhakti yogis are particularly attentive to grace, the divine energy that awakens and nourishes prema, or spiritual love. Divine grace is imperceptible to the senses, yet it is always within us, around us, and accessible to us if we tune into the correct frequency.

Bhakti yoga teaches that everything originates from the Supreme, even our bodies and the power to think, speak, and move. A practitioner of bhakti wants to express gratitude for these facilities by engaging them in service to the Supreme. Bhakti, in the end, is simply a desire to love and know God, and when that desire is strong enough, every action that follows becomes a heartfelt offering in his service.

In the Bhagavad Gita (7.3), Krishna tells us, "Among thousands of souls, one may endeavor for perfection. Yet of those who have achieved perfection, hardly one knows Me in truth." Realized knowledge of the Absolute, God, is called, in the Gita, "the most secret of all secrets" and is considered the privilege of a rare few.

Why is knowledge of God so secret? Why doesn't every soul see the Supreme Soul? It can't be because knowledge about God is difficult to find. There are hundreds of millions of copies of the Gita, Bible, Koran, and other holy books in print around the world. Literacy rates are on the rise, and even in places where literacy is low, missionaries provide information about God. More and more people have access to sacred texts and the education to read them. How is it, then, that so few people end up understanding God?

One reason is that most people are exposed only to the external features of religion and never find their way into its essential purpose. People are taught to see God as their order supplier and redeemer from sins. Many pray in the mood of bargaining with God: "If you give me success, then I'll believe in you," or "Make this person love me and I'll stop drinking," or "Give me good grades and I'll worship you every day," or "Cure my illness and I'll make a donation."

According to the bhakti school, this type of relationship between suppliant and order supplier is a step toward God and may inspire one toward religious practice and a moral life, but it is fairly low level of relationship, and if people don't get what they ask for, they can feel frustrated or lose faith.

As faith develops, we stop trying to make deals with God and look for a deeper exchange, one in which we see him as our dearest friend and begin to trust his direction. If we continue along this path, it's only a matter of time before trust becomes love. For true love to awaken, we need to rise to a state where we approach the Supreme for love untainted by selfishness or material expectations. Jesus highlighted this devotional spirit in his prayer, "Let not *my* will, but *your* will, be done."

When the motivation for our devotions surpasses material desires altogether, we will discover the most secret of all secrets—the intimate truth that the Supreme Being reveals when we surrender in love, unconditionally. At that point, we will know that God is both all powerful and our intimate best friend, and trust that he will always take care of us. This realization naturally frees us from fear and awakens the ecstatic love in our soul.

In contrast to conceptions of God as a harsh or fear-inspiring entity, bhakti texts mainly depict the Supreme as an affectionate, compassionate being who cares profoundly about the welfare and happiness of every soul. And how could it be otherwise, as all souls are inseparable parts of his own potency? When we embrace this beautiful and loving idea of God, our own instinctive loving nature emerges, and this in turn impels us toward a deeper, more intimate relationship with the Supreme Beloved.

For this type of spiritual evolution, grace is essential. We cannot attain divine love by our own efforts alone; we need help. Without grace, we may learn many things about the Lord and his creation, but we won't be able to really live what we know. It's not possible for the finite to know the infinite completely, but by grace, the infinite allows himself to be known. We draw grace to ourselves when we take our spiritual development seriously and sincerely try to cultivate the character traits, especially humility and a service attitude, that lend themselves to that development.

By definition, grace is the extension of God's hand even though we don't deserve it. It is the transcendent, ever-existing expression of the divine's love, and like the sun, it spreads its rays impartially. It shines for each of us, and when we open our hearts to receive it by living in a way that will draw that grace to us, the Supreme Being bestows it, because it is his desire that we taste the sweetness of his infinite love.

Grace carries us through and then beyond life's impediments and provides a level of satisfaction so high that it puts all material pleasure to shame. Although this grace is causeless, we still need to be receptive to it if we want to fully receive it. When, by our free will, we venture out of the dark cavern of ego and into the sunshine of loving, humble service, we open ourselves to the light of grace and realize the most secret of all secrets: God's love. My guru, Prabhupada, explained that divine love (prema) is very rare, but Krishna, the Supreme Person, gives it easily to those who sincerely want it more than anything else.

## A PILGRIMAGE WITHIN

The bhakti tradition encourages us to deepen our connection with the sacred within ourselves by visiting holy places. Although sacred spaces can be in our own homes or in local gatherings, going on pilgrimage to historical holy places is especially potent. There we can put all worldly concerns aside, at least for the time being, and fully tune into the spiritual energy there. Pilgrimage is a special opportunity to receive the blessings of saints and deepen our relationships with like-minded people who walk with us on the pilgrimage of life.

# PRACTICE 2

## SPIRITUAL RELATIONSHIPS, SPIRITUAL COMMUNITY

*The Supreme Lord said, "I am very much pleased by the friendly relationships among you. All of you are engaged in your occupations with devotion. I am so pleased with your mutual friendship that I wish you all good fortune."*

—BHAGAVATA PURANA 4.30.8

Years ago, when I was living in the Himalayan forest caves, I rarely saw other human beings, but in my solitude, I contemplated my relationship with the environment that supported me: the mountains, sun, and moon, the animals, birds, reptiles, trees, and local herbs. Through the primal nature of these associations, I learned much about the basic nature of all relationships. The nomadic monkey tribes were especially instructive. They traveled in groups, searching for food and shelter. Mothers doted on their babies, cleaning them, breastfeeding them, and carrying them wherever they went. The juveniles played together, swinging from branch to branch with incredible verve, while the older males scouted for food. Smitten, maturing males wooed the females, and it was common to see two rival males competing for the attention of a particular female. It didn't take much to note the parallels between monkey and human behavior, especially when two tribes fought over food-rich territories.

Like humans, monkeys attempt to settle their differences first with psychological warfare and posturing. In the world of monkeys, that takes the form of screeching, baring of fangs, and aggressive leaping, all of which stops just short of actual physical assault. As long as one party backs down, violence is avoided.

At times, though, the skirmish escalated into a vicious battle of biting, scratching, and kicking. Add sophisticated weaponry, and you have the basics of competition in human society.

I found it fascinating that I could contemplate the nature of human relationships when humans were so far away. It made me conscious of how critical relationships are to our lives. People can bring us the brightest of joys or the darkest of sorrows. They can elevate or degrade us, enlighten or bewilder us.

I also learned from monkey society that individuals are stronger in a group than alone. This realization helped me to appreciate how important we are to each other. When a group has a shared interest in enlightenment, the members help one another focus on living a life of spiritual and moral integrity.

Healthy relationships are hard work. Those who put in that work usually learn to see things not through the eyes of ego but with humility, which makes apparently insurmountable differences seem insignificant. The narrow mind will call a pebble a mountain, but those whose minds are broad will see the pebble for what it really is. When we cultivate relationships with this awareness, we can dismiss petty differences and focus on higher, unifying purposes. This is both the meaning and value of spiritual community: bolstered by the strength of others who share similar values to our own we find it easy to remain focused on what truly matters.

In the Gita, Krishna describes spiritual relationships like this:

*The thoughts of my pure devotees dwell in me, their lives are devoted to my service, and they derive great satisfaction and bliss from enlightening one another and conversing about me.*

—BHAGAVATA GITA 10.10

Spiritual communion is a beautiful medium through which to realize and share divine love. The heart of such relationships is seva, the spirit of service, ultimately the drive to serve the Supreme. My teacher was once asked, "Are you the guru of the whole world?" He looked down and replied softly, "I am everyone's servant, that's all."

In the early days of the Krishna movement in the West, despite his being a saint and scholar, Prabhupada shopped, cooked, and cleaned for his disciples, even though most of them were fifty years younger than he was. When they moved in with him, he waited patiently in line for his turn to use the bathroom. Later, his disciples began to show him more deference, but his spirit of selflessness didn't abate. Although he no longer had to clean up after them, he traveled extensively to help them and anyone else who would hear his message of love of God. He established over a hundred centers and communities in twelve years, writing over sixty books that sold in the tens of millions and attracted thousands of devoted students. But he asked for nothing for himself. He dedicated himself only to sharing his pure love for Krishna, the Supreme Beloved, with the rest of the world.

In the Bhagavad Gita (18.68), Krishna declares, "For those who explain this supreme secret among devotees, devotion is guaranteed, and at the end they come back to me. . . . There is no soul in this world more dear to me, nor will there ever be one more dear."

The bhakti texts tell us that even a moment's association with a saintly person can open the doors to spiritual perfection. A proverb says, "Show me your friends and I'll tell you who you are." As far as possible, we should keep company with saints and saints in the making. Such community is invaluable to our spiritual progress.

## DAILY CHALLENGES WITH FRIENDS AND FAMILY, AND IN THE WORKPLACE

Maintaining our spiritual awareness is challenging. How do you stay spiritually conscious when you're at work? What about when you're with friends or relatives who have little interest in your spiritual path? How do you offer others positive energy without being affected by all the negativity around you?

The bhakti tradition teaches us to maintain balance in our relationships and in how we use our time. Meeting regularly with like-minded friends allows us to wrap ourselves in spiritual armor. This armor protects us from becoming frustrated or bewildered by negativity. It empowers us to be respectful, kind, and faithful to our values and helps us to grow even in apparently unfavorable circumstances. Being with people who share our spiritual aspirations charges our spiritual batteries. So no matter what shape our day takes, we should cultivate close, caring friendships with those who understand and support us.

Prabhupada used to tell his students that choosing a devotional life was like declaring one's independence from *maya*, literally, "that which is not." If we really want to be free, we have to be prepared to confront the forces that bind or distract us. This includes struggling to overcome our baser tendencies toward selfishness, egoism, and hypocrisy while reaching for love, truth, and spiritual joy.

## HOW TO SUPPORT A HEALTHY SPIRITUAL COMMUNITY

A beautiful etiquette taught in the bhakti tradition supports healthy spiritual community: when we meet someone senior to us, we offer our respect and our service. We should honor our elders or any others who have been blessed to excel on the spiritual path, and do so without envy. Regardless of how far along the path we are, we should always be open to receiving inspiration and guidance from more accomplished spiritualists.

When we meet those newer to spiritual life, we should offer them care and affection. There's no room for condescension. Rather, we are called to be encouraging, supportive, and helpful, conscious that whatever progress we've made has been possible only because of those who helped us along the way.

What's the best way to cultivate spiritual relationships? Bhakti saint Rupa Goswami suggests six simple ways:

1. Confidentially reveal your mind to your close friends.

2. Listen to your friends when they open themselves up to you.

3. Be giving; give gifts.

4. Receive gifts from friends with gratitude.

5. Offer friends sacred food (prasada). Eat with your friends. Be hospitable and invite them home for meals. Be supportive.

6. Graciously receive sacred food from your friends. Affection is reciprocal.

These exchanges are ways that any friends share affection. When they are centered on a shared interest in devotion to the Supreme Being, they deepen one's bhakti. If we don't build affectionate relationships with other spiritually minded persons, we risk building them with those whose habits and values are not conducive to our spiritual health. What makes spiritual relationships so fulfilling is that they connect us to the source of all pleasure and love.

## THE ESSENCE OF SPIRITUAL COMMUNITY: "I AM THE SERVANT OF THE SERVANT"

The Gita (6.9) tells us that advanced spiritualists regard "honest well-wishers, affectionate benefactors, the neutral, the envious, friends and enemies, the pious, and the materialists all with an equal mind."

Relationships, like life, are full of complexities. For our practice, it's good to develop an equal, balanced mind when dealing with others. As servants of the Supreme, we are servants of each other. Sri Chaitanya taught a beautiful meditation: think of yourself as a humble servant of the servant of the servant of God's servants. He taught that we should be "humbler than a blade of grass and more tolerant than a tree." Humility, tolerance, patience: choosing these over ego when dealing with others helps us and pleases God, the Supreme Father, because any parent is pleased to see his or her children getting along.

But getting along takes sacrifice. The word *sacrifice* has a number of definitions, but in the context of love, we take the definition "to make sacred," and we do this by centering our relationships on mutual spiritual interests. When spiritual ideals form the foundation of a relationship, the relationship can survive whatever challenges may arise. The more we strive to improve ourselves spiritually and support our friends in doing the same, the more our relationships rise to a level beyond the reach of superficial disagreements and ego-driven agitation. The surface of a river changes with every breeze, but if we dive deep enough below the water's surface, we'll find a place of calm.

## Don't Criticize Others—for Your Benefit and Theirs

Criticizing others is often like pointing out the dark spots on the full moon. The full moon is resplendent and radiates volumes of soothing moonlight. Yes, it has a few spots, but why focus on those when the moon is so brilliant and beautiful and beneficial? Everyone has faults, but more important, everyone has a beautiful soul. We have the power to choose whether to focus on people's virtues or their faults—to fill ourselves and them with positive or negative energy.

Jesus told his disciples: "If you are about to offer your gift to God at the altar and you remember that your brother has something against you, leave your gift there and go and make peace with your brother. Then come back and offer your gift to God."

When Jesus was asked by his disciples how many times we should forgive a trespasser, they repeated that earlier teachers had said seven times. Jesus, however, suggested that we forgive seventy *times* seven. To be that forgiving takes a strong spiritual foundation.

It's said in yoga circles that we see everything according to our own mental state. My guru's teacher, Sri Bhaktisiddhanta Saraswati, used to say, "I see faults in others because I am honeycombed with faults." When monks in his ashrams fought, he sometimes sat them down facing each other and had them recite the good qualities of their opponents. Upon reminding themselves of the other's virtues they could recognize how proportionately small their rivals' faults actually were.

Sri Bhaktisiddhanta once sent a group of disciples to a distant city to teach bhakti. They had almost no money and knew no one where they were going. Within a couple of years, they had inspired thousands of people to help build their mission, and gradually they constructed a beautiful temple, as their guru had requested. But several weeks before Bhaktisiddhanta's arrival to inaugurate the temple, the project leaders noticed a young monk socializing with a young woman in a way that was inappropriate to the rules of the ashram. When the project leaders chastised him, the young monk was so disheartened that, without saying anything to anyone, he left the ashram.

When Bhaktisiddhanta arrived, thousands of townspeople were joyfully singing Krishna's names in kirtan in front of the new, elegantly decorated temple. A sumptuous feast had been prepared for thousands of guests, and a festive spirit prevailed. Sri Bhaktisiddhanta looked around and saw everything and everyone. The disciples smiled in anticipation of his pleasure. But instead, his face registered concern. He asked for the young monk. The faces of the project leaders sank. There was no way to hide what had happened, and they told their guru the story while Bhaktisiddhanta looked soberly into their eyes.

He said, "This temple, these practitioners, the wonderful food and decorations you have arranged: none of it matters to me as much to me as that monk. He may have made a mistake, but there was no reason to break his heart. I will not be satisfied until you bring him back."

The leaders were mortified. The young monk had not merited much regard in anyone's eyes, but they saw their teacher had a higher vision. They searched everywhere for the young monk and eventually found him working in a clock repair shop. On hearing his teacher's response to his leaving, the young monk wept and packed his bag to return. When he arrived at the temple, Bhaktisiddhanta welcomed him home. Only after reconciliation had taken place between the project leaders and the young monk could the joyous festival continue.

Sri Bhaktisiddhanta, like all other great teachers of bhakti, wanted his disciples to understand that as we devote heart, mind, and soul to Krishna, as we strive to awaken our love for him, we should also learn to offer love and respect to one another. He said it takes tremendous effort to bring one soul to spiritual life. Why should we discourage a sincere person who happens to commit a mistake along the way?

Caring for each other with patience, tolerance, and humility is part of what it means to walk a spiritual path. Bhaktisiddhanta showed compassion and the willingness to nurture what's good in others and not unnecessarily focus on "spots." And by the way, this monk later became a great spiritual leader.

## HAVE PATIENCE, WITH WISDOM

But what about seriously offensive behavior? Do we overlook it in the name of tolerance? Forgive it? What is a spiritually healthy response to such behaviors?

There is nothing spiritual about allowing abuse to occur. Forgiveness does not mean ignoring abuse or letting it go unaddressed. It is not a spiritual quality to remain passive where action may be required to protect the innocent or rectify serious offenders. To apply the balance between justice and compassion requires spiritual maturity and attention to the particulars of a situation.

There are so many things in life we are powerless to change: the way others treat us, the weather, the course of a disease. Challenges of all sorts cross our path no matter how hard we try to avoid them. Still, we have freedom in how we respond. Reinhold Niebuhr's famous "Serenity Prayer" comes to mind: "God, grant me the serenity to accept the things I cannot change, the courage to change the things I can, and the wisdom to know the difference."

Good character is a necessary foundation for meaningful, sustainable relationships and for a healthy community. My teacher once said, "Philosophy without good character is practically useless."

## SPIRITUAL FAMILY VALUES

A healthy marriage is a pathway to spiritual perfection. When we see our family in this light, with devotion to the Supreme Being at the center, caring for family members becomes a meaningful part of our yoga practice and a great learning experience.

Bhakti teaches married people to see their spouses, children, and other family as beloved children of God, brought together for a sacred purpose. Nourishing the bodies, minds, and souls of loved ones is an integral part of responsible spiritual practice.

Partnerships are sacred. Both partners should regard each other as a beloved child of God placed in one another's care. Romantic attraction comes and goes, but a substantial relationship built on a foundation of shared spiritual ideals and respect, loyalty, and devotion to each other endures and is priceless. A fulfilling marital partnership needs both partners to express their appreciation for one another through kind words, helpful actions, and dependability in both good and hard times. All human beings need to feel appreciated, and this is especially true of family members. The demands placed on a partner's time by work, children, or other responsibilities can lead one or both persons to neglect spending quality time with the other. Such neglect can lead to a breakdown in the relationship or even to emotional abuse, a serious transgression that carries karmic consequences. By contrast, caring spiritual relationships nourish and empower both partners.

Children too deserve special attention. We have a great responsibility when we become parents. Parents are caretakers of their children, responsible for nourishing them with God's love, guiding them by their good example and values. Children have a moral and spiritual right to that loving guidance. We may not realize the consequences of neglecting our children until it's too late. Children deprived of consistently expressed love often try to compensate for the lack of the attention they crave by rebelling in one way or another, turning to intoxicants, risky sexual behaviors, questionable friends, or even criminal activity. Feeling neglected, children may suffer from low self-esteem or depression, conditions that can cripple them for life.

In an ideal household, all members consider themselves servants of the Supreme and approach their roles as husband or wife, mother or father, sister or brother, daughter or son, with a view to the welfare and happiness of the others in the family. The bhakti culture considers that any home based on these virtues becomes a *tirtha*, or holy place.

Fidelity is at the core of any good marriage, and that is why most marriages start with some sort of vows. It is not easy to follow vows over an entire lifetime—vows are continually tested—but staying true to our promises is one way we express integrity. So, what's the secret of success? We should stay focused on the higher aspirations of our relationships. We should be prepared to humble ourselves, to admit our faults and honestly address them and learn to grow beyond them. We should always remember that we have a spiritual responsibility to our family members and explore every possible way to remain united for our higher purpose.

Families sustain a spiritual foundation in these traditional ways:

- Creating a sacred space in the home, where family members individually and together can perform spiritual practices.

- Creating a mood that the home is God's personal property.

- Praying together to stay together.

- Having good, spiritually minded friends to invite them home and visit their homes.

- Performing devotional service together as a family in your home, place of worship, or community.

- Practicing love and respect for each other and exemplifying this culture for the children.

- Forgiving and forgetting and being tolerant, patient, grateful, and humble—and teaching these qualities to ones children.

- Giving family members the benefit of the doubt. Being careful about passing negative judgments. Rashly blaming others is often a symptom of our own insecurity, immaturity, or selfishness.

- Seeing all family members as beloved children of God. If we love God, we will love those whom God loves and express it through our words and actions.

The essential principle is for each of us to focus on the higher purpose and broader picture of our relationships, try to find unity in our diversity, and be the best we can be. Sometimes we require accepting our family members for who they are despite our differences, while we ourselves faithfully adhere to the values we hold sacred.

## THE SECRETS OF THE REDWOODS

Every year I travel to Northern California to spend a day with a close friend. Together we roam Muir Woods, a sanctuary of enormous redwood trees, where we share our hearts and thoughts. As we walk, we inevitably look up at the towering redwoods, so tall they hardly allow a ray of sun to reach the ground. Their thick bark tends to absorb sound, enveloping us in silence.

One day we happened to come across a group of tourists gathered around a park ranger, who was explaining the secrets of the forest, and we stopped to listen. The redwood and sequoia trees, he explained, are the largest trees on the planet. Many of the trees in Muir Woods are hundreds of years old. Yet their root systems tend to be shallow, and with the loose soil and hilly terrain, the trees have little support. Still, over the centuries, these trees have endured massive windstorms, frigid blizzards, and devastating earthquakes. With only shallow roots, how do they keep standing?

The park ranger explained the underground secret of the redwoods: their roots reach outward and tightly wrap around the roots of other redwoods. The embrace of their roots creates a permanent bond. In this way, the trees support one another. Even the newest sapling is sheltered, as the ancient giants extend their roots and protect the new tree's roots. In this underground root network, all the redwood trees in the forest are directly or indirectly connected to one another. Their strength is in their unity. It's unity that empowers them to grow, even in the face of adverse conditions.

Here in Muir Woods, Mother Nature is teaching humanity a lesson critical to our well-being. Despite our shortcomings and differences, our strength lies in caring for one another. We need to reach out with the roots of our affection and embrace one another with a commitment to share, care, and support. Self-absorption exiles us to the shallow soil of our own limitations, dependent only on our deceiving ego. When we can stop thinking of "me" and "mine" and instead think of "ours," our roots will hold strong in the soil of love, trust, and grace, reminding us that in giving we receive.

## ⊱— PRACTICE 3 —⊰

### CHANTING THE HOLY NAMES OF GOD

*O King, for great yogis who have completely renounced all material connections, for those who desire all material enjoyment and for those who are self-satisfied by dint of transcendental knowledge, constant chanting of the holy name of the Lord is recommended.*
—BHAGAVATA PURANA 2.1.11

The most revered practice leading to an ecstatic love for the Supreme is kirtan—chanting hymns, prayers, or the holy names of God. According to the bhakti tradition, the Supreme Being manifests himself in his names, and to those who chant these names sincerely, he reveals his beauty, sweetness, power, and love. The sacred literature tells us that even the most misguided persons with the most degraded habits can become world spiritual teachers if they purify their consciousness by chanting God's names.

The bhakti literature proclaims the chanting of the Divine names to be "the prime benediction for all humanity" because, more than any other spiritual process, the chanting has the power to cleanse the mind and awaken the soul's dormant love for God. Chanting is easy; anyone can do it. We're living in a time the Vedas call the Age of Kali (an age characterized by forgetfulness of the true self and subsequent quarreling and hypocrisy), and it is said that in this troublesome age, the Supreme Being invests "all potencies in the sound vibration of the holy name" in order to attract our hearts.

Chanting God's names transcends all sectarian boundaries. Scriptures the world over have revealed many of the Supreme's names to humanity. Krishna, Jehovah, Christ, Yahweh, Allah, Narayana, Rama, Govinda: any revealed name from a genuine spiritual tradition is invested with grace, and chanting any or all of these names connects us with the Supreme. I found it interesting when a prominent Catholic priest inquired from my teacher, Prabhupada, how devout Christians could deepen their love for God. Prabhupada recommended that they sincerely chant the names of Christ and live with good character, according to Jesus's teachings.

In Sanskrit, the holy names are referred to as *nada-brahman*. *Brahman* refers to the Supreme, and *nada* literally means "a stream"—in this case, both a stream of sound and a stream of consciousness. The sound vibration of the holy names is transcendental, meaning that it flows first along the lower levels of consciousness (sensual, mental, and intellectual) and then floods the soul with awareness. This is why chanting is given prominence in India's spiritual traditions, and the Sanskrit texts often describe spiritual sound as the most effective way to awaken divine consciousness.

Everything in the material world is made up of sound. Molecules vibrate at particular frequencies. Material sound is the subtle background of temporary matter. The higher sound of the holy names has the ability to pierce through matter and nourish the soul, which is of the same spiritual nature.

Much can be said about the power of spiritual sound vibration. An analogy explains how chanting revives our original consciousness. When a raindrop falls from a cloud, it is pure water and you can see through it. However, when it mixes with the earth, it loses that natural transparency. When the impurities are removed through filtration, the raindrop returns to its original clear state. Chanting God's names is compared to the filtering process; it purifies the consciousness, returning it to its original pure, transparent state.

## How to Chant

There are two basic ways to chant: *japa* and kirtan. Japa is a more private meditation on a mantra, whereas kirtan refers to singing the mantra or devotional prayers, often with others. During japa, you recite the holy names softly to yourself or, if you can remain focused, silently in the mind. Japa is intimate and personal, and in the solitude of japa, you can offer your heart's deepest feelings as you connect with the Supreme through transcendental sound. All that japa requires is that you focus your attention on the divine sound vibration. When your mind wanders, you simply bring it back to the sound.

Divine mantras consisting of God's names are perfect and complete sounds. Approach them with a clear and humble heart.

To practice japa, many practitioners choose to sit in a comfortable position on a cushion on the floor or in a chair that supports good posture. Others prefer to pace while they chant. Japa is commonly practiced with a *mala*, or strand of beads. It is ideally practiced during early morning, when the world around you is quiet, making it conducive to concentrate. But japa can be done any time, even without beads. No matter what you're doing, you can chant japa in your mind or quietly to yourself.

Kirtan is an activity that can be done alone or with others, with or without musical instruments. It may be a soft, calm call for grace or a lively, spirited celebration of love. It can be performed while sitting, walking, or dancing. The happiness you feel when chanting with others will inspire your absorption in the mantra. The bhakti scriptures especially recommend congregational chanting, because it unifies the hearts of the participants and purifies the world.

In chanting the holy names, one's material qualifications or disqualifications have no relevance. As the sun of the holy name rises in the heart, it dispels the darkness caused by false identifications. In kirtan you can express love for the Supreme Soul and to one another, soul to soul. The depth of absorption possible when chanting as a united group, and the ease with which you find that unity, many hearts and voices joining as one, has tremendous power to generate extraordinary feelings of spiritual joy and invoke a shower of grace.

When divine sounds or holy names are given for repeated recitation, they form a mantra. The word *mantra* comes from two Sanskrit root words, *manas*, which means "mind," and *trayate*, which means "to deliver" or "to free." Repeating a mantra frees the mind from anxiety and illusion.

But which mantra should we chant? It is said that the Vedas are a "wish-fulfilling tree" that aids people to achieve whatever they desire. The Vedas contain mantras to help people achieve better health, more wealth, a loving spouse, children, and better overall enjoyment. They also contain mantras to help people attain more subtle material enjoyments, like yogic or mystical powers to manipulate matter. And, of course, they contain mantras for those interested in spiritual realization, whether that's liberation from matter or divine love of God.

One mantra in particular, known as the maha-mantra, or "great mantra," includes the powers and benefits of all the other mantras and is especially recommended for this Age of Kali. Countless enlightened saints and aspiring spiritualists from a wide variety of spiritual traditions in India over the centuries have chanted this mantra as their main discipline. The Vedic literatures, and the Upanishads in particular, declare that this mantra is the perfect spiritual method for the times in which we live—an age of quarrel and hypocrisy. The mantra is:

*Hare Krishna Hare Krishna*
*Krishna Krishna Hare Hare*
*Hare Rama Hare Rama*
*Rama Rama Hare Hare*

In this maha-mantra the word *Hare* invokes Radha (Hara), or the Supreme Feminine, who bestows intimate spiritual love. *Krishna* is a name of the Supreme meaning "the all-attractive one." *Rama*, another name of the Supreme, means "the reservoir of all pleasure." The maha-mantra serves as a prayer: "O Radha, O You who bestow grace, O Krishna, O Rama, please engage me in Your loving service."

There are numerous statements both in the sacred literature and by saints describing the blessings one receives by chanting the maha-mantra. Prabhupada wrote on this topic in *The Topmost Yoga System*:

> The transcendental vibration established by chanting the *maha-mantra* is the sublime method for reviving our transcendental consciousness. As living spiritual souls, we are all originally Krishna conscious entities, but due to our association with matter from time immemorial, our consciousness is now adulterated by the material atmosphere. The material atmosphere, in which we are now living, is called *maya*, or illusion. *Maya* means "that which is not." And what is this illusion? The illusion is that we are all trying to be lords of the material nature when actually we are under the grip of her stringent laws.

Chanting the maha-mantra is a process for reviving this original pure consciousness. By chanting this transcendental vibration, we can cleanse away all misgivings in our hearts. The basic principle of all such misgivings is the false consciousness that I am the lord of all I survey.

Krishna [or divine] consciousness is not an artificial imposition on the mind. This consciousness is the original natural energy of the living entity. When we hear the transcendental vibration, this consciousness is revived. This simple method of meditation is recommended for this age. By practical experience also, one can perceive that by chanting this maha-mantra, or the great chanting for deliverance, one can at once feel a transcendental ecstasy coming through from the spiritual stratum. This chanting of the Hare Krishna mantra is enacted from the spiritual platform, and thus this sound vibration surpasses all lower strata of consciousness—namely, sensual, mental, and intellectual. There is no need, therefore, to understand the language of the mantra, nor any need for any intellectual adjustment for chanting this maha-mantra. It is automatic, from the spiritual platform, and as such, anyone can take part in vibrating this transcendental sound without any previous qualification.

Chanting takes one to the spiritual platform, and one shows the first symptom of this in the urge to dance along with the chanting of the mantra. Even a child can take part in the chanting and dancing.

Prabhupada next shows us how we can access the deep power of the mantra:

These three words—namely Hara, Krishna, and Rama—are the transcendental seeds of the maha-mantra. The chanting is a spiritual call for the Lord and His energy, to give protection to the conditioned soul. This chanting is exactly like the genuine cry of a child for its mother's presence. Mother Hara [Radha] helps the devotee achieve the Lord Father's grace, and the Lord reveals himself to the devotee who chants this mantra sincerely.

In this connection there is a beautiful story from the holy place of Vrindavan. About five thousand years ago, a jackal was drinking water from a lake. Among animals, jackals are rarely respected. You often hear phrases like "the courage of a lion," "the strength of a bull," "the memory of an elephant," "as graceful as a deer," or "the voice of a nightingale," but who wants the qualities of a jackal? Comparing someone to a jackal, that scrawny, wolflike scavenger with the eerie night scream, is considered an insult. Jackals also feed on corpses.

So one day, in Vrindavan, some children saw a she-jackal lapping water from a pond, and laughing, they began to beat her with sticks. The jackal cried in agony, but the children kept beating her. Then some of the children picked up stones and hurled them at her. Trying desperately to escape, the jackal finally found a hole in the ground and huddled inside. Still the children did not relent. They wanted this jackal to suffer. So they screamed harsh words into the hole and then set a fire around its circumference, hoping to smoke the jackal out so they could continue to beat her. The terrified jackal shrieked in pain.

At that time, Radha and her friends were walking some distance away and could hear the jackal's cries. Feeling compassion, Radha told her friend Lalita, "No one should be suffering like this. Go bring that person to me." Lalita found the children around the hole with their sticks and sent them home. Then she put out the fire. Reaching into the hole, she pulled out the jackal and brought her, trembling, to Radha. The weeping jackal bowed her head at Radha's feet. Radha knelt down and petted the jackal on the head and accepted her as her own loving associate. She gave that jackal life's perfection, pure love for God.

The jackal is like the illusioned soul, and the children are likened to the three types of misery one meets in material existence: miseries caused by one's own body and mind, by nature, and by other beings. The jackal's cry was a humble calling out for mercy. When we chant Radha's holy name (Hare, in the maha-mantra) with the kind of sincerity the she-jackal felt, Radha will give us her heart. No sincere soul will ever be denied Radha's grace.

## How to Chant with Heart

Sri Chaitanya composed a verse that is the life and soul of bhakti yogis and the essence of chanting with heart. Chanting with this mood is where the fullest blessings of chanting are to be found:

*One who thinks oneself lower than a blade of grass, who is more tolerant than a tree, and who does not expect personal honor but is always prepared to give all respect to others can very easily and regularly chant the holy name of the Lord.*

— Sri Chaitanya, *Chaitanya Charitamrita: Antya-lila* 20.21

On my own spiritual quest, the Hare Krishna maha-mantra has come to protect me at times when I was in the greatest physical, emotional, and spiritual need. Long ago, I didn't even know what it meant or where it came from, but still, I felt its power whenever I sincerely chanted.

Bhakti transforms the heart. Deep within the heart of each of us lies a seed of divine love waiting to sprout and fulfill its potential. Chanting the names of God nourishes that growth. Gradually, the seed sprouts, springs up, and blossoms into the everlasting flower of divine love.

# ◆─ PRACTICE 4 ─◆

## HEARING FROM SACRED LITERATURE

People love to be entertained. How much of our energy and time do we spend watching movies and television, listening to music, reading books, and gossiping? What if we devoted that time and energy to hearing stories and teachings that offer enlightenment? Bhakti scriptures call this type of hearing *shravana*.

The practice of shravana is as simple as dedicating quality time to reading sacred literature and attending or hearing recordings of talks that discuss transcendence and inspire devotion. With today's technology, transcendental sound vibration is easily accessible anywhere at any time. Shravana refocuses our priorities, purifies the heart, and attracts divine grace. When such transcendental sound is energized with the subject of unconditional love for the Supreme and received from pure sources, it nourishes the seed of devotion within us and can transform our lives. The purer and more realized the source, the more powerful the effect.

Since childhood I've loved to hear meaningful stories. I found everything I could dream of when I discovered the *Bhagavata Purana*, also known as *Srimad-Bhagavatam*, an ancient Vedic text that weaves together fascinating stories with the philosophy of divine love.

How the *Bhagavata Purana* was once heard is itself an enlightening story. Long ago, a group of sages assembled in a forest called Naimisha. There they saw into the future and pondered the effects of a world where people would turn away from their own hearts, disregard the needs of others, and destroy the environment that was sustaining them. They knew this climate of internal discontent would give rise to hatred, wars (fought even in the name of God), pollution, disease, and anxiety, and they were moved by compassion.

One morning, as the sun cast its first rays into the quiet forest of sprawling banyan trees, the sages sat near the bank of the Gomati River. They recognized that humanity is one family and that the responsibility of holy people is to unite and serve the society as elders, dedicated to providing both example and direction. Wanting to bring about real change, they remained there for years, absorbed in meditation, ritual, and prayer. Although wise and experienced, they were confused as to what was most beneficial.

So they approached their elder, Suta Goswami, knowing him to be a gentle soul who had received his gurus' blessings; he was a sage free from vice and learned in the scriptures. On behalf of all human- ity the sages said, "O Suta, we live in a difficult age, when people are quarrelsome, their minds always disturbed, and their attempts at spirituality often leading them to division and pain. There are many types of spiritual practices, philosophies, and scriptures. What is the essence of dharma, and what can we do to bring the ultimate good to all of humanity?"

Suta Goswami answered in what is now a series of verses recorded in the *Bhagavata Purana* that forever serve as a guiding light for those who wish to walk a spiritual path. One verse in particular encapsu- lates the heart of Suta's teaching:

*The supreme dharma for all humanity is that by which people can attain loving devotional service (bhakti) to the transcendent Lord. Such devotional service must be unmotivated and uninterrupted to completely satisfy the self.*

—BHAGAVATA PURANA 1.2.6

When I first heard a saint speak this verse, I gained a profound understanding of just how inclusive bhakti is. Suta boiled all spiritual instruction down to one principle, love, and recommended unconditional, uninterrupted loving service to the Supreme Person as the essence of all spiritual instruction for the ultimate good of humanity. This love is dormant within all of us. Earlier, I defined *dharma* as the defining substance in a thing that gives it its identity. Well, our dharma is loving service. We can reawaken to it through shravana.

Suta continued:

*By regular hearing about the Lord and rendering service to great souls, all that is troublesome in the heart is eradicated and pure bhakti (loving service) is established.*

—BHAGAVATA PURANA 1.2.18

## HEARING FROM A SPIRITUAL TEACHER

Dating back to ancient times, the word *guru* has signified a spiritual teacher or master, a person capable of guiding others to awaken to their eternal self. In one of its meanings, *gu* signifies "darkness" and *ru* "to remove." There is a verse that yoga teachers often recite as an invocation before their classes that captures this meaning:

*om ajnana timirandhasya*
*jnananjala shalakaya*
*chakshur unmilitam yena*
*tasmai sri gurave namah*

*I was born in the darkness of ignorance and my spiritual*
*guide (guru) opened my eyes with the torchlight of*
*knowledge. I offer him my respects and gratitude.*
—BHAGAVATA PURANA 8.1.11, 8.3.25

In the traditional exchange between gurus and disciples in the bhakti line, the guru's responsibilities include instructing the student, caring for the student's spiritual well-being, and guiding him or her on the path toward liberation from bondage and suffering. The disciple's responsibilities include asking sincere questions about his or her spiritual advancement, applying the guru's teachings with sincere dedication, and assisting the teacher by rendering service. The guru should be learned in scripture and a living example of what the scripture teaches, and the student should be willing to take the precepts of devotional life seriously. If both guru and disciple are qualified in this way, the transfer of knowledge is effective.

If we want to pursue any field seriously, be it medicine, music, martial arts, physics, or whatever else, we benefit by having a teacher experienced in the field. This is all the more true for becoming a spiritualist, because the principles and practices of spirituality are far deeper and more subtle than those of any other field. Practicing spirituality without a proper guide may leave us lost in the plethora of available philosophies and practices. It will be difficult to make substantial progress.

The bhakti tradition teaches that we all have a personal relationship with the Supreme and that reviving that relationship is life's ultimate goal. At present, though, we're full of misconceptions about ourselves. We identify with the body and mind and our social standing, for example, and have acquired deep-rooted fears and desires. These block the natural flow of that relationship, just as plaque blocks arteries and restricts blood flow to the heart. We suffer from a plaque of false ego that blocks the natural flow of love from the soul into the heart and out toward the Supreme and the world. Gurus, like spiritual heart doctors, guide and train their disciples to remove that plaque. In this way, they act as transparent connectors to divine grace.

Most important, gurus exemplify timeless teachings through the authenticity of their words and their own authentic following. They should have spiritual and moral integrity and compassion. As such, the defining characteristic of the guru is not the ability to perform miracles or superhuman feats but to lead an exemplary life of selfless devotion under all circumstances and to inspire and empower his or her disciples to do the same.

An essential qualification of genuine spiritual teachers in the bhakti tradition is that they themselves are disciples of a qualified teacher from an ancient line of succession, where knowledge has been passed down through history. There are four such devotional lines of succession in the Vedic tradition. This is not so different from the traditions passed down through successions of teachers in many of the Eastern schools of music, natural medicine, or martial arts. This lineage of teachers is called a *parampara*. In India, parampara affiliation has always been the standard for spiritual movements. As the Gita (4.2) says, "This supreme science of the soul was received through the chain of disciplic succession [parampara]."

The principle of guru-disciple succession can be found in many great religious traditions. In India several successions are said to have started at the dawn of creation. Others began with the earthly appearance of a particular avatar or were given prominence by the teachings of a particular saint. Each guru in a succession is responsible for preserving and disseminating his or her tradition's teachings. By studying with a teacher from an unbroken line, we receive the original revelation, and by serving our teacher, we honor all the saints in that succession, and in all other true successions.

The parampara system is intended to protect knowledge from misappropriation and adulteration. The analogy is given of receiving a ripe mango from the top of a mango tree. Several people climb the tree and form a line. The person on top hands the mango down to the person below, who passes it down to the next person, until the mango reaches the ground unbruised.

Gurus are one of three complementary sources of spiritual knowledge that work in harmony to guide a student. In addition to the guru, there is the community of saintly teachers and serious practitioners past and present, and there are the scriptures. The guru connects us to the current of truth that flows through scripture, while the community of bhaktas confirms that truth by living its spirit. Together, these three maintain and safeguard the purity of spiritual teachings. If a spiritual teacher behaves or teaches in a way that diverges from the teachings of scripture or the example set by the lineage of saints, that person is unable to represent the flow of truth.

The bhakti tradition considers the Supreme Being to be the original guru, the eternal fountainhead of knowledge and grace. All other true spiritual teachers represent that one ultimate guru, the Supreme Beloved, who is seated within our hearts. In the ancient bhakti successions, human gurus are enjoined to see themselves as humble servants of the Supreme, not to claim that they themselves are the Supreme. Gurus serve society by sincerely representing the Supreme, repeating spiritual teachings in ways that are relevant to their disciples, and living exemplary lives, so the spiritual guide provides a connection to the eternal current of wisdom and grace.

There are two principle types of gurus: the *shiksha*, or instructing, guru, and the *diksha*, or initiating, guru. The shiksha guru inspires and guides us by his or her instructions and exemplary lifestyle. There may be several instructing gurus in a person's life. The diksha guru gives initiation into a parampara for a student who has been practicing for some time and wishes to deepen and formalize his or her commitment to the path. There is generally only one initiating guru.

In the bhakti schools in India, hearing sacred texts from authentic sources has always been given primary importance. And special reverence is accorded to the Bhagavad Gita: its universal message provides inspiration, faith, and practical guidance on how to live connected with the Supreme in every situation.

## ⊱— PRACTICE 5 —⊰

### WORSHIPING THE LORD, HOWEVER YOU KNOW HIM, WITH FAITH AND VENERATION

The dictionary defines *worship* in two ways: "(a) the feeling or expression of reverence and adoration for a deity; (b) the acts or rites that make up a formal expression of that reverence." Since we have spent a lot of time discussing the first definition in relation to bhakti, this section discusses the second.

Devotional ceremonies are designed to bring our attention to the presence of God within and around us and to infuse us with that spirit. When properly understood and performed, such worship leaves deep, positive impressions within the mind. A well-designed ritual takes the practitioner's body and mind through a series of steps that are simultaneously aesthetically pleasing and spiritually purifying.

In bhakti practice, such worship is called *puja*. Puja commonly consists of offering physical objects in a specific order and with specific prayers to the object of worship. Puja is not ritual in the way many people imagine rituals—that is, routine worship without much internal participation. All worship has the power to be deeply moving spiritual experiences, but routine ritualism, or ritual performed without the heart dimension, could become sectarian observances that can alienate thoughtful people.

Truly devotional rituals are not based on superstition or ungrounded sentiment. Puja is a way of connecting with the transcendental realm; it's a tool we can use to focus the mind in our sincere intent to love and serve the Divine. As a tool, it provides us with the language to help direct our thoughts, and it engages the body in a meditation by having us perform a series of actions. In its most enlightened form, puja translates the idea of devotion into an action of devotion. The spiritual energy we generate during puja can stretch beyond the limits of time and space and transmit blessings and grace into the world.

Puja is a form of meditation—a way of absorbing body, mind, and words in devotion and aligning ourselves with the Supreme. It shapes the mind to reflect the soul's true nature. Those who perform puja find themselves cultivating gratitude and love and a strong desire to transform their lives into fully spiritual expressions.

You can think of a devotional ritual as an envelope you use to send a message to the supreme object of your love. An envelope is only as valuable as its contents. So what message would you like to send in your ritual-envelope? Would you use your puja to placate the Supreme Being? Get something you want? Make an unselfish offering of love? The answer to this question is critical, as it determines whether your ritual-envelope is material or spiritual, empty or valuable. Jesus warned against empty rituals done "according to the letter of the law but without understanding the spirit and power behind it."

All day long, our senses and mind are bombarded by images that reflect the materialism that surrounds us. On top of that come the worries and pressures of modern life. For bhakti yogis, the experience of attending or performing a puja infused with beauty and devotion—whether it's a temple ceremony, a ritual sanctifying an event like a marriage, or a simple meditative ceremony in the home—can be a refreshing way to leave our troubles behind and reconnect with our spiritual essence.

## DEITIES: IDOLATRY OR SACRED WORSHIP?

*One should worship the Deity form of the Supreme*
*until one realizes the Supreme Being's presence in one's*
*own heart and in others' hearts as well.*
—BHAGAVATA PURANA 3.29.25

Perhaps one of the more complex bhakti practices to comprehend is deity worship, which takes place in temples and yogis' homes. In Sanskrit, the deity is called an *archa-vigraha*, literally, "a shining form." My teacher, Prabhupada, used the English word *deity* to refer to this sanctified form of the Supreme in order to differentiate it from an idol.

Some Westerners are confused and even alarmed by the practice of deity worship common to Hinduism, Jainism, Buddhism, and other Eastern spiritual traditions because they mistake it for idolatry. Many Eastern traditions, however, consider deity worship a highly respected part of yogic science. All of India's spiritual traditions agree on this point: the Supreme Being is unlimited and independent, so he can appear according to his sweet will in any way he chooses, including in the form of a deity that may be made of stone, metal, earth, wood, or in the form of a painting.

Like most other scriptures of the world, bhakti texts do not advocate idolatry—the worship of arbitrary forms invented by the imagination or approached without pure spiritual intentions. Scripturally prescribed worship of authorized deities, on the other hand, is highly respected. If the deity is made according to authorized guidelines and God's presence is invoked by an enlightened guru, the Supreme Being will appear in that form to accept the worshiper's prayers and offerings and facilitate his or her meditation. The Supreme reciprocates with the purity of the worshiper's intent. You can think of the deity as a government-approved mailbox. Not just any box will do. Letters need to be dropped in a mailbox provided by the postal service in order to reach their destination.

"I am the source of all spiritual and material worlds," Krishna declares in the Bhagavad Gita (10.8). Everything emanates from the Supreme, and if he chooses, he can appear through his energy as a deity to help us remember him. As electricity flows into a light bulb to radiate light, so the Supreme can manifest his presence in a deity. Electricity is invisible, but we see it when it energizes a light bulb. In a similar way, the Lord may appear in the tangible form of a deity to help us see and feel his presence.

In several religions, devotees focus their prayers, rituals, and devotion on particular objects: Catholics use crucifixes or statues of Mary and baby Jesus to help them commune with God. The Eastern Orthodox Church uses icons. In the cathedral of San Damiano in Assisi, St. Francis, at a crossroads in his life, prayed to Jesus for direction. The painted wooden form of Jesus on the crucifix hanging above the altar spoke to him: "Francis, my church is in ruins.

Repair it." This was a moment of complete transformation for St. Francis, and it's what prompted him to abandon his life as the son of a wealthy merchant and commit himself to reviving the devotional spirit of the Church. This powerful historical event is just one example of how God, in an apparently material manifestation, reciprocated with a sincere devotee.

When we display photos of beloved family members, those images are more than paper to us, and looking at them invokes affection. Having a deity is not so different. These inner mysteries in the bhakti tradition become clearer as devotion deepens.

## THE MOOD OF WORSHIPING THE DEITY

*Arati* is a popular daily ceremony performed in Indian temples. It embodies the mystery of deity worship. During the ceremony, the worshiper offers the deity various items. The Bhagavad Gita explains that the world is composed of eight basic elements (earth, water, fire, air, and space, and on the subtler level, mind, intelligence, and ego), and each item offered during the arati represents one of them. Arati is meant to be an offering of all creation back to the Supreme Being, its creator. It is an act of gratitude and an expression of our desire to be in harmony with his will. Arati is meant to be a reciprocation of love, as when a child cooks a meal for his or her parents with the ingredients the parents have provided.

The worshiper begins the arati by waving incense before the deity. Later in the ceremony, a flower is offered. Both these items represent the earth, which is characterized by its fragrance. Then a small vessel, often a conch shell, is filled with water and offered. The quality of water is taste. A small flame represents fire, which has the quality of sight. A fan, often fashioned from peacock feathers or a yak's tail, is offered, representing the element air, whose characteristic is touch. With each article, the worshiper recites a mantra, and throughout the arati, a small or large bell is rung. These sacred sounds, which vibrate though space, constitute the offering of space, whose characteristic is sound. Remaining absorbed in the arati experience is an offering of the mind, concentration on the details of the arati is an offering of the intelligence, and the service mood with which the objects are offered is an offering of the ego. Thus arati engages every sense: sight, smell, sound, taste, and touch. And through the offering to the deity, the whole being takes part in offering the creation back to the creator with love and gratitude.

Aratis, commonly performed at dawn and dusk, can transform the worshiper's way of thinking. Thoughts of the temporal world are set aside, and worshipers move deeper into single-minded remembrance of the Supreme Beloved. Their eyes see the beautiful deity form, their ears hear the sound of the bell and, since arati is often accompanied by kirtan, the singing of the holy names. Their bodies sway to the melodic kirtan. Once their minds have left behind the challenges of the world, for a brief time at least, their soul is home again.

One of my dearest friends and someone I venerate as a truly saintly person is Yamuna Devi, who was born and raised in Oregon. At a young age, she dedicated her life to serving our guru. She gave her heart to devotion to Krishna, and she put her soul into everything she did, mastering every art she pursued in service. In 1969 she and George Harrison of the Beatles became friends. George told Yamuna that with her voice, she could become one of the greatest female vocalists of her time, and he recorded her on Apple Records. After singing on a single that became number one in England and other parts of the world and with a career ready to take off, she decided to reserve her singing voice for her beloved Radha and Krishna. Prabhupada called her singing a "symphony of pure love."

She also became a master cook and wrote an award-winning vegetarian cookbook that was rated number one internationally. Everything she did—her sewing, calligraphy, gardening, speaking, and especially her puja—was incredible.

In her home she spent hours a day making sacred offerings to her deities. Her altar was magnificent—not filled with expensive things, but with love woven into every intricate detail. Through her puja and chanting, she saturated her home and herself with bhakti. Everyone who met her or witnessed her puja—whether they were priests or atheists, hippies or Hell's Angels, rock stars or villagers, grandparents or teenagers—was deeply moved. Upon witnessing the gravity of Yamuna's character, wisdom, and love and seeing her devotion to her deity, even skeptics were transformed and had to admit that God was present. Seeing this, I too was transformed.

## How to Set Up an Altar

For those who are inspired to do so, it is simple to set up a place for puja in one's home or even one's workplace. First, find a place that can be reserved exclusively for your altar, where you can focus on your spiritual practice. It may be as simple as a table or a shelf, or you can have an elaborate altar built. Next, place a sacred object or objects that will help you connect with God, according to your spiritual tradition. This could be a painting or carving, for example. You might place photos of your guru here, or of saintly people you admire, or of a holy place you revere.

An altar allows you to find a place of refuge where you are free to focus on your internal journey through prayer, meditation, or chanting. In this sacred space, you can also practice meditational worship (puja) by offering whatever pure objects may be available: pure foods, fragrant flowers, incense, or other items. Actually, the heart is meant to be an altar within the temple of the body, where we offer our love to the Supreme.

The type of worship I have just described helps us connect to that sacred space within and allows us to express our love on an altar in our homes.

## WHEN RIVERS MEET

Sweeping down from the glacial peaks of the Himalayas through the vast forests and past the mountainous villages and caves and hermitages of the yogis, the rivers Ganges and Yamuna finally reach the Indian plains. The two rivers then flow east through seemingly endless agricultural fields, past quaint farming villages, and through bustling towns and populated cities. By the time the rivers reach their destinations, tens of millions of people daily will have bathed in them for hygiene and spiritual purification.

Nearly a thousand miles from their starting points, the two rivers converge at a holy place and embrace like lost lovers, while from below, the river Saraswati meets them. This place is Prayag, near Allahabad, in north central India. Every twelve years, throngs of the faithful gather there for the Kumbha Mela, the world's largest religious festival. In 2013 an estimated 40 million people bathed at the confluence on the day of the dark moon in January, and an estimated 80 million people came to Prayag to bathe, meet holy people, and perform their rituals during that month.

Prayag is the also the site of a fifteenth-century dialogue between Sri Chaitanya, an avatar of Krishna, and the bhakti saint and Sri Chaitanya's disciple Rupa Goswami. Prior to this meeting, Rupa had been a fabulously wealthy minister to the king of a vast kingdom. Just before this historic meeting, he had renounced everything and come to Prayag as an ascetic in search of divine love.

In that holy place, Sri Chaitanya explained to Rupa the path of bhakti, comparing the spiritual aspirant to a gardener and our dormant love to a seed buried in the field of the heart. Bhakti yoga is the art of cultivating that precious seed of devotion.

Bhakti yoga starts when we appreciate the devotional qualities in others. Such appreciation creates faith in something beyond our ordinary lives and encourages us to seek the association of those who can inspire us to go deeper. By the grace coming through those who have made some progress on the path, the seed of love of God in the field of the heart begins to stir, and we begin to want a spiritual practice as well as to live a life harmonious with our practice.

Sri Chaitanya told Rupa that spiritual practices are the water and sunshine that nourish the seed of devotion. He presented an elaborate explanation of the philosophy and practice of bhakti. Rupa Goswami recorded these practices on palm leaves and then bound the leaves into a book, *Bhakti-rasamrita-sindhu*, that has served as the guidebook for countless bhakti yogis from all walks of life over the centuries. In 1970, my teacher wrote a summary study of the book in English, now available as *The Nectar of Devotion*.

## ADDITIONAL PRACTICES

We have already discussed five potent forms of spiritual practice. Let's now explore five other practices. All are really different types of meditation, and if we practice them sincerely, the seed of devotion in our hearts will sprout and grow into a magnificent tree, on which the fruit of full self-awareness and ecstatic love of God will ripen.

### — PRACTICE —
## REMEMBERING THE DIVINE

We've already examined the importance of chanting the holy name and hearing from sacred literature, both ways to increase our meditation on the Supreme. The strength of these two practices is that they help with absorbing the mind in remembering the Lord. We may remember the Divine by meditating on a mantra, chanting the holy names with others, studying sacred literature, performing puja, or simply seeing God's hand in our daily activities. The impressions our spiritual practices create in the mind are meant to help us increase our meditation on him at all times. Such remembrance is the core of meditation in the bhakti tradition.

Just as a mother thinks lovingly of her daughter when she sees her daughter's shoes, so we can recall our soul's Beloved in everything we encounter in life. As the mind becomes more focused through chanting and self-study and as these practices awaken our love for the Supreme, so it will be natural that we begin to see everything in relation to him and never forget him. The bhakti tradition says that Krishna attracts our minds like a magnet attracts iron filings. Bhakti yogis consider this attraction to be the hidden treasure of all spiritual disciplines—the confluence where the rivers of all spiritual practice ultimately meet and are fulfilled.

Bad habits and negative thought patterns create latent impressions (samskaras, in Sanskrit) on the subconscious and are therefore difficult to break. Bhakti offers us ways to transform them. By turning our attention, as far as we are able, toward meditation on the

Supreme, who is all pure, we are purified. Such remembrance controls the mind not by merely negating thoughts but by transforming what we think about from material to spiritual. When advanced in meditation, a bhakti yogi's thoughts flow toward the Supreme like a smooth, thick, uninterrupted stream of honey.

## AN ANCIENT TALE OF A PRINCE

The *Bhagavata Purana* tells the story of the small child, Prahlad, who exemplified a simple method of remembrance. Prahlad's father was a powerful king and hated the concept of God, thinking God to be the ultimate obstruction to his tyranny, which was based on manipulation, exploitation, and terrorism. In his warped mind, worship of God was the seed of all evil. He could barely tolerate his son and heir's devotion toward such an enemy. When the boy challenged his conceptions, he realized that Prahlad would probably grow up to be his enemy too, so he decided to kill him.

The king devised a series of execution methods. First, Prahlad was thrown into a pit of venomous serpents. When that failed to kill him, the king had him sit on the lap of his sister, who had the power to withstand fire. Prahlad survived; the sister did not. Later, he was thrown off a cliff. When all other means failed, the king mixed poison with Prahlad's food. Little Prahlad never prayed to his Lord Krishna to be saved. Rather, he simply remembered Krishna with gratitude and love, and Krishna always protected him.

When Prahlad's father was finally slain, Krishna offered Prahlad any perfection he desired. Prahlad replied that he did not want anything, as he was satisfied simply to remember the infinite sweetness of his Supreme Beloved. "But," he added, "if it pleases you, please forgive my father for his countless atrocities and give him liberation from all suffering forever, in the bliss of your abode."

## A MODERN TALE OF A BUSINESSMAN

One of my dear friends, Hrishikesh, is a leading industrialist and philanthropist in India. At one time, his family managed one of the most successful companies in the country. Over the years, however, due to changes in government policies and shifts in the economy, many other companies in the same field went out of business, and after his highly revered father retired, he was practically alone in leading his company.

He spent years struggling under massive debt, complicated legal issues, and aggressive attacks, yet he always had time to help people in need. With great care, he personally reached out to serve thousands of people without expecting anything in return, not even credit for his selfless service. As he gradually lifted his company out of its turmoil, he provided shelters for widows, cared for the sick and dying, sponsored education for children, counseled impoverished families on how to improve their economic status, provided for monks in ashrams, and inspired incredible spiritual programs. He did all this with grace, dignity, and heart-melting humility. Like a lotus flower rising from the depths of a polluted pond, he remained peaceful and loving while providing hope and joy to those around him. I once asked him how he does it. With an innocent twinkle and a serene smile he told me, "By remembering all the blessings Krishna and saintly people are giving to so many people." His humble reply helps us remember what's truly valuable and reminds us of Krishna's assurance in the Bhagavad Gita: "Always think of Me, and you will come to Me without fail."

In whatever situation we may find ourselves, we can remember our higher purpose in life through these practices and find meaning, shelter, and joy.

## ⟞  PRACTICE  ⟝
### PRAYER, OR COMMUNION
### WITH THE DIVINE

Prayer is key to devotional practice, because prayer carries our intent, our aspirations, and our will to love. It's a line of communication with the Supreme, a way to cultivate an actual relationship.

Does the Supreme hear our prayers? Bhakti yoga teaches us that the Supersoul dwells in each of our hearts as our friend, witness, and benefactor. He never leaves us. Therefore, we can both reach out to him and reach him at any moment, in any place, under any circumstance. He hears and sees everything. Certainly he hears our prayers.

Sometimes people wonder: If God already knows everything, why bother to pray? The answer to this question speaks to the heart of devotional practice: it is the exchange of affection that holds meaning. Love is not predicated on who knows what or by who is right or wrong. Those who love want to communicate with each other. Those who love want to put their beloved's interests before their own. A child plucks a flower from the mother's garden and offers it to her mother. Why bother, since the flower already belongs to her mother? Prayer, like that flower, is how we express gratitude for the life we've been given. Through prayer, we tell the Supreme Beloved that we want to be near him in good times and bad and that we wish to know him. Perhaps in our prayer we tell him we're confused or happy or angry or feeling humbled. Perhaps we share our weakness and ask for strength—his strength—or just want to know that he's there with us. Whatever we say in our prayers, prayer is an opportunity to commune with the Divine.

Many people say they don't know how to pray, but prayer has no particular formula. You can draw on the words of sacred texts or the prayers of saints to form your prayers, choosing words that resonate with your feelings, or you can pray in your own language, with your own words. The key to prayer is to speak with sincerity, gratitude, honesty, and humility.

In a broader sense, prayer is not just the words we speak to our Beloved; it includes living prayerfully, mindfully aware of his presence. It's a frame of mind that we weave into everything we do. Work, service to family and society, study, spiritual practices — everything becomes energized by divine communion.

In the beginning stages of devotional life, you may find yourself praying for what you need or want. Although this is only a beginning communication, not yet based on a deeper love of the person we're approaching, it has the virtue of acknowledging a divine presence in our life. As you mature in bhakti, you will find yourself beginning to approach the Supreme not as someone to do your bidding or fulfill your needs but as the object of your service and love. Mature prayer expresses appreciation for both fortune and misfortune. Mature prayer asks not for material assistance but guidance and purity of purpose. The most mature of all prayers asks for the privilege to serve and love unconditionally, to be an instrument of divine grace in the world.

When faced with painful circumstances, a bhakti yogi asks the Lord how he or she should respond to the situation: "What will please you, my Lord? Let me grow in wisdom, become purified, and do your will." There may be some value in asking why something is happening to you, since the more we understand things, the more we may be able to guard against painful circumstances happening again. Still, the more important consideration in the mind of a bhakti-infused lover of the Supreme is, "How can I use this situation to serve you?"

The essence of any devotional prayer, whatever its origin, is to humble oneself before the benevolence of the Supreme, to glorify, seek grace, and appeal to be allowed to serve with love.

Sri Chaitanya illustrated this mood in his simple prayer: "O my Lord, I do not desire to accumulate material wealth, nor do I desire beautiful women, nor do I want followers. I do not desire even liberation from birth and death. All I want is unmotivated loving service to you" (Siksastakam 4).

Similarly, here is one of my favorite prayers spoken by the saint Vritra: "O beautiful Lord, as baby birds that have not yet developed their wings always look for their mother to return and feed them, as small calves distressed by hunger await their mothers to come back and provide their milk, or as a morose lover longs for her beloved to finally return home after long separation, I always yearn to render loving service unto you" (*Bhagavata Purana* 6.11.26).

## ← PRACTICE →
### SELFLESS ACTS:
### LIVING IN SPIRITUAL HARMONY

To love means to serve. The innate nature of the soul is to serve the Supreme with unselfish love. This loving service, by its own nature, extends to all God's children just as feeding the stomach nourishes all other parts of the body. Our greatest fulfillment is in the joy of selfless service.

Generally a servant is thought of as someone doing something low or pitiable. Hardly anyone wants to be a servant. But contrary to this common use, sacred texts declare the position of servant of God and kindness to others as an esteemed aspiration. Soon after I came to the path of bhakti, I wrote a letter to my mother in Chicago and then signed off, "Your Servant, Richard." Alarmed, my mother wrote back, "What happened to you? Why are you demeaning yourself by calling yourself a servant?" In my next letter, I signed off, "The servant of your servant, Richard." Seeing that, she decided not to pursue the topic, fearing, I imagine, how I might degrade myself further if she did. In time, though, she came to deeply appreciate that this mood of servanthood was an exalted aspiration. Actually, it was from my mother and father and their example in my life that I learned so much about unselfish loving service. When I finally returned home after my long journey to the East, I found my mother, who loved to cook for our family, had acquired a small library of vegetarian cookbooks. Although in 1972, vegetarianism was considered a radical choice (and incomprehensible to her), she loved me, so she learned to cook what I liked to eat. That small gesture still fills my heart with warmth.

Bhakti yoga teaches that to serve the Supreme Being is the dharma of every soul. Forgetful of that true self-interest, we choose to channel our natural propensity to serve into the service of temporal things that cannot and will never fully satisfy us.

Still, selfless service is how we express love. Parents express their love for their children by incredible self-sacrifice and service for years at a time. Friends and siblings convey love through all kinds of service to each another, helping each other whenever they are in need: perhaps driving, counseling, encouraging, watching each other's children, or being there to help in so many other ways. Spouses share their life goals and help each other achieve them, and like friends, they remain faithful to and supportive of each other; often raise children together; and when not directly together, serve each other by serving their children.

They give and take, and their relationship strengthens because of it. Love for humanity is expressed by serving people in need, and love expands to inspire us to serve beings outside our own society or species.

The spirit of service reaches its pinnacle when we decide to express our love to the Supreme Being. The relationship we have with God is the essence and origin of all other relationships. Directing our serving propensity to pleasing the Supreme is a way of living fully in yoga and includes all other expressions of love.

## THE TALE (AND TAIL!) OF HANUMAN

The *Ramayana* is the history of the avatar Rama, who was playing the role of a human prince. One of Rama's beloved devotees was Hanuman, who appeared as a hero in the Vanara race, a race of divinely empowered monkeys who lived in the forests of India. Hanuman exemplifies the spirit of devotional servitude, the spirit that characterizes bhakti.

The *Ramayana* tells us that the tyrannical king Ravana abducted Rama's wife, Sita, and imprisoned her on his island-kingdom of Lanka. Hanuman and a band of Vanara warriors were sent to search for Sita. When they arrived at the seacoast and learned that Ravana had taken Sita to an island eight hundred miles off the coast, they lost heart.

But Hanuman, his heart swelling with love for Lord Rama, was unstoppable. His enthusiasm to serve his Lord was so intense that even an obstacle the size of the ocean couldn't discourage him. He climbed to the top of a mountain, chanted the name of Rama, and leaped. Alone, surviving life-threatening encounters as he flew across the ocean to Lanka and facing both obstacles and dangers when he arrived, Hanuman finally found Sita weeping in separation from Rama under a tree in a walled garden. To encourage her and prove he was Rama's emissary, Hanuman presented Sita with a ring that Rama had given him for her and spoke sweet words reassuring her that Rama would soon come.

Hanuman eventually allowed himself to be captured so he could meet Ravana face to face. He was beaten, bound with ropes, and humiliated on his way to the throne room. But despite all that, he fearlessly admonished the evil king, whom he called a feeble coward, and offered ways the tyrant could be redeemed. Ravana, outraged, decided to torture Hanuman by tying oil-soaked rags to his tail and lighting them on fire. But Hanuman saw every situation as an opportunity to serve his beloved Rama. He broke free from his restraints like a true hero and jumped from rooftop to rooftop with his blazing tail, sending everything he touched up in flames. After setting the city on fire, he jumped into the ocean to extinguish his tail.

Finally, after another daring leap across the ocean, he returned to Lord Rama, reported Sita's condition, and gave Rama her message. Overwhelmed by Hanuman's service, Rama trembled as he expressed his inability to repay him. "All I have to give you," Rama said, his voice choked with emotion, "is myself." With these words, Rama embraced Hanuman to his heart as both wept in divine love for each other.

For Hanuman, pleasing Lord Rama was the ultimate perfection of all of his desires. He had surrendered his free will to the highest cause: the pleasure of Rama and compassion for those who were suffering. Hanuman remains in constant absorption in his meditation on serving Rama.

As I write these words, my mind travels back two decades to a meeting I had at Harvard University with Diana Eck, a renowned scholar of world religions. At first we spoke of theologies Eastern and Western, but when I mentioned Hanuman, Dr. Eck's eyes lit up.

Our scheduled half-hour visit was greatly (and gratefully) extended as we both marveled at Hanuman's incredible will to serve.

As we gain a deeper understanding of our inherent spiritual nature, we appreciate that serving others for God's pleasure is the most valuable gift of life. With this awareness we can recognize opportunities for seva (divine service) with our families, friends, and society wherever we may be. Even a small thing, when done in this spirit, is an exalted accomplishment. Look for, value, and respond to such opportunities, and then see how miracles unfold in your heart.

## ← PRACTICE →
### THE ULTIMATE SPIRITUAL FRIENDSHIP: FRIENDSHIP WITH THE DIVINE

*Life after life, may I be connected*
*with Krishna in this friendly attitude.*
—PRABHUPADA, PURPORT OF BHAGAVATA PURANA 7.5.23

In the Bhagavad Gita (5.29), Krishna tells us that he is everyone's most intimate friend. "A friend in need is a friend indeed." A true friend is one who will be there at both our best and worst times. From his side, the beloved Lord remains forever in our hearts, day after day, birth after birth, whether we worship him or deny him. He never abandons us, and the moment we turn to him, he's there. At the time of death, when our need for him is the greatest, if we remember our dearest friend and want his company, he escorts us to our spiritual home.

As our bhakti practice develops and our sense of service expands beyond reverence to intimacy with the Supreme, feelings of friendship toward him may awaken. Everything with him becomes sweeter as focus on his all-powerful, majestic nature is overwhelmed by an ecstatic, spontaneous exchange of love in friendship. We then not only feel cared for by our Supreme Friend but we find ourselves his well-wisher, wanting only to see him happy. The spontaneity of friendship with God comes from deep spiritual realization and harbors no pretense; but we can catch glimpses of it even in our present state as we learn to trust the Supreme more and more.

## — PRACTICE —
### SELF-SURRENDER: OFFERING ALL OF ONESELF

Self-surrender means to offer body, mind, words—our life—to the will of the Supreme. Words like *surrender*, which usually connotes capitulation and defeat, often sound frightening. But surrender to the Supreme Beloved is really victory of the true self over the false self, the ascension of soul over ego. Surrender for those on the path of devotion means to give oneself completely to transcendent love.

Surrender is at the heart of most spiritual traditions and is, at times, exemplified in extreme ways just to give us a glimpse of the depths of a devotee's heart. In the Bible we find Jesus in the olive grove at Gethsemane. Knowing his crucifixion was near, he prayed, "Father, if you are willing, remove this cup from me; nevertheless, let not my will, but your will, be done." There is a parallel to this in the Old Testament: Abraham accepting the Lord's order to sacrifice his beloved son Isaac. Both acts of surrender were glorious, inspiring millions of people to the present day.

The Vedic scriptures too have countless stories of surrender, including those of kings and queens, ascetics, mothers, children, and working people who have dedicated body, mind, and words to the loving service of their Beloved. Here is the story of

Draupadi, from the Bhagavad Gita, which is embedded within the text of the 100,000-verse epic, the Mahabharata. Draupadi's story is pondered by scholars and ascetics and also by children — it's a favorite bedtime story!

The story takes place in a magnificent palace. There, the most powerful royal warriors had assembled, unaware of Prince Duryodhana's evil plot. Duryodhana was ablaze with envy toward his cousins, the five Pandavas, because they were the rightful heirs to the throne he coveted. The Pandavas' father, the king, died when they were children, and Duryodhana's father usurped the throne for his son. Duryodhana's father was blind and therefore considered not fit to rule, but he was nevertheless able to exploit the Pandavas' vulnerability and plotted with his son to humiliate and discredit the Pandavas, exile them, and ultimately murder them.

In this particular story, Duryodhana wanted to hurt the Pandavas in an especially painful way by dishonoring their wife, Draupadi. (Draupadi was married to all five of the Pandava brothers, but that's another story.) Duryodhana coveted her, so he sent one of his brothers, a powerful warrior, to enter the women's quarters and drag Draupadi by the hair into the assembly where her husbands were being cheated of everything they owned. Like a rabbit caught in the claws of a tiger, she was unable to free herself. Duryodhana ordered his brother to strip Draupadi in front of her husbands and the council in order to show that he was making her a slave.

For a virtuous woman, this public shaming was more painful than death. The members of the assembly shouted cruel words at her that pierced her heart like burning spears. She pleaded for mercy, but the warriors present just laughed.

Feeling powerless, she collapsed. Duryodhana's brother again grabbed her long black hair and yanked her to her feet. Then, taking

hold of the end of her sari (saris are six feet of cloth that are wrapped
to cover the body) and with lust in his eyes, he prepared to disrobe her.

Her large, lotus-shaped black eyes, glazed with tears of desperation, implored her heroic husbands to save her. Sitting on the side-
lines, they hung their heads, hearts pounding with rage and anguish.
They too were prisoners of fate and could do nothing to protect her.
She then turned toward the throne, but the usurping king ignored
her. She cried out for help to the noblemen, but either they were
obligated to follow the king's lead or they were themselves intimi-
dated by the evil prince. None would meet her eyes.

As Duryodhana's brother started tugging at her clothes,
Draupadi began to speak a frenzy of condemnations, calling the
warriors debased cowards with no character. But she was alone and
in danger. Frantically, she tried to pull her sari tighter around herself with her soft fingers, but it was futile. The warrior played with
her like a cat with a mouse. Draupadi despaired. In that state, she
realized that only God could save her. She threw up her arms as a
gesture of surrender, and with tears of sincerity she cried out with
an emotion straight from her heart, beseeching the Lord to accept
her as his own regardless of what happened to her in this uncertain
world. From her heart of hearts she cried out her Lord's beautiful
names: "O Govinda! O Krishna!"

The Lord, who ordinarily will not interfere with the doings of
humans, could not resist her love. He took the form of sari cloth. Because
Krishna is unlimited, Draupadi's sari became unlimited. Although the
warrior pulled on her sari with all his strength, he couldn't remove it:
however much cloth he managed to strip from her was replaced by the
Krishna-sari, and Draupadi remained covered. But he did not give up,
and Draupadi spun like a top, her arms raised high and her heart chanting the Lord's names. Duryodhana's brother pulled until the assembly

hall was filled with fabric. Eventually he fell exhausted to the ground. Draupadi, however, remained in the loving embrace of her Dearmost.

He whom when Moses petitioned him had appeared as a pillar of fire to save unarmed Israelites from a pharaoh's army now appeared as a never-ending sari cloth to save Draupadi. Both examples show that the Lord responds to the sincerity and humility with which we approach him. Even if the physical body may succumb to external circumstances, the true blessing of self-surrender is the soul's eternal freedom in God's limitless love and the awakening of our love.

Although these stories give us historical examples of surrender in extreme circumstances, this spirit can be applied in our everyday lives by making the will of the Supreme our priority and recognizing that we are simply caretakers of what is, after all, his property. Surrender means to use everything in harmony with his will. Imagine how liberating this is to the spirit when we stop trying to control what isn't ours with our misguided ego. Imagine how little we would then be driven by selfishness and anxiety.

Sometimes we may feel that our spiritual growth is impeded by our past behaviors. But whatever we have done or not done in the past is forgiven if we release our past bad habits and offer our hearts in surrender. This is beautifully revealed in a statement Lord Rama makes in the *Ramayana*: "If a person comes to Me saying, 'I am yours' even once, with all sincerity, then I shall give that person protection from all danger forever after. This is my solemn vow made here before you all. Even if Ravana, my archenemy, himself came to me, I would not refuse him."

The Bhagavad Gita tells us that the Supreme Being reciprocates not according to our material qualifications or disqualifications but in relation to the sincerity of our surrender. There's a story about an event that took place in fifteenth-century South India that illustrates this truth.

Every day, erudite scholars gathered in the courtyard of a temple to study and debate philosophy. In a corner of that courtyard sat a solitary man dressed in simple clothes. He was uneducated and obviously didn't fit in with the esteemed gathering. Each day, the scholars watched him struggle just to read the Bhagavad Gita. His pronunciation was a mockery to the assembly. Clearly he was illiterate. Still, he cried tears every time he picked up the book. Was he mad? The proud scholars scoffed at him.

Then one day, the Krishna avatar Sri Chaitanya visited the temple and saw this man staring at his book and crying.

"What are you reading?" he asked.

The man looked up. "I cannot read properly, so I do not really know what the text says. But my guru told me to come to this courtyard daily and read aloud the entire seven hundred verses of the sacred Gita. Sometimes I think I say the verses right, but other times I know I'm saying them wrong. I don't know how to do better. But I continue because I'm just trying to please my teacher."

"But why are you crying?" Sri Chaitanya asked.

The man sighed. "As I read, in my mind I see Krishna, who is all-beautiful, speaking to his devotee Arjuna. Krishna is the all-powerful God, yet he has accepted the humble role of a charioteer just to show kindness to his faithful devotee. I cry with joy to think of God's love for his devotees."

Sri Chaitanya lifted the man to his feet and embraced him. "You," he said, "are a true scholar of the Gita, for you have realized its conclusion."

Surrender involves the will to try to please the Supreme Beloved with a sincere, humble, grateful heart.

Each one of these primary bhakti practices, if done sincerely, can bring us to a state of perfected love. Still, among these practices, chanting, either aloud or quietly, enriches all other practices and is in itself a complete offering.

All bhakti practices are built on a foundation of integrity, enthusiastic effort, and sincere intent. Practice bhakti sincerely and you will realize that God's love is in you and all around you, and you will see the whole world in the light of that love.

# Leading a Spiritual Life

*Adversity is the first path to truth.*
—LORD BYRON

## OBSTACLES TO THE PATH

It's possible to transcend the world even while living in it. After all, it is here in this world, with all its ups and downs, that we have our chance for enlightenment. I meet all kinds of people in my travels, from billionaires to the destitute, from professors to the illiterate, from the upright to the immoral, and each of these encounters has shown me that no one is exempt from the challenges of living in the material world, no matter what path they're on or how spiritual they are. Our greatness is not measured by how long we live or how many things we accumulate but whether we live with integrity despite the changing weather.

*If you lose your wealth, you have lost nothing;*
*If you lose your health, you have lost something;*
*If you lose your character, you have lost everything.*
—WOODROW WILSON

194 THE JOURNEY WITHIN

A successful spiritual life is measured by the quality of our character and how well we've learned to love unconditionally and be loved unconditionally. But it's not easy. The world doesn't make it easy.

It's inevitable that we'll face obstacles as we step onto a spiritual path, coming both from ourselves and from the world. It can be disorienting to learn that everything we assumed we knew about the world and ourselves isn't as true or meaningful as we thought. How do we navigate through obstacles and still embrace spiritual transformation? We start by briefly exploring some of the main obstacles to practice, which can be sorted into three broad categories: inertia, laziness, and distraction.

The dictionary defines *inertia* as "a tendency to do nothing or to remain unchanged." It relates to two sides of a coin: having fixed habits and routines that stifle our progress and not being able to relinquish them and not having the self-discipline to step forward and create new habits even when we want to. Sometimes progress requires that we leave unfavorable habits behind. But as the saying goes, "Old habits die hard."

The momentum of past tendencies directed toward something that is contrary to our spiritual progress tends to inexorably drag us from our real goals. But we can answer the call for positive change by filling our lives with alternatives that lift us away from unfavorable habits, and thus we can rise above all the excuses the mind provides for clinging to them. Krishna gives Arjuna a formula for overcoming inertia in the Gita (2.59): "The embodied soul may be restricted from sense enjoyment, though the taste for sense objects remains. But, ceasing such engagements by experiencing a higher taste, he is fixed in consciousness."

Inertia is sometimes fueled by laziness in our practice. Laziness in the spiritual sense may leave us actively attentive to our mundane responsibilities but procrastinating our spiritual needs. Constructing a building without investing in a solid foundation may serve our short-term goals but not offer much long-term stability. A child may see going to school as impeding his fun, but if he has good parents, they will have a higher, long-term plan for his happiness. Similarly, if we do not actively invest in our spiritual growth, our quality of life remains shallow and vulnerable to life's uncertainties and to the demands of the senses. Yet even when we know all these things, we still live in a demanding world and are accustomed to value what we see as tangible results, blurring focus on our internal needs.

Distraction is another primary obstacle to practice. We are diverted at any moment in countless ways: from within by our mind and senses and from without by people and things, events, and circumstances. Weapons of mass distraction constantly bombard us. To capture our attention, the media invests huge resources in ads for entertainment of all sorts, and with the advancements in technology—the Internet, smart phones, smart TVs, and all sorts of other handheld devices—these influences are becoming more invasive. Those who have a strong spiritual connection can learn to use these devices to their advantage, but for most of us, they all too often divert us from our life's purpose. If we're not careful, distractions big and small will invite us to spend a moment with them and then take us for a long ride.

Obstacles to practice are overcome by sincerity and determination. Keeping company with inspirational, exemplary people nourishes determination, as does reading enlightened literature and hearing uplifting recordings. By giving quality time to spiritual practices, we tap into our inherent determination. We each have the power within us to overcome challenges. We need to recognize that power and strengthen it by exercising it for our own benefit. Every time we make a choice to exercise our divine nature, our spiritual determination grows stronger. However, each time we choose to serve our unfavorable tendencies, our determination weakens. It's said that "God helps those who help themselves." With a positive attitude empowered by faith, we can overcome obstacles and attract a higher power.

## OBSTACLES TO FAITH

Let's now explore obstacles to faith. The experience of feeling betrayed could be a serious test of our faith—betrayal in relationships, when we betray ourselves and when our bodies betray us through illness.

When we put trust in people and it is betrayed, it can deeply hurt both emotionally and spiritually. This can happen to anyone and in ways we may never expect. It may come, in a sense, as the suffering or death of a well-wishing loved one, or it may come upon us in more antagonistic ways, such as the disloyalty of a spouse, the upheaval of a divorce, or when a friend or family member breaks trust. We can feel betrayed too when we encounter envy or unkindness or abuse, whether in our private life or within a community, or by heartbreak when a spiritual leader disappoints us by inappropriate actions. All of these can afflict faith.

People are prone to feel betrayed by themselves just as much as by others when they face their personal failings, shortcomings, or mistakes, especially when these failings affect their relationships, vocation, or spiritual efforts.

Illness is also a common, and at times serious, obstacle to faith, particularly when it is prolonged. It can lead one into such despair that a person may challenge, "Why does God deny me my health?" The emotional storm induced by any of these betrayal experiences can lead us to question our faith in the Supreme, or even the heart of our relationship with him (Does he care about me?) or to blame him for our pain.

By keeping company with people who have strong faith and by cultivating our personal inner connection through philosophical understanding and spiritual practice, we gain a broader perspective of people and events and what they really mean to us. Instead of blaming other people or even God, we can learn to transcend apparent contradictions in the heart by seeing through the eyes of love and forgiveness. I remember visiting Ram Das some time after his stroke. He was sitting in his wheelchair, eyes glistening with gratitude. He told me how he viewed his condition: "Like a father affectionately caresses his child, God caressed me with a loving *stroke* of grace." I found his realization both heartwarming and profound.

As we progress on the spiritual path, we gain beautiful internal experiences that protect our faith from apparent contradictions and disappointments. When we are touched by divine love, our soul's true treasure, nothing will be able to deter us from serving that love. The light of grace protects us even in the darkest times.

In my many years of counseling people on the spiritual path, I've heard over and over again about the disappointment of feeling far from the goal and of the lingering of unwanted desires. If you feel this, evaluate how sincerely you are following your path. Are your meditation, chanting, prayers, and study regular and attentive? Are you striving to live with integrity, eager to respect and serve others? Bhaktivinode, a saint in the bhakti tradition, has recommended that at the end of each day we ask ourselves if, on that day, our love for God has grown and, if not, how we can improve.

Sometimes feeling far from the goal of unconditional love is a catalyst to appreciating the value of that love and not taking it for granted. The fire of yearning for God in separation can burn away attachments born of ego and open the door to intimate realizations. When we truly appreciate the limitless value of spiritual love, we can live our practice with enthusiasm and have patience that however long it takes to attain it is a small price to pay for it.

Still, even after knowing all of these things, for many people a very difficult obstacle to developing faith is what they see happening in the world. Events seem to contradict our intuitive reasoning or even what we understand to be the laws of karma. We want to think a benevolent, loving God controls the universe, but why do bad things happen to good people? What follows is a very personal story.

## WHEN BAD THINGS HAPPEN
## TO GOOD PEOPLE

One fateful morning, I read a disturbing headline on the Internet: "Nepal Plane Crash Kills 15, 7 from Mumbai" (*Times of India*, May 15, 2012). The news spread across the world through television networks, the Internet, and newspapers.

For a moment I wondered if I might know any of the casualties, but I dismissed that thought quickly. There are 15 million people in Mumbai. What were the chances that I'd know the seven who died during this plane crash? Still, my anxiety lingered.

Then I got the call that eight, not seven, members of my own spiritual family had lost their lives in that crash. My heart went numb. Each of the Mumbai dead was someone I knew and loved. These eight friends had been on a pilgrimage in the Himalayas. It's a difficult pilgrimage, and few people dare to make it. On the last leg of their journey, while flying over the snow-capped mountains, a strong wind blew their twenty-seat propeller airplane into the side of a mountain. It happened in the remote holy place known as Muktinath, "the place where one is given liberation." A tragic end for such a noble journey.

The next day while I was in New York City, I got a phone call from Mumbai. It was from a young woman in her twenties who has been like a daughter to me since she was a child. She lost her mother, father, and younger brother on that plane, and when she spoke to me, she was weeping uncontrollably. Finally, she blurted out, "I don't want to live anymore. Why them and not me?"

To be with my spiritual family, I canceled the rest of my American tour and returned to India. Each of the thousands of people in our congregation knew at least one of the departed souls intimately; they were special to all of us. The community immediately began supporting the affected families in an incredible display of love and service.

One of the victims was Taruni, a charming fourteen-year-old girl who drew everyone's affection. She had been on the flight with her mother. I named her on the day of her birth. Whenever I saw her, I felt blessed with joy. I had seen her just a month before her passing away. I was leaving a birthday gathering, on my way to the Mumbai airport, when Taruni shyly approached me, her mother at her side. They knew I would be gone for several months, and Taruni tearfully handed me a delicate jasmine flower and said, "I will miss you so much, so much, so much." Now my heart echoed her words.

During Taruni's memorial service, media vans covered three blocks of the street outside her home. She had been a child star in several Bollywood movies, adored by the nation for her sweetness. Amitabh Bachchan, perhaps the most popular actor in India, with whom Taruni had costarred, wrote, "I am shocked and deeply grieved by the tragic end of Taruni. She was an exceptional child. Please, God, may this not be true."

Although Taruni had been showered with media attention and fame at an incredibly young age, she had remained humble. She loved Krishna and her friends and family as if she were everyone's daughter. I couldn't imagine the grief of her father, an old friend of mine, who in this tragedy lost his only child and his wife.

On arriving in Mumbai, I found beauty in the exceptional outpouring of support from the congregation toward the affected families. Their homes were filled with friends who cooked and cleaned and consoled and shared their love by singing kirtan together. It seemed that the passing of these dear souls united the hearts of the community members. When nothing else makes sense, sometimes compassion can touch us to the core.

Still, besides the outpouring of compassion, the pain of the community was profound, and the shock of suddenly losing eight members overwhelming. I found that bewilderment gnawed at the hearts even of our seasoned spiritual practitioners. Everyone wanted to know why this had happened. I could see the question in their eyes. So I spent my days giving talks on finding grace in the face of tragedy and consoling the families of the deceased. Intense grief is like a fortress wall, difficult to penetrate with words alone, but shared sorrow can help make those words more meaningful.

So, why *do* bad things happen to good people?

People are inclined to categorize whatever happens to them or in the world into tidy logical or philosophical boxes. While that may satisfy the intellect, it doesn't always reach the heart. Spiritual knowledge is not just about *knowing* but *transforming*. While grieving for the loss of our beloved members, our congregation hoped to learn and grow from the tragedy. So before answering the important question of why, we started with beautiful remembrances of each of the departed souls, reflecting on what we lost by their departure and what we had gained by everything they had given us. We reflected on how rare and unique each person was, and on the blessings their eternal souls gained through their devotional lifestyles.

Then we turned to the question: Why? And inevitably, we turned to the sacred literature for perspective. The *Bhagavata Purana* tells the story of Bhishma, grandfather of the Pandavas, heroes of the Mahabharata. On his deathbed he mused aloud to his grandchildren about why their lives had been so difficult. They were, after all, intimate devotees of their Lord and personifications of morality, honesty, and devotion. Why did they have to endure exile, defamation, assassination attempts, and the murder of their loved ones? Why *them*?

Weeping, he told them that no one can know the plan of the Lord. "Even though great philosophers inquire exhaustively, they are bewildered. . . . In my opinion, this is all due to inevitable time, under whose control everyone in every planet is carried, just as the clouds are carried by the wind."

With these opening words, Bhishma gives us a glimpse into the depth of the subject he is about to address. Basically he's saying that it's difficult to know why good people suffer because the answer is beyond what we can see. But Bhishma went on to explain that when we understand the larger picture of reality, we realize that the Lord's grace on any soul is always perfect. However, in the harsh light immediately following a tragic incident, even great philosophers are often "bewildered."

While it's tempting to focus our thoughts on how a particular body is affected by specific events or to look for someone to blame, the enlightened mind sees an immortal soul passing through a fleeting moment of tragedy or death on its timeless journey toward spiritual freedom.

Along the way, each person's unique perspective will affect his or her outlook on what's good or bad. We've all looked back at particular moments in our lives and understood how things that seemed bad at the time turned out to be blessings, and even how things that appeared to be good turned out to be curses. Stretch this continuum of good and bad out over this one lifetime and beyond and you'll see a general pattern of progress. It's natural that we tend to limit our viewpoint at any given moment to our present state of mind without considering the overall benefit an event may have to the soul. We can't see the full picture because our limited mind and senses can't see too much of the past or almost any of the future. But we can understand from enlightened people that God's grace awaits us in every situation, and we will recognize it if we open our hearts to it.

Though the general Vedic way of evaluating destiny is to look at cause and effect (karma), the Bhagavad Gita explains life from an even broader perspective. The nature of everything in the world is temporary and constantly changing, the Gita tells us. Therefore loss here is inevitable for everyone. The Gita says:

*From the highest realm in this material world to the lowest, all are places of suffering. But one who attains My abode never takes birth again in this material world.*

— BHAGAVATA GITA 8.16

The Gita also tells us that the spiritual abode is within each of us. It's our home, the place of our real comfort. The Bible echoes this truth: "Make your treasure not in this world where thieves plunder, rust corrodes, and moths destroy, but in the kingdom of God. The kingdom of God is within you."

See the bigger picture. For the imperishable soul, this lifetime is like a single pencil point in a long line of many lifetimes with dots extending to eternity. If we can't see beyond the present moment, we've missed the point.

We may never fully understand why tragic things happen to people, but there are three things we can know for sure:

1. Because everything is temporary, the material world is a place of eventual suffering.

2. We are souls whose existence stretches beyond the ever-changing conditions of this world. We are actually eternal. When we realize this, we become joyful.

3. Grace is behind everything that exists. If we take shelter of grace, in the course of time, we will recognize the source of grace, the Supreme Being, our eternal friend. He will shelter us from life's storms. Krishna promises his protection in the Gita (2.20, 9.34):

   For the soul there is neither birth nor death, nor having once been does it ever cease to be. . . . Being completely absorbed in me, surely you will come to me.

There is a place in the heart that is accessible only by faith, trust, and love. In this sacred space within us, the heart accepts what the mind and intellect may not be able to understand as they witness the endlessly changing universe.

For the mourning family and friends of those who died in the plane crash, connecting with this sacred inner space was a community effort, much like the embracing roots of the redwood trees. Over the next few days, several small memorials and funerals took place, culminating in a large memorial service at our Mumbai temple. Thousands came together throughout the day to share their memories of the departed souls and offer their songs and prayers for those souls and their families.

At that larger service, my message was simple: "These souls have moved on to a higher place, so we should rejoice for them and celebrate their lives. Yet we are now bereft of their physical association. Let every tear we shed tonight be a tribute of love and gratitude to their beloved souls. Those tears will nourish the flower of divine love in our hearts and keep us connected forever."

## TRANSFORMING FEAR

When tragedy strikes innocent people, it confuses us. The world may seem cruel and meaningless, and we can lose faith. As we make a deeper spiritual connection, however, our perception of life and the world transforms. This happens by the power of grace. What was once invisible to us becomes seen. The preponderance of the laws of karma will recede into the background as an infinitely higher reality moves into the foreground. The story of life even in apparently ugly times becomes beautiful when we tune into this shift in perspective. The darkness of illusion is dispelled as we step into the light of grace, a light that shines inside and outside everything and everyone but which we so often fail to see. Grace is supremely powerful yet infinitely soft, sweet, and gentle. Being touched by it gives us the eyes to recognize that beyond life's unpredictable circumstances, the loving hand of the Supreme Friend is within our reach. That hand is there to protect, empower, and shelter us and, ultimately, to offer us freedom. Trusting such benevolence can lift us above fear.

## FAITH IS MORE THAN A BELIEF

The spiritual path requires an investment on our part: reasonable, soundly rooted faith. Faith isn't about being "religious"; it's really a change of consciousness. It's not so much about understanding what happens after death as it is about transforming yourself now. It isn't about what you believe (beliefs are changeable) but what you trust with your intelligence, your intuition, and your heart. From the devotional viewpoint, faith is a conduit by which we become linked with God, with each other as spiritual beings, and with the world.

Faith by this expanded definition helps us see that the world transforms for us, not against us. It helps us understand that grace is a power higher than the laws of nature and is always awaiting us when we orient ourselves to receive it. Still, it is helpful to understand the subtle mechanics of creation — that there are laws of nature that hold us responsible for our actions, or what the ancient texts of India call the laws of karma and what Jesus referred to when he said, "As you sow, so shall you reap." At the same time, we are never without hope and support as we pass through the sunny and stormy seasons of life. Faith allows us to see that both the happiness and suffering are not random but helpful to our development as spiritual beings and to understand that we are free to choose progressive development or something else.

## KARMA

The word *karma* literally means "action." The law of karma refers to our actions and the reactions we set in motion when we do something. India's spiritual traditions consider the law of karma a natural law, similar to the law of gravity. That is, it's a law that acts irrespective of whether one believes in it or not.

Acts of kindness offered to others tend to attract acts of kindness to ourselves; malicious actions tend to do the opposite, and we feel pain.

Of course, our experience in this world often shows us the opposite: good people suffer and bad people go unpunished. But all actions have corresponding reactions, and all reactions are fulfilled in time. Whatever action is performed is like planting a seed that will eventually grow to produce a corresponding reaction. A seed may lie in the ground for some time, but when conditions are right, it will sprout and grow. We can't always predict when this will happen.

The principle of karma is simple, but the details of how it operates are complex.

One of my own experiences provided me an analogy for understanding how to effectively process the concept of karma. Some years ago, I contracted malaria. I couldn't trace when the infected mosquito had bitten me, and I therefore had no way to know where I was at the time or even where I was bitten. Neither could I discern which mosquito bit me. But my symptoms were clear: I had been bitten by a malaria-carrying mosquito and now had to take the proper treatment. I also realized I should be more careful in the future; for instance, when I am now in infested areas, I try to sleep under a mosquito net.

We may not be able to trace the specific reason for our suffering, but we can ascertain that at some time we have acted in a way that sowed the seed that grew into our present condition. We might have committed that action in this life or another. It doesn't really matter. What matters is recognizing our symptoms, taking the proper treatment now, and being careful to avoid reinfection in the future.

Faith opens one's eyes to the idea that the world transforms for us as opposed to against us. The philosophy of karma is not meant to induce depression or an unhealthy guilt; it is provided to help us grow emotionally and spiritually in whatever our situation is by taking responsibility for our choices and then gaining wisdom from whatever ensues. With this understanding, let's briefly explore ways we can benefit from this vision.

Think of karma as an aspect of the universe that realigns itself in response to how we live in the universe. That is, for every action, there will be a corresponding reaction. Because life is a long continuum of actions and reactions, our results include both joy and suffering. Both can bring wisdom if we open ourselves up to our responsibility for our actions and we desire that wisdom. Making wise choices in our personal behavior, especially in how we treat others, is often a good place to start when thinking of how to apply the concept of karma to better ourselves.

## THE INNER EFFECT OF KARMA

According to the law of karma, there is a progression that leads to and perpetuates suffering:

1. The seed of suffering is ignorance of our true nature as a loving servant of the Supreme Being.

2. From ignorance of the self, we seek pleasure outside our true nature and develop selfish desires.

3. Selfish desires impel one to engage in immoral activity.

4. Immoral activity produces two types of reactions: manifest and unmanifest. Manifest reactions are those we are suffering now, and unmanifest reactions are those that lie in wait, like a seed, for the proper moment to germinate. These will eventually grow and bear the fruit of physical or emotional suffering.

It's crucial to understand that by engaging in immoral activities, we strengthen the inner selfish desire and exacerbate the inclination to engage in those same suffering-producing activities again and again.

Our thinking shapes our behavior, and our behavior in turn shapes our thinking, so the more we think we are getting away with selfish behavior, the more we will repeat it. Selfish thoughts beget selfish actions, which beget more selfish thoughts. It's not hard for this cycle to turn into addiction. Every cigarette I smoke will increase my smoking habit, and the more my body craves nicotine, the more I'll obsess about smoking. If you look at it, you'll see that many actions you perform follow this thinking-acting-thinking cycle, or the cycle of habituation.

On the positive side, this means that we can focus on the types of thoughts and acts that bring us "good" karma and avoid the thoughts and acts that bring us "bad" karma. If I make a habit of being kind, compassionate, and loving toward others, I'll reinforce those thoughts and behaviors until they become second nature. Similarly, if I cut down on my smoking, eventually the storm of withdrawal will pass and my smoking habit will gradually disappear. Of course, some habits are harder to establish or break than others, but it's universally true that we are creatures of habit and habits can be changed. This means that unmanifest negative karmic consequences can be mitigated or reversed through sincere reformative effort and positive experiences enhanced by good thoughts and actions.

Every time we give in to anger, greed, or the cravings of the mind and senses, we're watering the roots of those behaviors. Strong roots make strong, branching plants, so the chance that we'll give in to our cravings increases. If we curb those tendencies, however, and choose instead to act in a way that builds physical, emotional, and spiritual health, we'll also build spiritual stamina and the strength to resist temptation in the future. The obstacles to healthy behavior are different for each of us, but the general principle applies to everyone: replace behaviors that impede growth with behaviors that nourish it, and the flower of self-realization will bloom.

Just as a tailor fashions a glove to fit the shape of a hand, nature, in conformity with the law of karma, provides the soul with a body that perfectly fits the desires stored in the mind and the nonmanifest karma from previous lives.

Still, in our exploration of the self, the critical point to realize is that karma never touches the atma, or soul. It is the body and mind that experience good and bad karmic reactions. Karma is a material law that functions in the material sphere. It does not affect the eternal self.

This means that nothing we do is either so good or so bad that it can change who we really are: an eternal loving servant of the Supreme Beloved. As I have explained, the dharma of something is that thing that cannot be taken away. You can't separate heat from fire and still have fire, and you can't be separated from your nature of eternal loving service to the Supreme no matter what you do. What we can do is speed up or delay realization of our true nature through our thoughts and behavior. We can choose to fall deeper and deeper into the darkness of forgetfulness, or awaken to the light of truth.

## THE SOUL IS UNTOUCHED

*As the moon on water appears to flicker,*
*so too the soul who identifies with the body.*
—BHAGAVATA PURANA 3.7.11

If the pains and pleasures of karmic reaction do not touch the soul, then what does it mean to feel pain or pleasure and what does it mean that we are held responsible for our actions?

Pain and pleasure affect a soul influenced by the false ego that identifies with the temporary body and mind. It's as if we're living in a dream that never seems to end. The *Bhagavata Purana* (11.11.2) describes the condition: "Just as a dream is merely a creation of one's intelligence but has no actual substance, similarly, material lamentation, illusion, happiness, distress, and the acceptance of the material body under the influence of illusion are all creations of God's illusory energy. In other words, the soul's illusory identification with material existence has no essential reality."

Imprudent choices implicate us in particular karmic reactions, including rebirth in another material body. So although karma does not affect the eternal self directly, it does prolong suffering in the dream of misconception. As long as our actions are selfish, we remain in an environment that facilitates selfish behavior.

The yoga texts state that human beings have been given the priceless gift of free will, which can be exercised to do great good or great harm. But with the blessing of much free will comes responsibility. A human being can choose to be a saint or a criminal or anything in between. We are responsible for the consequences of our words and actions.

I once knew a wealthy father who left his two sons equal shares of his estate before he died. One followed his father's guidance and bought a beautiful home, got married, and raised his family there. The other fell in with bad company and ended up investing part of his father's money in a narcotics deal. He thought it would help him get even richer quickly. He was caught and has now spent the greater part of his life in prison: he's still there, thirty years later. He chose to turn a blessing into a curse. He didn't have to make the choices he did, but making them left him with these devastating consequences.

Let's now hear about someone who turned a curse into a blessing. I met a woman who was horrifically abused and neglected as a child. Unable to cope with her misery, she became addicted to drugs during her teenage years and supported her habit with theft and prostitution. As the years passed, she came to the point of total desperation and realized she had to change or die. She got herself into rehabilitation, which changed her life. Now she helps other drug addicts make the same leap. She believes that everything she endured as a child and her subsequent addiction has given her profound insight into why abuse victims find their way into addictive behaviors, empowering her with compassion. This woman chose to transform a curse into a blessing, and she now offers the same opportunity to others in a way that hardly anyone else can do. She is grateful for her experiences, no matter how difficult they were at the time.

Once we act, we're bound to the karmic reactions of our choices, just as once we board a plane to Chicago, we can't change our destination midway. But once we're on board, as well as when we reach our destination, we can make new choices that will allow us to sow the seeds of a more beneficial future. To a significant extent, we are the makers of our own destinies.

## MISCONCEPTIONS ABOUT KARMA

Unfortunately, many people who know something about the science of karma misunderstand its spirit. When they face difficulties, they think their suffering implies that they are bad people, and so they hate themselves, which makes matters worse. However, as I explained to Dorothy in the airport in Florida, awareness of karmic principles should foster a desire for wisdom and humility, not impel us to beat ourselves up with guilt.

What's the difference between humility and self-flagellation? Humility is self-awareness. It gives us a modest and realistic view of ourselves that neither inflates our ego nor deflates our self-esteem. With humility we no longer see ourselves through the lens of our insecurities. Humility should lead to a healthy questioning of ourselves, which leads to following that "still, small voice" of conscience. And that leads to self-acceptance and tolerance, compassion, and forgiveness of ourselves and others. The most humble are the most self-aware. So awareness of how karma works not only leads us toward wholesome thoughts and actions, but equips us with the tools necessary to maintain a stable self-confidence in response to the inevitable challenges of life.

Ultimately these teachings are given to help us recognize the true beauty and greatness of who we really are in relation to the Supreme, the world, and all others. It is said, "Humility is not to think less of yourself but to think of yourself less."

Some say that knowledge of karma makes people fatalistic and justifies being unproductive, lazy, or indifferent to the suffering of others. After all, if everything is predestined, why should we try for anything? But nothing in the concept of karma supports this misconception. In fact, it's quite the opposite: knowing that a situation has its origin in something other than chance is a strong impetus for change. Eighteenth-century British statesman Edmund Burke said, "All that is necessary for the triumph of evil is that good men do nothing." Proper understanding of how the universe operates should soften the heart, not make it more callous.

## SEEING BENEVOLENCE IN THE LAWS OF NATURE

The actual benefits of understanding nature's laws, including the law of karma, are realized when the understanding is applied to improve one's quality of life, not to judge ourselves or others or to make blanket assumptions about one another's suffering. Here is a meditation, drawn from the realizations of ancient sages on the inherent benevolence of nature's laws. This meditation offers a grateful, positive view that takes us beyond the world's often harsh realities.

The law of karma acts like a fever. Karmic reactions purge what is unhealthy in the world, just as a fever in the body burns up harmful bacteria. If you want to understand the law of karma, you have to look beneath the surface of how the world operates.

Karma is not just a mechanical law; it's responsive and dynamic — nature's way of restoring health. What feels like punishment is actually for our ultimate benefit. This natural law is essentially an expression of Mother Nature's love and will ultimately heal us if we respond well to it.

Don't measure the law of karma with eyes that see only the immediate, viewing only what affects the body and mind, no matter how ruthless or unjust things may appear on the surface. We have to take a broader view: we are eternal souls in need of healing and focus in order to regain our spiritual health.

## KARMA AND BHAKTI YOGA

Bhakti yoga is a practice that takes us beyond karma and frees us from both manifest reactions and those lying in seed. Bhakti is based on living true to oneself, in harmony with nature and her source, and reconnects us to the current of grace, allowing the endless cycle of karmic action and reaction to, in time, finally come to an end. Words and deeds offered in devotional service produce no karma at all, but nourish the seed of pure love.

Through bhakti, we gradually perceive God's love all around us and we embrace our life's circumstances as opportunities for progress on the journey within. With this vision apparent curses change into living blessings. Coming to these realizations is a gradual process. In the beginning stages, we receive a dose of grace — enough to open the heart and awaken us to loving devotion. As we begin to practice in earnest, the soul's inner nature will burn through all our misidentifications and, like fire, burn off all the habits and mentalities that hinder our progress. To the degree that we are attached to these things, we may feel some pain. But as our devotion burns brighter, the complicated, intricate conditionings, the karmic shells we've spent lifetimes developing, are eventually burned away completely and the soul shines forth.

The more the soul shines through, the more we will see through the eyes of grace. With a grateful heart, we will take whatever life gives us and use it to serve our Beloved. If life takes something away, we will see the hand of our Beloved. As the bhakti saint Bhaktivinode wrote, "All the troubles encountered in my Beloved's service shall be the cause of great happiness, for in his devotional service joy and sorrow are equally great riches, for both destroy the misery of ignorance." The idea that bad things happen to good people is true only on the surface. Underneath we will find the benevolent arms of grace waiting to embrace us and welcome us home.

# Growing Through Adversity

*One of the greatest tributaries of the river of*
*greatness is always the stream of adversity.*
— CAVETT ROBERT

## VARSHA'S JOURNEY

How can we enter into a happy, fulfilling life when so many harsh experiences conspire to bring us out of that blissful realm of consciousness and into the painful realities of the world around us? How can we grow to see crisis as part of the spiritual journey? How can we avoid becoming bitter and instead continue to grow, even in the face of tragedy or extreme adversity? Here is the story of an ordinary family and how they found shelter from extreme tribulation by seeing through the eyes of gratitude.

In India in the mid-1980s, when our Mumbai community was still very young, I used to visit a medical student named Vishwarupa, his wife, Brajeshwari, and their daughter, Rupa, in their small apartment. Often they invited professors, doctors, and friends to gather for spiritual discussions.

By 1999 Vishwarupa was a senior administrator in our community hospital. Soon after, Brajeshwari was diagnosed with cancer. She was able to go into remission through prolonged treatment. Several years later, Brajeshwari and Vishwarupa realized their long-cherished dream for a second child. Rupa was overjoyed. "I always wanted a little sister or brother," she later said. "It took fifteen years, but I finally got my wish. I just couldn't wait!"

Brajeshwari was in labor. As she approached the time for delivery she blacked out. The labor pains stopped and she vomited. Doctors put her on oxygen and rushed her to intensive care. An hour and a half later, the labor resumed and she gave birth to a baby girl. They had already chosen her name: Varsha, "shower of grace."

Vishwarupa rushed to the delivery room. There he was told that Varsha didn't breathe for three minutes after her delivery, a dangerously long time. Unaware of the complications, Rupa embraced her father in great happiness. She finally had a sister.

Varsha was taken to the natal intensive care unit (NICU), where she was given oxygen. After some time she started to cry, something she hadn't done in the delivery room, but her crying was severe and forced, and the doctors couldn't explain why. They brought her to Brajeshwari to nurse, but she only cried louder and more strongly. Her right hand flailing in circles indicated to the doctors that she was in pain.

A few days later, Varsha suffered a multiorgan failure. Brajeshwari stared at her baby through the NICU window, then ran back to her room and cried. In her heart, she knew that even if Varsha survived, she would never be normal. And who would take care of this sick child, she wondered, if her cancer returned?

"At that moment," she later told me, "I realized that Kṛishna had sent this child to us. But why? She was no ordinary child. What were we supposed to understand from her birth? It was confusing, and we felt total despair."

Our Mumbai community rallied to her support. Feeling their love reinforced Brajeshwari's conviction that there was more to her daughter's condition than tragedy and sadness. "This child was mysteriously bringing our whole community together," she said. "My helpless little girl was helping us to always think of Krishna, to see what was happening as a blessing as well as a challenge. Those feelings lessened the sadness. Little by little, I began to feel more inspired to perform the service that was in store for me whichever way things went."

Varsha did survive that first crisis, and four months later the doctors performed an MRI scan. The result was heartbreaking: 40 percent of Varsha's brain had been destroyed at her birth. She would never talk, sit, or walk, and she would likely never be able to control her muscle movements.

Brajeshwari and Vishwarupa looked to me as their teacher. When they asked me for a spiritual perspective, I agreed with Brajeshwari that Varsha was a special child whose very existence required mature spiritual insight. The Supreme Being had entrusted his dear daughter to their care, and in doing so he was giving them an opportunity to cultivate unselfish love for the soul dwelling in that challenged body. I asked them to try to feel grateful for the gift of this special service. Medical science had reached its limits in treating her, and either the world was a heartless place or they needed to find a greater meaning through faith.

Brajeshwari and Vishwarupa agreed. The universe was not cruel and purposeless. They knew that from so much of their own life experience. Seen through the eyes of devotion, having such a soul as their child was a blessing. If they took good care of her, no doubt deeper realizations and understandings would emerge.

Vishwarupa later told me, "It was wonderful that we were able to see the materially worst event in life from a transcendental viewpoint. Something tragic took on great meaning for us."

Life was not easy for them. Varsha couldn't sleep, and Brajeshwari and Vishwarupa were up for hours as the baby cried, swinging her in a blanket until she finally stopped.

When I visited them, Varsha was often crying, her small round face contorted by an agony that no one except perhaps her mother could fathom. The baby had no power to express herself other than by crying, and she never would. Her mother remained gentle and loving despite that, holding her baby in her affectionate embrace and rocking her as often as she could, kissing her forehead and whispering sweet mantras and songs in her ear, knowing all the while that her little daughter would never be all right.

"Whenever married friends of ours had a child," Brajeshwari recalls, "they would derive such pleasure from talking about their baby—how the baby said a first word or took a first step or learned to play. But when we saw Varsha's MRI, we knew there would never be such moments for us. Varsha's life would probably be short, and there would be no walking or talking or playing. It took time for us to come to grips with our own grief. The circumstances were extreme, and I struggled to find solace in my faith and in prayer. I struggled to embrace a higher knowledge in the face of a heartbreak that seemed out of my control. I felt so vulnerable and unprepared, but eventually things became clearer for us. First, we believe in the soul, so we knew this would be Varsha's last birth in the material world. She was helpless, which meant she could not create any karma; nothing that would keep her in this world. Then we also saw proof that this child was special. Everyone around her was always chanting for her, offering their blessings, and, as she has grown, she is clearly blissful when there is kirtan, chanting, and many devotees around her."

Fifteen-year-old Rupa shared her mother's feelings: "I thought that I would play with my sister, walk with her, run, have fun with her. But now I know that it is not possible. Now that I know she may only have a short life, I have decided to keep aside my own desires of enjoying certain activities with her. I want to serve her and help her to be as happy as possible and to support her spiritually instead of expecting pleasure out of her."

Rupa discovered that her sister liked it when she imitated the sounds of birds, so to please Varsha, Rupa regularly went to the forest to learn the songs of various birds. Seeing her sincerity, the Lord has gifted Rupa the ability not only to sing like the birds but to sing devotional songs and melt the hearts of all who hear her.

"In a way, people outside this experience can never understand why we consider ourselves privileged," Vishwarupa says. "Does believing as we do make it all right that Varsha has such suffering? Of course not. But I can tell you that the devotee community has done what medical science could not. They have brought her happiness. They know how to see beyond her imperfect body to the spark of consciousness within, and they relate to her: we relate to her on that level. I have seen children with a similar condition who do not have that kind of support Varsha has and I feel for them. Varsha is blessed, and so are we."

I find it inspiring to see a family, in the face of extreme adversity, embrace their life with a deeper insight and love than they thought they had. All of us, through life's circumstances, can choose to connect with a power beyond our own by embracing the truth that the Supreme Being's grace is always accessible. This family chose to see adversity not as the consequence of a cruel, purposeless universe but as an opportunity to offer selfless love. Tragedy strikes so many, but so does grace. When you look at your life, try to turn whatever appears tragic in it to you into a beautiful expression of gratitude toward the Supreme. Vishwarupa and Brajeshwari have become grateful to have Varsha as their daughter, and Rupa feels grateful for her little sister. It is beautiful to watch how the family has come together and how much joy they feel in serving her. Theirs is a joy of selfless giving.

## SPIRITUAL LIFE IN A MATERIAL WORLD

Even before achieving full self-awareness, it's possible to refine how we process life events. People immersed in their conditioning and people who have learned to see beyond body and mind to the soul confront the same problems and dilemmas. The difference is how they respond. Those immersed in their conditioning think, "Here is my bad luck again, coming to make my life miserable." But wisdom cultures around the world teach us to think, "Here is my hard luck again, coming to help me cleanse my misconceptions and to grow." The difficulties of this world won't disappear when we reach full self-awareness. Rather, devotion will equip us with a deeper level of perception: we will see the hand of the Supreme providing us opportunities for growth even in the most desperate of circumstances, and in the course of time, when our spiritual connection is deepened, we will be truly free.

## THESE ARE TIMES . . .

At the start of the American Revolutionary War, the better-trained, better-organized, and better-armed British military was crushing the untrained, loosely gathered, and poorly armed American militia. In 1776, Thomas Paine wrote a series of pamphlets called *The American Crisis* that inspired hope and kept the militia fighting even during the darkest hours of the war. I reproduce his words here because they are applicable to spiritual seekers in their own dark hours:

> These are the times that try men's souls. The summer soldier and the sunshine patriot will, in this crisis, shrink from the service of their country; but he that stands it now, deserves the love and thanks of man and woman. Tyranny, like hell, is not easily conquered; yet we have this consolation with us, that the harder the conflict, the more glorious the triumph. What we obtain too cheaply we esteem too lightly: it is dearness only that gives everything its value.

In spiritual life, as in war, we stand against the tyranny of material conditioning on the battlefield of the mind. Our adversary, the false ego, is not easily conquered, but the prize is our spiritual freedom, and it is the dearness of that freedom that gives the struggle its value. We may face powerful opposition: feelings of spiritual emptiness, crises of faith, the loss of taste for our practices, the fear of rejection. We may sometimes think that despite all our struggles we've made little spiritual progress. We feel vulnerable and weak even after years of practice. And that's a good thing. Only when the ego becomes exposed can we know how to use our energy to combat it more effectively. Knowledge is the fire that burns away the weeds of selfishness so the flower of the soul can blossom.

I often meditate on how words from the wise help me see the inherent potential in every situation and alter my perception of my own challenges. When the renowned sculptor Michelangelo was asked how he was able to carve such beautiful works of art, he said that the form he was carving was already in the stone; he simply had to chip away everything that obscured it. We are works of art and we're already "there in the stone." We already contain within us the potential for selfless love and complete fulfillment. For the wise, the difficulties they experience are not so much karmic results of past misdeeds as the Supreme Sculptor helping us chip away at everything that obscures us—the layers of illusion and misconception that cover our beauty. The more the soul becomes uncovered, the more ability we'll have to "see the invisible, feel the intangible, and achieve the impossible."

Part of that seemingly impossible task is moving the weed-like ego aside so that the seed of divine love will grow in a heart softened and fertilized by gratitude and humility, watered by spiritual practice. In a grateful heart, the tree of love will root deeply and hold forth even in the stormiest of weathers.

## LESSONS FROM TREES

Accepted by the bhakti tradition as the avatar of divine love, Sri Chaitanya took the role of a saint in fifteenth-century Bengal. Scriptural prophecy, history, and a long tradition of saints support his divinity. He taught that divine love is accessible to those who are "more humble than a blade of grass, more tolerant than a tree, and ready to offer all respect to others while expecting none in return." By cultivating these qualities, the heart becomes a fertile field where the flower of divine love can blossom.

Now let's take a closer look at the tree analogy and how the tree tolerates inconvenience for the welfare of others. Trees stand directly under the burning summer sun even as they provide shade for those similarly afflicted. In the frigid winter, the ice-covered trees provide us with their wood, which keeps us warm. In the dry season, a mango tree, even though not having been watered for months, provides a juicy fruit to quench our thirst. When a tree is cut down, it sacrifices its body without protest, providing lumber for building and wood for heating. In this sense, trees symbolize service to others.

## THE GIANT SEQUOIA

A few years back, I gained a penetrating insight from a tree. With a busload of teenage pilgrims, I traveled high up into the Sierra Nevada Mountains of California to Kings Canyon National Park, home of the second-largest tree on earth, a sequoia called "General Grant." The General is forty feet in diameter. It would take twenty adults holding hands to circle its base. If you hollowed it out, you could fill it with 159,000 basketballs or enough gasoline for a car to circle the world three and a half times. By some estimates, the General has been standing for 1,700 years.

If you look up its trunk, you'll see that a large segment of its bark is charred black from countless forest fires. These fires killed smaller trees, but this giant sequoia endured. It occurred to me that the will to grow despite the heat of adversity is necessary if one wants to thrive. If we withstand the temptation to give up when we fail or are dishonored or betrayed, and if we want spiritual growth, we'll survive, thrive, and deepen in wisdom and devotion.

The scorch marks on the General Grant tree are battle scars, you could say, but they're also ornaments, and that's how they've been recognized. Great souls don't seek praise, but sometimes their virtues get recognized. This tree was finally awarded for its long life in 1926 when President Calvin Coolidge proclaimed the General Grant the nation's official Christmas tree. In 1956 President Dwight D. Eisenhower designated it a national shrine and a living memorial to those who gave their lives for their country. From the General Grant tree, we can learn to accept praise graciously, remain firmly rooted, and continue to grow no matter what.

Not far from General Grant is General Sherman, the world's largest tree. It has been standing for more than 2,200 years. The General Sherman was alive during the fall of the Roman Empire, the Mongolian invasions, the American Revolution, and the American Civil War. Indeed, the Sherman tree was standing long before Europeans set foot on American soil. How big is this tree? If the trunk of the Sherman were filled with water, there would be enough to provide a full bath to each member of a family of six every day for twenty-seven years. A six-foot-tall human looking up at the General Sherman is proportionately equal to a mouse looking up at a six-foot-tall human. It's sobering to think how our perception of reality is so relative to where we stand in the world and how tall we are!

I asked the teenagers I was traveling with, "If General Sherman, who has lived so long and seen so much, could give humanity a message, what would he tell us?"

After several humorous remarks from the boys, Laxmi, a fourteen-year-old girl, spoke up. "I hear the tree crying out to us: 'Why do you humans waste your time fighting and obsessing over superficial things? Your lives are so short. Focus on what's really important: your spiritual relationships.'" Laxmi spoke with such feeling that I almost felt the tree speaking through her.

## The Blessing of a Forest Fire

*Every adversity, . . . every heartache, carries with*
*it the seed of an equal or greater benefit.*
—Napoleon Hill

*One's greatness has to be estimated by one's*
*ability to tolerate provoking situations.*

—Prabhupada, *Krsna: The Supreme Personality of Godhead*

The redwoods taught me yet another valuable lesson. This was in Muir Woods, near San Francisco. I learned that during the early 1900s, there had been hardly any new growth among redwoods for fifty years. No one knew why until finally it was revealed that park rangers had been too efficient in their work: they had successfully put out all the forest fires. It turned out that redwoods need a periodic fire to clear the way for their seeds to sprout. Here was a graphic example of how good intentions without proper knowledge can create setbacks.

In his book on fire ecology, *Wildfire: A Century of Failed Forestry Policy*, George Wuerthner demonstrates the need for this balancing act in nature and how it works. The small, oatmeal-grain-sized redwood seed is embedded in a very hard, dry cone and cannot be freed without some sort of intervention. The heat of a forest fire cracks open the cone and releases the seed, which then falls to the ground. The fire burns away brush and shrubs so the seed can reach the soil and take root. When the seed sprouts, too much sun can kill it. Ashes from forest fires cover the seed until it has time to grow. Fire enriches the soil with necessary nutrients.

Once the sprout begins to grow, it needs abundant sunlight. That too is aided by fire, which has already cleared away plants and small trees that block the sun. The fire of adversity in our own lives facilitates our growth when we learn what nature teaches us through the redwood tree.

# THE SEED OF DIVINE LOVE

Sri Chaitanya taught that the seed of divine love is already living in the heart of every being, but it's covered by the hard cone of false ego—that ego that wants to control rather than serve, exploit rather than love. This ego covering is very difficult to break, but break it we must if we want to release the seed of ecstatic love and let it grow.

The bhakti tradition tells us that it's possible to break the hard cone of ego only by the grace of the Supreme and his loving servants. How do we access that grace? We have to really want it. In Sanskrit, this intense yearning to love and serve the Supreme is called *laulyam*. The fire of difficult times can lift us up out of complacency and intensify our yearning for the power of divine grace.

Many of us are encased in a hard cone of spiritual complacency. The fire that breaks that cone is a burning sincerity. Sincerity is often precipitated by the fire of difficult times. Crises can sharpen our focus on what's really important, and when we turn sincerely to the Supreme at a critical point, the experience of the crisis can burn away our obsession with the trivial.

When I was twenty-nine, two doctors told me I would die from an incurable disease within six months. Suddenly many things no longer mattered. I found myself aware of what was essential to me: my relationship with God and with those I loved, and my health. Drinking almost a gallon of water a day and following a strict diet for a year cured me. That ordeal left a significant impact on my consciousness that stays with me today.

If we adopt a grateful, tolerant attitude that reminds us that we're never abandoned and always protected, then whatever painful events we may have to face, as undesirable as they seem, will clear us of unnecessary attachments and nourish the seed of love in the soul.

# A Nazi's Transformation

I'd like to share a story that shows how even during one of the most savage and heartbreaking periods in world history, helpless people surrounded by cruelty, torture, and death chose to see an opportunity to connect with grace.

This story was told to me by one of my dearest friends. His father had been an officer in the Nazi SS. He was dispatched on murderous missions and helped to manage concentration camps. From time to time, one of his fellow officers noticed something peculiar. Outside the walls of a gas chamber, in a holding tank, were drawings of butterflies. What did they mean?

His curiosity was aroused. Finally, he asked a condemned Jew about it. The tortured, emaciated victim gazed down at the filthy, bloodstained floor, shook his head in grief, and said nothing. Then he looked up and directly into the eyes of his captor, his face shining with hope. In a whisper he revealed the secret of the butterfly.

A caterpillar crawls in the dirt, eats debris, and at any moment can be trampled to death or eaten alive by birds. Then the struggling little insect is imprisoned in a cocoon. But through that ordeal, the caterpillar is transformed into a butterfly, free to fly in the open sky. It then lives on a diet of pure nectar.

"Some of us believe," the Jewish prisoner told the Nazi, "that despite all your cruelties, through our faith in God, our souls will be liberated, like the butterfly, into a land of freedom where we will drink nectar from the flowers of God's grace. And you will suffer for your atrocities when our suffering is over."

The officer was taken aback. When my friend's father heard this story from his fellow officer, the bubble of propaganda he and his nation had been fed about how Jews are dangerous subhumans burst. He suddenly saw his own insanity in having bought into such an idea and what he had done in service to the Gestapo. He realized that the people he was murdering were special, sensitive people with profound insight, and for the rest of his life he experienced horrific nightmares and felt a bitter repentance.

His son, like so many other Germans of his generation, rebelled against his parents' ignorance and searched frantically for meaning and truth. Eventually he found the path of bhakti. He and I are best friends. He is the son of a murderer of Jews, and I am the son of a Jew whose uncles, aunts, and cousins were tortured and exterminated by the Nazis. But our hearts are one in affection.

We need to rise above the atrocities of the world. Like-minded, caring people can unite beyond sectarian issues and call out for real change based on the real self. In whatever role you find yourself—mother, father, politician, farmer, entertainer, shopkeeper, industrialist, student, or priest—listen for the call to open and cleanse your heart and to share the wealth of truth with the world by your words and example. The world craves such leadership. The Gita (3.21) says, "Whatever action a great person performs, common ones follow. And whatever standards they set by exemplary acts, all the world pursues."

Become an enlightened leader. Be active in the world, but rise above all selfish misconceptions by choosing to keep the roots of your values sheltered in the soil of integrity and grace.

# Living Consciously and
# the Art of Dying

*In the spiritual endeavor there is no loss or diminution, and a little*
*advancement on this path can protect one*
*from the most dangerous type of fear.*
—Bhagavad Gita 2.40

## THE PASSING OF TWO GREAT SOULS

Please hear the humanly painful yet spiritually beautiful stories of two of my dear friends who walked through what is seen by most people as life's most fearsome gateway, death, in a state of liberation and love.

My dear friend Kunti was a single mother of two. Although her life was difficult, she was kind, cheerful, and full of love right until the end of her life. She had cancer. In the last stages, she was paralyzed from the waist down and her body was thin and pale, yet her smile radiated throughout the room. Those who came to see her during that time said she gave them light and hope.

She was special, and a television station in Idaho heard about her through word of mouth. When the television producers met her and witnessed the dignity with which she was accepting death, they produced a series of shows showing how spirituality brings peace, wisdom, and joy even at such a difficult time.

People who came to console Kunti left inspired by her. She enlightened them in a gentle, natural way and even helped them solve their problems, even as hers was unsolvable. She loved to chant Krishna's names and read sacred literature, especially the Bhagavad Gita and *Bhagavata Purana*. She spent time praying intensely for her children. Through her words and example, she touched her daughter's heart, and her daughter, who was in her twenties at the time, remained at her bedside until the end.

One morning as the sun was rising, I came to see Kunti. She exclaimed, "I am so grateful for everything I have been given in life and especially now. Some people think I'm on my deathbed, but I feel as though I'm being blessed by the hands of my beloved Lord. As I read our guru's books, I feel that he is speaking every word directly into my heart. I feel his love and Krishna's love like never before, and I feel my own love washing away all the pains and sorrows of this world. It's beautiful. I would not change my place with anyone else." Hearing her, I realized that she had what everyone is really seeking: hope and joy.

The last wish Kunti expressed to her daughter was that she use her beautiful voice to bring people closer to God. Kunti left this world with dignity, grace, and love. Inspired, her daughter, Karnamrita, has become a well-loved kirtan singer, performing all over the world. She dedicated her first CD to her mother.

Sometimes God teaches the world lessons through those who love him. In 2005, my friend Bhakti Tirtha Swami called me. Born John Favors in a Cleveland ghetto, he became a civil rights activist in the 1960s, then graduated from Princeton University, and later became the one of the first African Americans to be ordained a swami in the Vaishnava bhakti tradition. He authored a number of books and traveled the world, extensively sharing his knowledge and inspiration. Among the thousands of admirers who sought his spiritual guidance were Nelson Mandela, Muhammad Ali, and Alice Coltrane. Now, in a small home in rural Pennsylvania, he was dying of melanoma. By the time he called for me, his leg had been amputated and his body was full of tumors. For the last two months of his life, I sat at his bedside, and we shared our hearts as we discussed realizations, philosophy, and spiritual stories. One day in his final week, he was in so much pain that his emaciated body began to shake uncontrollably. He couldn't focus on our discussion, so I softly chanted Krishna's names to him.

Then, before my eyes, his face began to glow and his eyes sparkled as he burst into a gigantic smile. "It doesn't get any better than this," he said.

"What do you mean?" I asked.

"I am feeling Krishna's love so deeply today while tasting his name. I can see and feel the beautiful place where I'm going. I am so grateful."

A few days later, I held his hand as he moved out of his body to his cherished divine home, while hundreds of his friends and students filled the house, all of them chanting, crying, and praying. It was one of the most beautiful experiences of my life. So much love filled the room.

During the eight weeks I spent at his bedside, our singular purpose was to help each other remember Krishna with love and gratitude. During that time, I came to understand the unimaginable extent to which friends could love each other when love for the Divine is at the core of their relationship. I miss him terribly and will always be inspired by what can only be described as a glorious life and death that was not without pain but was also beyond pain.

# DEATH AND LIBERATION

The departure of my friends has brought me both heartbreak and gratitude. The heartbreak comes from being left behind without the continued joy and inspiration of their physical company. The gratitude comes from the memory of their loving friendship and the gift of faith their lives offered me. Death is a subject that most of us would like to push back into a hidden corner of the mind. But sacred texts and saintly teachers remind us that it's wise to remember our mortality. That's easy to do if you just look around you in the natural world.

One afternoon while I was sitting on a sandy bank of the Ganges River, I gazed into a cloudless blue sky. There, a hawk soared on currents of air, wings extended. His reddish-brown feathers shone in the sun as he circled lower and lower, finally coming to hover just a few yards above me. I could see his glistening yellow eyes scanning the river.

Suddenly he plunged headlong into the Ganges. A frantic underwater skirmish ensued, and he emerged moments later with a flapping fish, about a foot long, held tight in his talons. The fish squirmed desperately as the hawk carried him high into the air and then disappeared into a nearby forest.

That fish had known nothing but life in the river and had been living it that day like any other day. In an instant, it was ripped away to meet death.

We too live with little awareness that at the least expected moment, a crisis can disrupt our lives or death can snatch us away. Every day we hear about serious reversals, even death, happening to people. We see it all around us. Still, it's rare to find people who live with an awareness of their mortality and who really believe death could happen to them.

This spiritual complacency is something we need to guard against. It's not that we should be paranoid or pessimistic; rather, we should be realistic and aware in a positive way. Awareness is crucial to our well-being. If the fish had swum deeper, the crisis-bringing hawk would not have reached it. This is a metaphor for spiritual life. Obviously no one can hide from the eventual death of the body or from the possibility that he or she will have to face a serious challenge. But if, like the fish, we dive deeper into our connection with the Divine, we will find an inner reality so satisfying and supportive that we will be able to greet all life events, including the inevitable end of the body, peacefully and with realization that we are eternal, undying souls. This is the place beyond fear.

Even though bhakti texts celebrate the eternal life of the soul, they contain very detailed descriptions of what happens to the soul at the moment it leaves the body. Such teachings are meant to remind practitioners that every moment is precious and that spiritual development, or the life of the soul, should be taken seriously. It's the only life that lasts. Life is meant for self-fulfillment (we are, after all, pleasure-seeking beings), but when we spend precious time on superficial, fleeting experiences, it's easy to forget the hawk of fate flying just above us. Therefore bhakti sages and all others who walk a spiritual path advise that we live each day with quality, as if it were our last.

## LIVING WITH AN AWARENESS OF BOTH MORTALITY AND IMMORTALITY

In the epic Sanskrit text the Mahabharata, a celestial being asks a wise king, "What is the most amazing thing?" The king replies: "That people see death everywhere yet think, 'This won't happen to me.'"

But who is it saying, "This won't happen to me"? Is that person a destructible physical organism, a body? Or do we inherently know that we are indestructible? Facing death compels us to think of difficult questions like, "Who am I?"

One of the physicians from our Mumbai hospital's emergency ward once told me that when patients are rushed in on stretchers, she often hears them say, "I never thought this would happen to me." Hardly anyone does.

The Bhagavad Gita teaches us that the core problems we face in this material world are birth, old age, disease, and death. All four are inevitable. When children are born, there is only one thing we can predict with absolute certainty: someday they'll die. Why do we fear something so inevitable? What is it in us that makes us want to escape death? And what happens to us after death? Do we simply cease to exist, like a cloud that dissipates and vanishes in the sky?

The bhakti saints and scriptures tell us that the reason we have an instinctive longing to live is because the soul is eternal. Old age and death are foreign to our nature. The permanence of life and the impermanence of matter are the central teachings of nearly all the wisdom cultures in the world, and enlightenment consists in understanding these two truths and how they should change our outlook and behavior.

## WHAT HAPPENS AT DEATH?

Many eastern wisdom texts agree that at the time of death, the soul travels to another destination, a process often called transmigration or reincarnation. At that time, the gross elements of the body—the body's earth, water, fire, air, and space—return to their source. The temporary "car" we traveled in during the body's life is thus recycled while the passenger moves on.

Sri Krishna describes the critical moment of death in the Bhagavad Gita: "Whatever state of being one remembers when he quits his body ... that state he will attain without fail." Human life is like a class with an exam at the end of life. Careful preparation optimizes our ability to graduate. The school of life provides opportunities for growth in wisdom, and death is the final exam. The state of our consciousness at that critical moment determines our soul's next destination.

This means that our desires, attachments, thoughts, words, and deeds shape our consciousness throughout life, including at the moment of death. And our state of consciousness at the end of this physical lifetime determines where we'll take our next birth. In another verse of the Gita, Krishna says, "Those who at the end of life quit their body remembering me at once attain my nature. Of this there is no doubt." If we remember the Supreme with love at the time of death, we will graduate from the school of life and never have to take birth in the material world again; the soul will return to the spiritual world. This remembrance of God at the time of death is natural when we sincerely cultivate God consciousness in life.

We often hear of accounts of near-death experiences in which people see the events of their whole life flash before them like a movie. The Vedic literature also describes this phenomenon. We should be vigilant to live in such a way that when it's our turn and if we see that playback, we'll see our spiritual connection rather than things we regret. The spiritual capital of a life lived consciously will provide the currency that will take us to a higher spiritual destination.

Although dying is often painful and almost always difficult, for those who have disengaged from the fears and ambitions of an egoistic life and turned their hearts to the Divine, death is also a release. At the time of death, you close your eyes and then open them again and you are home.

## REMEMBERING WHAT IS IMPORTANT

*This human form of life is a most valuable asset for the living entity who can utilize it for solving the problems of life.*

—PRABHUPADA, *BHAGAVAD-GITA AS IT IS*

"The preciousness of time" is a Hindu children's story that happens to be a favorite among many adults as well. Narada had a disciple named Kailash. When Narada asked him to please take his spiritual life more seriously since time was passing quickly, Kailash replied, "Yes, I will, but I have to finish my studies first." Narada left him in peace.

Some years later he returned and made the same request. Kailash was a little more apologetic. "Yes, you are right. I should focus on my spiritual development, but I just got married and have to build the business to support my family."

When Narada returned a few years later, Kailash had children to raise and then, years later, grandchildren. "Just one more thing I need to do, then I'll be ready," he kept saying.

Later, when Narada again returned, Kailash's children broke the news that their father had died. As Narada walked away, disappointed that he had failed to help his disciple, a dog ran up and barked, "Narada, I'm Kailash."

His compassion aroused, Narada said to the dog, "It's not too late. I'll help you. Please take your spiritual life seriously."

"Yes, I will, but can't you see that my children and grandchildren aren't taking care of my estate? Let me guard it for a little more time."

Narada returned one last time only to find that the dog had died. To his surprise, he heard his disciple's voice through the hiss of a snake in the grass. "I'm Kailash. Yes, let me take my spiritual life seriously—I know you've come to help me—but I need to attend to a just a few more matters. I have to protect my family's crops from thieves and predators. Honestly, I'm almost done."

Narada loved his disciple, but sometimes love requires firm action. He walked up to the door of the house and told Kailasa's now aging children that there was a poisonous snake in their yard. The men rushed out with sticks and began to bash their father.

Kailash cried out, "Narada, I'll take my spiritual life seriously! I'm ready. Save me!"

Time and tide, as they say, waits for no man. How long will we procrastinate? All we really have is the here and now. Death doesn't care if you've finished everything. When your time's up, you have to move on. So if you had to strip your life down to essentials, what would be important to you? While performing our duties in the world, these essentials should not be neglected.

## Nothing Is Random About Who We Are

❧

*The living entity in the material world*
*carries his different conceptions of life from*
*one body to another, as the air carries aromas.*
*Thus he takes one kind of body and again*
*quits it to take another.*
—Bhagavad Gita 15.8

It's natural to wonder where the soul goes when it leaves the body. In India, most people accept the idea of reincarnation, the repeated cycle of birth and death. In the West, however, I am frequently asked whether we have only one chance to determine our destiny, or if there's a heaven and a hell, or why so many people are born into situations they haven't chosen.

Like the law of karma, specific details pertaining to the transmigration of the soul, or what we call "reincarnation," are far from simple to understand. For thousands of years, the teachers of Eastern spiritual paths, along with many monks and mystics from the West, have explained transmigration in all sorts of philosophical texts. Enlightened masters as well as avatars like Buddha and Rama, who have changed the course of history with their wisdom and compassion, have taught the principles of transmigration.

I mentioned earlier that each of us is born with particular characteristics, from the color of our hair to our talents and disabilities. We're also presented with an array of opportunities. Although people often tell their children that they can be anything they want to be, that's not always *completely* true, because our karmic history may limit our achievements in the material sense, although with faith, determination, and grace, we may overcome insurmountable material obstacles. Still, someone who is born colorblind, for example, will not be able to become a pilot. But he or she can be something far more wonderful spiritually than that person can imagine. Who we are and who we become is not based on chance but on how we choose to interact with nature's laws.

## THE EVOLUTION OF CONSCIOUSNESS

A common theory in science discusses the evolution of matter (and of bodies, or species). This theory posits that nature uses natural selection and the cells' tendency to mutate, and a lot of time, to generate improvements in the bodies of the various species. Gradually primitive species become more complex life forms, culminating in the human being. Members of a species that fail to adapt in order to survive will fail to spread their genes and eventually die out.

The theory of evolution is often considered to be in conflict with theism, but let's take a closer look. There are ideas shared by both, but the primary disagreement between the theists and the atheistic version of evolution is in their understanding of the origin of the universe. Theists attribute the original cause and catalyst of development to a Supreme intelligence rather than chance or an inconceivable event in cosmic history.

The Vedic perspective also addresses the idea of evolution, but not just the evolution of matter. Rather, it discusses the evolution of consciousness. I've described how in the soul's bound state, it is encased in matter, with which it identifies. Souls living in the most primal bodies have basic awareness; they distinguish between themselves and "other," between food and nonfood. The Vedas call this *annamaya* ("consciousness"). From these primal species, the soul moves upward until it reaches the human form, where the body allows for highly developed discernment. The evolution of consciousness culminates when the soul realizes its inherent spiritual nature beyond matter and achieves the liberated state of a fully spiritual life.

From this perspective, bodies are simply vehicles that souls use to fulfill their material desires and experience the dualities of material nature, such as pleasure-pain or heat-cold. When one vehicle is no longer capable of supporting life, the soul abandons it in what we call death and moves into a new vehicle to continue its journey. Without spiritual awakening, we can carry on like this endlessly, moving up and down through the species according to our desires and karmic reactions. But the moment the soul becomes interested in self-realization, the end to this cycle of repeated birth and death is in sight.

## THE WHEEL OF LIFE: SAMSARA

Anyone familiar with yoga or Buddhism has probably heard the word *samsara*, literally "a wandering through," which refers to the repeated cycle of birth, growth, dwindling, and death and is compared to a constantly revolving wheel. The wheel of samsara revolves endlessly, and souls get trapped on it due to their attachments. But they can also rise above it.

How does the soul reincarnate, or wander through, in this cycle? The Bhagavad Gita explains that in each life, our actions are like deposits we make into a karmic account. At death, the soul sheds its old body and is drawn toward a new one according to its desires, attachments, and attitudes both from the life it is leaving behind and whatever karmic investments it has made in prior lives. We can see the soul "transmigrate" even while it's in its current body: the body changes from infancy to childhood to adolescence to adulthood, it becomes an old adult, and eventually it breaks down and dies. But it is the same self that is passing through all those states.

The transformations we go through in a material body are predictable: we're born, we grow, we spend some time maintaining, some of us produce offspring, we deteriorate, we die. The cells that make up our body die continually and are replaced, so in effect, we generate an almost entirely new body every seven or eight years. If you've recently become my friend, you may not recognize a photograph of me as a child; my body was different then. But I recognize myself in those photos because I've witnessed the many changes my body has gone through up until now. In that sense, a seventy-year-old has already "transmigrated" a number of times since birth.

At death, there is another transformation: the soul leaves one body and moves into another. The Gita (2.13) says, "As the embodied soul passes from childhood to youth to old age, the soul similarly passes into another body at death." What we call death is the moment the soul leaves the body.

We have two kinds of material bodies. One is the gross body of flesh and blood, and the other is the subtle body of mind, intelligence, and false ego. The ego, the subtlest element, covers the soul with forgetfulness of its true spiritual identity. In that state, the soul seeks satisfaction through the mind, the body, and the senses. The soul becomes so absorbed in this pursuit in each life that it develops deeply ingrained habits and ways of thinking. At the time of death, these habits become criteria for the creation of our next body. The Gita tells us that as a breeze carries pollen from one flower to another, so the state of mind we have developed carries us toward our next birth, where we can continue to pursue whatever we've identified as happiness and suffer from whatever obstructs our idea of happiness. Thus from the Vedic perspective, the variety of bodily forms and the varieties within each bodily form are not a product of random chance but a result of the past choices each soul has made.

The Vedic text *Padma Purana* states that there are 8.4 million forms of life in the world. These include varieties of aquatics, plants, insects, reptiles, birds, animals, and human beings. Human beings have the special ability to reason, which allows us to question our place in the universe and realize our full spiritual potential. So when a soul finally takes birth in the human form, it has an opportunity to transcend the wheel of samsara.

As material attachments continue into the next life, so does spiritual progress. In each successive birth, we pick up where we left off. Sometimes we meet someone we consider an "old soul," and this is usually based on the perception that that person has a deep wisdom and even spiritual maturity. Such qualities are accumulated over lifetimes. Imagine a child prodigy like Mozart, who composed his first symphony at eight years old. Where did his musical development come from? The *Bhagavata Purana* has a number of accounts of child prodigies in the spiritual field—children like Prahlada, who exhibited a pure state of consciousness from the age of five and who became a great spiritual teacher.

On the spiritual platform, whatever we gain is not lost; we will begin our next life with all the realizations and spiritual merits from our past life, and these realizations and merits will gradually come to our awareness at appropriate times. Of course, we can always choose another direction, and instead of continuing our spiritual development, we can forget about it. While our "spiritual bank account" will then remain dormant, the account never depreciates nor are the funds lost. Bhagavad Gita (2.40) states, "In this endeavor there is no loss or diminution, and even a little advancement on this path can protect one from the most dangerous type of fear."

Let's celebrate a truth that brightens our lives: the soul is eternal. It never dies. Spiritual realization is never lost. If we continue on the path, appreciating the good fortune that allows us to continue, we will inevitably succeed in becoming happy to the core of our hearts.

*By My grace you will pass over all the obstacles of*
*conditioned life and will attain transcendental peace*
*in the supreme and eternal abode.*

—BHAGAVAD GITA 18.58

# How Unseen Forces Impel Us

*Material nature consists of three modes—goodness, passion, and ignorance. When the eternal living entity comes in contact with nature, he becomes conditioned by these modes.*

—Bhagavad Gita 14.5

What are the unseen material powers in the universe that drive us to act in ways sometimes against our better judgment? The Bhagavad Gita talks about the three *gunas*, literally "ropes" because of their binding nature. These invisible powers, or gunas, are also referred to as "qualities" or "modes." According to our frame of mind and our choice of words and actions, we tune into a particular guna or a combination of gunas and come under their influence.

The first of the three is *sattva*, goodness. The Gita describes it as "illuminating," meaning that people strongly influenced by this mode lean toward purity, knowledge, peacefulness, and happiness. The second, *rajas*, the mode of passion, compels us to work hard and achieve as much as we can; it increases our taste for challenge and reward. The third, *tamas*, the mode of ignorance, pulls us toward envy, hate, anger, apathy, indifference, depression, and, in its more lethal stages, madness and suicide. The Gita (3.5) says, "All are forced to act helplessly according to the qualities they have acquired from the modes of material nature—and no one can refrain from acting even for a moment."

People respond to situations based on how they are influenced by the modes, so different people respond to, or even witness, the same situations differently. The three modes pervade all matter in both its physical and subtle forms. Just as the three primary colors—red, yellow, and blue—mix to produce a wide spectrum of other colors, so goodness, passion, and ignorance blend in this way and produce innumerable combinations of influences on the things we see and our behavior and attitudes in relation to them.

Some of these influences are easy to see, such as on food. The Gita (17.8–10) says, for example, "Food in the mode of goodness increases duration of life, purifies existence, gives strength, health, happiness and satisfaction. Such food is juicy, wholesome and pleasing to the heart. Foods that are too bitter, too sour, too salty, too hot, or too pungent are in the mode of passion. Foods that are stale, decomposed, or putrid, or a product of bloodshed are in the mode of ignorance."

The Gita analyzes a number of items or acts—for example, how we give charity. Charity given without expectation of return, with the intention of genuinely helping someone, is in the mode of goodness, but charity performed for one's own gain, whether that gain is profit or prestige, or charity given in a grudging mood, is in the mode of passion. Giving something impure or without considering what effect the gift will have, or a gift that benefits no one, is made in the mode of ignorance.

A place can also be influenced by the modes. A library is a place where the mind can be calm and concentrated, so it's designed to be clean, quiet, and well lit, all *sattvic* qualities. Try studying in a *rajasic* place, like the floor of the New York Stock Exchange, or in a *tamasic* place, like a smoke-filled and raucous bar. We're influenced by our surroundings because we're influenced by the modes. It's natural to seek out places conducive to what we're trying to accomplish at any given moment. Few people will go to a bar to meditate. Rather, people look for somewhere natural and green, or at the very least clean and peaceful. That's because generally such spiritual practices are sattvic.

It helps to perform spiritual activities in a sattvic environment because such an environment is conducive for a clear head and heart.

The mixture of modes in us reflects our interests and aspirations in past lives as well as the choices we've made in this one. With observation and reflection, we can identify which modes are affecting our behavior most prominently.

But most important, it is the intent behind one's actions rather than the actions themselves that primarily define their quality. Therefore, it is best not to judge others by what they do too quickly. External appearances can be misleading. Hard work, for instance, is not necessarily in the mode of passion; it is the selfish or materially attached objective behind the work that qualifies it as rajasic.

Goodness is characterized by preservation, passion by creation, and ignorance by destruction. Thoughtful people balance their passions with goodness to create healthy, beneficial results. And they guard against allowing their passions to be influenced by the mode of ignorance, creating unhealthy, destructive consequences or habits.

## THE VALUE OF THE MODE OF GOODNESS

The mode of goodness is a gateway into spiritual life, from where we can transcend the material influences altogether. The Bhagavad Gita (14.26) defines a liberated soul as someone who has risen above all three modes: "One who engages fully in bhakti, unfailing in all circumstances, at once transcends the modes and comes to the level of Brahman (spiritual liberation)." Patanjali's *Yoga Sutras* confirm this conclusion: "Ultimate liberation is when the modes return to their original [latent] state, when the power of consciousness is situated in its own essential nature."

So how do you stay connected to the mode of goodness? Try to keep your space clean, eat pure foods, spend time daily hearing from books of wisdom, and seek regular association with those whose minds are simple and pure. No matter how busy your schedule, set aside time every day for spiritual practice. You may not be able to isolate yourself completely from the lower modes, but if you live a life centered on your spirituality, you can inoculate yourself from their effects.

The practice of bhakti yoga, in which thoughts, words, and actions are engaged in a spirit of devotion to the Supreme, transcends the modes and is beyond matter and time.

# TIME

*Forget the past that sleeps*
*And never the future dream at all*
*But act in times that are with thee*
*And progress thee shall call.*
—BHAKTIVINODE THAKUR, *"SARAGRAHI VAISHNAVA"*

In balancing your life, it's helpful to understand the dynamic force that sets the modes in motion and perpetuates their influence on creation. That force is time.

Colloquially we tend to speak of time in measurements: seconds, minutes, hours, days, years. The wisdom texts of the East, however, speak only briefly of how time is measured and instead refer to it as a force of nature—a commanding influence that pushes us ever forward.

Time is mystical. It erodes mountains, evaporates oceans, obliterates planets, extinguishes the sun, and presides over every being in creation from the womb to the tomb. Nothing and no one can alter it for even a moment. Conquerors, billionaires, champions, and geniuses: all must eventually accede to it and surrender everything they've accumulated. No scientific achievement or technological breakthrough can alter it. Beauty cannot seduce it. Bribes cannot entice it. Brains cannot deceive it. Entire military arsenals can't stop it. Yet time is elusive. It can't be seen, touched, tasted, smelled, or heard. With every tick of the clock's second hand, time is plundering our lives like a master thief.

More than two thousand years ago, there was a wise and resourceful minister, Chanakya Pandit, whose practical guidance enabled Prince Chandra Gupta to singlehandedly overthrow a tyrant and establish the powerful Mauryan Empire. Chanakya is renowned for his insightful sayings. Here's one of them: "All the riches in the world cannot buy back even a single moment."

The present is all we have. It's in the present that we create our destiny; the future is created by the choices we make in the moment. The present has been shaped by the past, but the past is now gone forever. Better to focus on the moment we have with us now.

Children on the seashore labor hard to build castles of sand, but when evening approaches and the tide comes in, even their most frantic efforts to save their work can't protect it. Inevitably the ocean will swell in and roll over it and drag the castles back to the sea, leaving nothing but the raw ingredients from which they were built. Adult onlookers may be nonchalant when they see their children's efforts (and tears), but they may not consider that their own efforts are not much different. We all seem to spend our lives on the shore of birth and death building castles of worldly accomplishments in the sand of material existence. But at the dusk of life, the rising ocean of time will send its fateful wave of death and wash everything away. None of us is exempt.

*Time I am, the great destroyer of all the worlds.*
— BHAGAVAD GITA 11.32

All that exists is the here and now, yet the present disappears as soon as it appears, and in the process, our lifespan imperceptibly but steadily diminishes. The *Bhagavata Purana* (2.3.17) gives us warning, direction, and hope: "With every rising and setting of the sun we are one day closer to death. But for those who spend their life absorbed in service to the Supreme, every sunset brings them one day closer to their own eternal life."

The true value of a human life lies not in the number of years one lives but in the quality of one's consciousness and contributions. The oldest known tree in the world is in Sweden, a Norwegian spruce said to be nearly 9,200 years old. Such a life span is amazing to us, especially in comparison to our own, but even our brief life lived with a spiritual focus can be of tremendous value. As the *Bhagavata Purana* (2.1.12) says, "What is the value of a prolonged life which is wasted, inexperienced by years in this world? Better one moment of full consciousness." Jesus lived for thirty-three years, St. Francis for forty-four, and Sri Chaitanya for forty-eight, yet their contributions will remain forever.

True happiness is forever within us, but we have only the present moment to seek and find it. Every moment is a priceless blessing if we appreciate its potential by grounding ourselves in the reality of the timeless soul. Eternity is the experience of living joyfully in the continuous present moments of life.

As divine love awakens in us, we'll find ourselves living in a world far wider and deeper than the world of opinions. Unconditional love empowers us to view the universe from a compassionate perspective, wherein we realize the eternal nature of all souls who are struggling on a journey through the cosmic creation, trying to find their real home. Home is where we reunite with the grace and love of the Divine that is within us and in the background of everything that exists. If we are willing, nothing can obstruct that grace and love from finally drawing us home.

# Becoming One Through Love

*If one offers Me with love and devotion a leaf, a fruit,*
*a flower, or a little water, I accept it.*
—BHAGAVAD GITA 9.26

## THE BANANA SELLER'S STORY

Through bhakti we learn that all varieties of love have as their prototype and ideal model the personal love shared between the individual soul and the Supreme Soul. When we lovingly offer to the Supreme Beloved the best that we can and the best that we are, according to our capacity, whether it is a small offering or a large one, the Lord reciprocates by filling our heart with a satisfaction that nothing else can provide. This spirit of simple affection is the basis of our relationship with the Supreme, and it's also what makes our relationships with others satisfying.

A few years ago I visited the home of a multibillionaire. He poured his heart out to me. Financial pursuits had consumed all his time, he said. Even after becoming a billionaire, he confessed that in the end, he'd found happiness only in simple things: friends, family, charity, and his spiritual practice. These things don't have a price tag, he said, and success often spoils relationships by provoking envy, greed, and suspicion and by leaving one little time for the things that really matter. His wife added that before they had made their fortune, she had been happy with their simpler life, which carried none of the complications wealth had brought.

Because I'm a little known for telling stories, they asked me to tell them a story that might help them balance the crushing burden of corporate life with an understanding of what's really valuable in life. My mind went back to a quiet field of rice paddies I had visited a couple of weeks before. The area was dotted with small groves of coconut, mango, and banana trees. Goats wandered about, nibbling on the leaves. Women in colorful cotton saris knelt to collect kindling, piling it into straw baskets, and then heaving the baskets onto their heads to carry. Children laughed and played cricket. A small shrine in the field commemorated a man who had once lived there.

I shared with the couple a tale dating back five centuries, a story that, for me, expresses a powerful message. The story takes place in Navadwip, "the place of nine islands," West Bengal, and this rice paddy was near the banks of the Ganges, not far from where Sri Chaitanya was born.

Sri Chaitanya is an avatar of Krishna, and when he was young, he concealed his divinity and played among the people in his village like a human child. His family and friends called him Nimai because he was born under a neem tree. When Nimai was a boy, he used to buy bananas and banana leaves (used as dining plates in rural Bengal) from a seller named Sridhar. Sridhar barely made a living, sitting on a dusty roadside with some fruits and leaves displayed on an old cloth. Unlike other merchants, he charged his customers the lowest price he could afford. He mainly wanted to make just enough to survive so he could concentrate on something that was more important to him. Of the meager profits he earned, he gave the first half in charity as an offering to Krishna on the bank of the Ganges. He was free of any trace of duplicity, and his love for Krishna was simple and pure.

As an excuse to be with his devotee, Nimai came daily to Sridhar to bargain the price of his bananas. Sometimes Nimai would give half the price or Sridhar would just give them to him when the bartering turned to arguing. Sridhar didn't know that Nimai was his Beloved in disguise, but in his heart he felt a mysterious love for this boy, and he found himself longing for Nimai's arrival each day. The longer they haggled over the price, the happier Sridhar felt.

One day Nimai challenged Sridhar, "You're always chanting 'Krishna! Krishna!' but your life is miserable. Why worship Krishna? What's he doing for you?"

Sridhar replied, "I'm not starving. I may get a little or a lot. What does it matter? My body is covered and I am alive."

"But *look* at you," retorted Nimai. "Your clothes are in tatters. You tie the holes in them with knots because you can't even afford thread and a needle. And look at your body. It's so skinny. Your home is a grass hut with many holes. Your roof leaks. Just look around you. This town is full of atheists and people who pray only for their own benefit. They all eat and dress well and have fine homes."

Sridhar replied, "Kings may live in jeweled palaces and wear elegant clothes and enjoy splendid pleasures, and birds may live in a grass nest on a tree and wear the same feathers every day, but both still pass the time in the same way: trying to enjoy their lives. I am enjoying my life, and I'm perfectly happy."

Nimai challenged Sridhar further. "You can't fool me. I know you have a great treasure, but you hide it so you can enjoy it in secret.

You're deceiving the public, who think you're a poor man. One day I'll find your treasure and expose you. What will you do then?"

Sridhar replied, "I *am* a poor man. What you see is what I am. Why do you always fight with me? I live by selling bananas and banana leaves. What is it you want from me?"

"Donate some bananas, roots, and leaves," Nimai said, smiling. "Then I won't fight with you."

"Take whatever you want. Don't pay for anything. I don't mind."

Every day, Nimai ate his meals on leaf plates given by Sridhar. Whenever a wild squash grew from Sridhar's grass roof, he would send it to Nimai's mother to cook for him.

Years later, when Nimai became known as Sri Chaitanya, he revealed to his most intimate followers his identity as an incarnation of Krishna. One night, to please his followers, he freely gave each follower whatever boon he or she asked for. Sridhar was not present for this event at first, but Sri Chaitanya sent some of his followers to find him. When he arrived, Sri Chaitanya showed Sridhar his form as Krishna and asked him to request a boon.

Sridhar was overwhelmed. He said, "Lord, what will I buy from you? I do not want anything."

Sri Chaitanya replied, "I *must* give you a boon. Ask for whatever is in your heart. I will give you the fabulous wealth and property of a king!"

But Sridhar didn't want that.

"Then I will give you the mystical perfections that come only by prolonged yoga practice," Sri Chaitanya offered. "You will have the power to perform miracles."

"That will only be a distraction," Sridhar said.

"Then ask for something. I will free you from all suffering forever."

Sridhar bent his head low and said, "Please, I don't want that either."

"Then how about eternal residence in the spiritual world? That is the ultimate perfection. Please accept it."

"I don't want to do business with you, trading my heart for some boon," Sridhar said. "I've given you my heart freely. I want nothing in return but the chance to please you and serve your servants."

"Ask, ask," the Lord demanded. "For *my* pleasure, ask for something."

"If I must ask," Sridhar whispered, "you may give me this: I want that you will forever come to steal my bananas. In my heart of hearts, allow me to always remember that beautiful boy Nimai coming to steal my bananas."

Sri Chaitanya wept with affection. He kept the promise he had made Sridhar when he was a boy by revealing Sridhar's hidden treasure; he exposed the limitless wealth Sridhar secretly enjoyed in his heart: the treasure of pure devotion.

It doesn't matter if one is a billionaire or a banana leaf seller. The only indestructible treasure one can possess is love for the Supreme and an eagerness to serve him and his creation.

In India, those who renounce material possessions to fully live their spiritual practice are addressed as "Maharaja," "great king." This title might seem overblown for such people, but it's designed to help people remember what their greatest wealth and power is and to orient themselves accordingly.

In the Bible, Jesus says that if we make our treasure in this world, it will be stolen by thieves, eaten by moths, or corroded by rust, but if we make our treasure in the kingdom of God, there will be no such destruction. "Provide purses for yourselves that will not wear out, a treasure in heaven that will never fail, where no thief comes near and no moth destroys. For where your treasure is, there your heart will be also" (Luke 12:33–34).

By observing the dealings between Sri Chaitanya and Sridhar, we come to appreciate the beauty and simplicity of an unconditional love steeped in giving. Each wanted only the happiness of their beloved. This is the dynamic of love between the Supreme Being and the soul, and it forms the ideal for our relationships with one another.

After my story, my hosts escorted me to the dinner table, where we shared a sumptuous vegetarian dinner. After some light talk and laughter, they walked me to the door, where their chauffeur awaited. From the luxurious car I returned to my straw mat on the floor of our hot, crowded ashram. It was quite late. Lying down on the straw mat, I closed my eyes and relished the beauty of that day. It was neither his wealth nor my poverty that filled my heart with joy, but the opportunity to try to give something that I love so much to my hosts—or to anyone else.

## WHOM SHOULD I LOVE, AND HOW SHOULD I LOVE THEM?

*Dharma is defined as that which sustains—*
*the essence of something. Dharma is the eternal*
*essence of one's spiritual nature and function. The*
*dharma of the soul is the pure spiritual love for the*
*infinite Supreme Being. In other words, the soul's*
*dharma is bhakti, loving devotional service.*

—BHAKTIVINODE THAKUR

In bhakti, loving the Supreme Being is the deepest inner experience, and one can express it in this world through devotional service and compassion toward others.

As has been explained, there are several schools of Vedic thought, and they see the Absolute from different perspectives. The school of bhakti focuses on the intimate, personal nature of the soul's relationship with the Supreme.

This relationship is sometimes described through analogy. As sunlight is formed of rays radiating from the sun, so each soul is an individual spark of spiritual energy emanating from the Supreme Being. Because both the sun and each of its rays are of the same quality (each consists of heat and light), the soul is of the same quality as the Supreme. Like the Supreme we are *sat*, eternal; *chit*, full of knowledge; and *ananda*, blissful. In this sense we are not different from the Supreme Being. However, just as each ray of sunlight is but an infinitesimal part of the sun's actual power, so quantitatively we are only an infinitesimal part of the Absolute. The soul is simultaneously one in quality with and different in quantity from the Supreme.

The *Katha Upanishad* (2.2.13) says, "There is one eternal being, out of many eternal beings. The one eternal being forever sustains the many eternal beings (the souls) and is their original source."

In order to enjoy the ecstasy of pure, intimate, loving relations in eternity, both the soul and the Supreme are persons, and both are eternal. The goal of bhakti yoga is to reawaken awareness of our original healthy condition in which all of our relationships are based on our original selfless love.

It's often said that if two people love each other deeply, they become one. In bhakti theology the perfection of "becoming one with God" is to become so ecstatically immersed in love (prema) that your heart merges with God's love and you lose yourself in the happiness that love generates. The self is never actually lost, of course; what does disappear is the illusion that we were ever separate from our Supreme Beloved.

# DON'T THINK SMALL

Because form in this world is limited, people have a tendency to believe that something unlimited must be formless. This is what makes it difficult for some people to accept a personal conception of the Supreme. The abstract, formless concept of the Divine somehow seems more spiritual because we have no experience of unlimited form in the material world. Doing away with the notion of form in order to realize unlimited spiritual truth can be useful, but it's not the only way.

Here's an example. The walls of a room have form and are therefore limited in the sense that they occupy a limited amount of space. If we were to remove their form with, say, a wrecking ball, would their formless debris then be limited or unlimited? Obviously, they would still be limited: the debris is the same amount of matter as the original wall. So the mere removal of form doesn't make an object unlimited. What creates limitation is not form but matter. Any material object, with form or without, is always limited. The Supreme is unlimited not because he's formless but because he's not material; he's spiritual. The Supreme is beyond all dualities, including the duality of form and formlessness.

Although one may argue that form and personality limit the Supreme, it can be equally well argued that not having form and personality is limiting; that is, without form and personality, the Supreme is less than his own creation. A solution to this argument is to understand that the Supreme, being spirit, has an unlimited personality, form, and potencies. A simple example: our human eyes limit our vision; we can see only what those material instruments of sight have the power to encompass, which honestly, isn't very much. An eagle's eyes can see for miles, for example, and insects, with their compound eyes, can see in ways that the human eye cannot. Some people think that for the Supreme Being to be unlimited, then, he can't have human eyes or compound eyes, because that would limit him; instead he must have *no* eyes. However, bhakti philosophy explains that the Supreme's eyes, in contrast to our eyes, have the power to see everything at all times everywhere. His eyes are not the material, physical instruments we have to work with but are spiritual senses that do not depend on physical laws.

Similarly, people find personality to be limiting. Everyone we've ever known—be it our parents, friends, or world leaders—has personal frailties and shortcomings, so isn't it limiting to God to have a personality? Isn't personifying God anthropomorphism—attributing human qualities and form to something superhuman and unknown?

Ancient bhakti texts and teachers tell us that it's just the opposite: sentient form in this world reflects the personhood of the Supreme Being, not the other way around. The Bible says man is created in the image of God. The Bhagavad Gita provides the useful analogy of an upside-down banyan tree, which refers to a tree reflected in a lake. The material world is compared to the tree's reflection on the water: two-dimensional, without real fruit and thus a poor substitute for the original tree. In a similar way, the forms of this temporal world are derived from the original forms that exist in the eternal realm. The love that binds people together in this world is a reflection of the original love that binds the soul to the Supreme Beloved.

In my years of teaching, I have found that beneath the surface there's often a deeper objection to the notion of the Divine as a person. In our worldly experience, dealing with people can be painful. Our relationships with others are marred by betrayal, frustration, regret, or sorrow, and that doesn't foster enthusiasm for the prospect of an eternity of persons. Worldly encounters can lead people to believe that God's highest expression must be impersonal.

Forgetful of our spiritual nature, in a world of constant change, we become vulnerable to the agony of heartbreak. The misery of heartbreak is like no other because it frustrates our innermost purpose: to love and to be loved.

As a youth I listened to the blues; I felt a profound connection whenever I heard a musician express the grief of lost love. Each note, each word, sounded like a plea for relief. There's a remedy for almost every other kind of misery, but as Bobby "Blue" Bland sang, "When you got a heartache, there is nothing you can do." The origin of that yearning is in the soul's need to reconnect with its eternal Beloved.

Even if a relationship isn't marred by betrayal, neglect, or disappointment, it will inevitably end in death. Should eternal love not be devoid of anything that can be taken away? And isn't all love characterized by loss of one sort or another? It's understandable why people choose to avoid spiritual personhood.

## DIVINE LOVE SURPASSES MATERIAL LIMITATIONS

Let's explore how bhakti opens doors into a love that transcends the frailties of material life. All varieties of love have as their perfect prototype the personal love shared between the individual soul and the Supreme Soul. The health of any relationship in this world can be measured by how thoroughly it reflects the purity of its origin in that divine relationship. The Bhagavad Gita (15.7) says, "The living entities in this conditioned world are My eternal fragmental parts. Due to conditioned life, they are struggling very hard with the six senses, which include the mind."

Years ago, while suffering from typhoid fever, I was given a special insight into the human condition. Whatever I ate made me extremely nauseated, and I felt a fierce, stabbing pain in my stomach. It was a relief not to eat; at least then I wasn't in pain. But it was only when I recovered and was finally able to eat properly that I felt nourished and satisfied. I learned something precious from this: for a person with a disease, fasting may be good. But fasting can never compare to the satisfaction you feel when your body is healthy and you can eat.

Similarly, loving relations in this temporal world give some satisfaction, but they are vulnerable to egoism and complications, and inevitably they end. To negate our misconceived personhood and relationships is only a partial cure. This type of liberation frees us of suffering, but the bhakti texts tell us that there is something more.

Only loving devotion lets us realize the soul's complete fulfillment. It's natural that we're attracted to love, beauty, and pleasure, but it isn't until we connect those yearnings to the Supreme that we feel true fulfillment. Ecstatic love (prema) includes the peace of release from suffering. That peace is beyond material limitations, but prema, in its fully developed state, gives us a love that is spontaneous, reciprocated, and ecstatic.

But how can we love someone who's unlimited? Don't you have to know someone to love him or her? How can we, who are limited, hope to know the unlimited?

In reply, consider that the Supreme wouldn't be unlimited if he couldn't make himself known to us. We refer to this revelation as a soul becoming a receptacle for truth manifesting from the spiritual plane. Revelation comes from something higher than ourselves, descending through grace; it doesn't depend on our ability to reach it. There's no level of yoga skill or advanced stage of detachment or philosophical analysis or knowledge or good works that can ensure that grace descends on us. It comes only from the Supreme himself—as bhakti traditions say, "by his own sweet will." The Supreme reciprocates with the sincerity of our faith, love, and service by drawing us to him and drawing himself to us. Krishna says of himself in the Gita (10.10), "To those who are constantly devoted to serving Me with love, I give the understanding by which they can come to Me."

# Entering the State of Grace

*As one approaches me, I reveal myself accordingly.*
—BHAGAVAD GITA 4.11

## TARABAI'S GIFT

Divine love is an incomparable gift and one that may elude us even after a lifetime of spiritual practice. Such love is revealed only to those with a sincere and devoted heart, to those who love to serve. To bring us closer to this truth: sometimes little things in life open our hearts, and we come to appreciate that there's something more than just our day-to-day passions and sorrows. One of those things for me was an incredible encounter I had, again, in India.

One day, a dozen villagers took an eight-hour bus ride to personally bring me a gift. If you've ever ridden an Indian bus through the villages, you'll recognize how arduous this was for them. I wondered why they had done it.

When they arrived, they crowded into my small room, where we sat together on a straw mat on the floor. The women wore faded cotton saris, and the men worn grimy, baggy pants and shirts. Their faces, some scarred by smallpox, were weathered, and as they smiled,

I could see that many were missing teeth or had none at all. These were poor farmers; their livelihoods came from their small plots of land. Years of drought had dealt them a crushing blow. They toiled day and night on land that was hard and dry and produced next to nothing. Most of their wells had run dry, and they had to resort to hauling water in pots on their heads from miles away. Many worked in others' fields, and had to walk miles in the predawn to get to work, but they were given barely enough wheat to feed their families for the day.

As we sat, I reflected on how these poor people would celebrate a single good rainfall. But years passed and it never came. Some of them were my students. They had gone through a lot of trouble to bring me this gift, and I was excited to see what it was. It must be something amazing.

It was a gift of gratitude, they boasted, from Tarabai, a poor woman from their village. Tarabai had been too sick to make this visit. It was out of respect for her that they had agreed to present it. From a gunnysack they pulled out a grimy cloth sheet gathered and tied at the top with a bundle wrapped inside. One woman untied the knot, and ceremoniously put the gift on the floor in front of me. The villagers watched to see how I would react, hoping I was pleased. This gift was precious to them. If it had been diamonds, they couldn't have been more enthused. It was a gift of profound meaning, unlike anything I had ever received.

In my mind's eye, I could see the dirt roads that led to their village. I recalled a visit when a group of people from Mumbai and I had bounced and jerked along that road as our jeep hit one pothole after another. It took several hours to reach their isolated village, and when we arrived, we were greeted by the local people enthusiastically playing drums and cymbals and dancing. It was rare that outsiders went there, not to speak of an American-born swami. It was a bittersweet visit for me: their life was so obviously a struggle. But my hidden purpose in going was to meet with Tarabai.

I first met Tarabai at our orphanage in Mumbai. She was then in her fifties, but her rugged life had taken its toll and she looked much older. She was skinny, wrinkled, and gray haired, and she wore a faded old sari. Tarabai was a widow. Her husband, a poor farmer, had died, leaving her with three children and a small plot of parched land. To feed her children she worked slave hours. From sunrise to sunset, she carried on her head a heavy bucket of wet cement for almost a mile one way. Her bucket would then be filled with rocks for the return trip. It was a terrible job to do under the blazing Indian sun, and her frail body swayed as she struggled back and forth all day. She was paid in a crudely ground wheat flour—just enough to feed her children for the day. Yet she never complained or asked anyone for anything.

But as a mother, she grieved for her children. Because she was uneducated, she had no way to educate them or provide better for their basic needs. She had come to our orphanage to ask us to take her eldest child. Downtrodden as she was, she glowed with dignity. We agreed to take her son. Weeping, she embraced him. It was unbearable for her to leave him, but she knew it was his only hope to get an education. She turned to the principal and told him to make sure her son did plenty of chores to earn his keep. "He should not take it for granted or think he's a beggar," she said. He was ten, and the skinniest child I had ever seen. His thighs were barely the thickness of my wrist.

The boy was perfectly polite, though, and very sweet natured, and he seemed genuinely grateful to have been accepted. As the months passed, he began to work hard at school and was the first to volunteer for chores at the orphanage. My sympathy and affection for him grew. He took pains to learn English and would run to my room to share any new sentence he had learned. Everything actually seemed hard for him, but he worked harder than anyone else at everything he did. My concern for him, and especially for his mother, grew.

The day we visited his village, our footsteps on the path raised a powdery dust that parched my mouth, burned my nostrils, and irritated my eyes. On either side were barren, cracked fields. Here and there a few withered crops battled the drought, struggling to grow. The few trees that grew were practically bare.

Finally, we came to Tarabai's mud hut, surprising her. Perplexed but overjoyed to see us, she welcomed us with her palms pressed together and tears in her eyes. Her home was a single square room of about fifteen feet, with floor and walls of dried mud and a thatched roof. Not a single piece of furniture occupied the room, which held only a couple of metal cooking pots, a three-gallon earthen water pot, and a shin-high clay platform for cooking. She gathered twigs for fuel. Otherwise, there was only a simple altar with a photo of Krishna on it and an aged wooden trunk that held her family's clothes. She had no electricity, no running water, no plumbing. The family toilet was the open field.

Despite her obvious poverty, her home wasn't just surprisingly clean; it was immaculate. Every piece of metal shone. Every object was in its place. Regularly she washed the walls and floor and then plastered them with a thin layer of fresh mud, made with water she had carried from almost a mile away. Each morning she drew traditional designs on her floor and walls with colorful mineral powders. Her laundry and even the cleaning rags were meticulously folded and in their place. I can't remember ever seeing such a well-kept home. Despite her primitive facility and her excruciating labor to raise her children, she seemed to take great pride in being a mother and caring for her home. We could see it and feel it. Her home was filled with love.

When I praised her, she smiled shyly and replied in the local Marathi dialect, "This is Krishna's home. I love to clean it. These are Krishna's children. I love to serve them." It was clear she meant it.

One of my companions discreetly offered her some money to help ease her burden. She politely but firmly refused. She didn't want her children to grow up thinking they were a family of beggars who lived on charity. She wanted to teach them by her example that they should work for their sustenance with integrity and gratitude for whatever they were given by God. She felt that too many poor children were becoming beggars or expecting charity. Despite all the hardships she faced, that lesson was the principle of her home.

It wasn't long after my arrival at Tarabai's house that it filled with other villagers. The room was mildly lit by the afternoon sun streaming through a rounded hole that served as the only window. It was hot. Tarabai picked up a small fan made of dried leaves and rapidly whisked me with it. The villagers asked me to tell them a story. The scene reminded me of a story I love from the *Bhagavata Purana*. I told it sentence by sentence, allowing time for the translator. This is what I told them.

## A KING AND A POOR MAN

Some years before speaking the Bhagavad Gita, Lord Krishna and a group of sages visited the kingdom of Mithila. Two of his devotees lived there: one a poor householder of a priestly family (Brahmin) named Shrutadeva, who spent his time seeing to his family's needs, but earning just enough to sustain them each day. They were a happy family who enjoyed their love for the Lord.

The other devotee was the king, named Bahulashva, who lived with his family in luxury. Their love for the Lord and their citizens was pure. Both families made their distinct homes into abodes of devotion.

Pleased with both of them, Sri Krishna decided to travel a great distance to visit them. When he arrived, the whole town turned out to greet him, including King Bahulashva and the poor brahmin Shrutadeva. Both these devotees approached Krishna at the same time to invite him to their homes and please them, and Krishna accepted both invitations.

At the royal palace, Sri Krishna and the sages were offered solid gold thrones to sit on. The king bowed his head and presented fine garlands, exquisite garments, and jeweled ornaments. A sumptuous feast prepared by the king's top chefs was served on golden plates, and servants fanned Krishna with fine, silver-handled yak-tail whisks. The most talented musicians, acrobats, and actors staged performances. The king and queen offered heartfelt prayers, expressing how unworthy they were to host the Lord. "Because we are so engrossed in materialistic activities, you have mercifully come to save us," they said. There was, of course, nothing materialistic about them, because they thought of their wealth as sacred property entrusted to them for God's service and for the welfare of the citizens. They were genuinely humble and devoted.

As everyone leaned forward to hear the story, Tarabai served us cool well water in handmade clay cups.

I then turned to Shrutadeva's greeting of Krishna. Shrutadeva lived in a mud hut not so different from Tarabai's, but he received Sri Krishna with the same enthusiasm the king had. He and his family offered the best of what they had—not golden thrones but grass mats on the floor; not a gourmet feast but simple rice; no silver-handled yak-tailed whisks, but Shrutadeva fanned Krishna and the sages with the old shawl that he was wearing. Shrutadeva had no acrobats or court performers, but he entertained his guests by dancing and singing and twirling his cloth in the air. Like the king and queen, Shrutadeva and his wife offered heartfelt prayers. "You reveal yourself in the hearts of those who, with pure consciousness, constantly hear and chant about you, who serve you with love, and who speak about you with others.

"Although you live in every being's heart, you remain hidden from people disturbed by their own selfishness. No one can grasp you with their material power or knowledge or wealth, for you reveal yourself only in the hearts of those with sincere devotion. O Sri Krishna, please tell us how we can serve you and those you love."

Krishna told Shrutadeva and his family that what pleased him most was when his devotees remembered him with love and served his devotees and all others with care.

Krishna was equally pleased with King Bahulashva and Shrutadeva because they had equal devotion. He did not measure their value by what they possessed or by what they did not. After staying for several days in both homes, he and the sages departed.

——◦——

Tarabai's hut was quiet. As I sipped my water, only the drone of a bee and the buzzing of flies could be heard. In the distance, a cow mooed.

"Krishna is *bhava grahi*," I said. "He is not concerned with what's offered but with the intent behind the offering. Krishna is all-attractive, but he is all-attracted to our devotion. The depth of your bhakti can't be determined by your wealth or status or scholarship or beauty. None of these things matter. Sincerity is the only currency you can possess to attract Krishna's interest. In this story, both a wealthy king and a poor brahmin attained the same pure love because they had the same currency."

When I concluded, one of the farmers said that my story was about a king and a brahmin. He wanted to know whether Krishna would show people of low castes mercy—a good question, given that I was in India. In response I told them a children's story I once heard from my guru, which he told to illustrate that Krishna is not partial to worldly position.

———•———

Narada is a saint who can travel anywhere he likes by the power of mantras. He is known to visit the Supreme in the spiritual world whenever he likes. One day he met a scholarly brahmin who was expert in rituals and had many disciples. "When you see Sri Krishna," he told Narada, "please ask him when I will see him."

Later, Narada met an illiterate cobbler, who was banging away at a tack as he fixed someone's shoe. "When you meet Sri Krishna," he said, "please ask if this tiny soul will ever get His mercy."

When Narada met Sri Krishna, he posed both questions.

Sri Krishna replied, "Tell the brahmin that even after millions of births, he won't be able to see me."

Narada was confused. The brahmin was a pious man and attentive to his religious rituals. "And the cobbler?" he asked.

"The cobbler will see me in this very life."

Now Narada was even more perplexed. How could a low-caste cobbler be more deserving than a brahmin?

Seeing the question in Narada's eyes, Sri Krishna said, "If they ask what I was doing when you spoke to me, tell them I was threading an elephant through the eye of a needle."

Some days later, Narada met the brahmin lecturing on philosophy to an assembly of scholars. "When will I see Sri Krishna?" he asked.

"Krishna said you won't see him even after millions of births."

"What?" shouted the brahmin. "That's ridiculous. You obviously don't know who I am. You'll suffer for your audacity. People worship me. I don't believe you even saw Sri Krishna. If you really did see him, what was he doing?"

"He was threading an elephant through the eye of a needle."

"Impossible," blazed the brahmin. "You're bogus, a fraud. Get lost!"

Shortly after, Narada ran into the cobbler under a giant banyan tree. "Will my Beloved ever show me mercy?" he asked.

"You will see him in your present life," Narada replied.

The cobbler wept in gratitude. "Please, tell me, what was he doing when you met him?"

"Threading an elephant through the eye of a needle."

"Oh, how wonderful," the cobbler exclaimed.

"Do you believe such a thing is possible?" Narada inquired.

"Of course," the cobbler replied. "My Krishna can do anything. After all, he has inconceivable potencies." The cobbler then picked up a seed that had fallen to the ground from the banyan tree under which they sat. "Do you see this enormous tree?" he asked. "Well, Krishna put an entire banyan tree in this tiny seed, and in that tree are more seeds which will fill an entire forest with gigantic trees, so how hard is it for him to thread a mere elephant through the eye of a needle?"

---

I looked over and saw Tarabai listening with attention.

The lesson of this second story, I explained, is that we can study and learn the theory of something, but if we want to realize our knowledge, we need the grace of God, who reciprocates with our sincerity. Race, religion, nationality, social status, caste:

all these are external; Krishna reciprocates with the intention of our heart.

In the late afternoon, we were all invited to a larger hut for dinner.

## BACK TO THE GIFT

As the years passed, Tarabai's son grew to be a natural leader for his companions at the orphanage and a favorite of his teachers. He wasn't particularly gifted academically, but he excelled because of his sincerity, diligence, and graciousness. In the public school he attended, he was first in his school for studies and went on to receive a number of scholarships.

Back in my room, all these memories flashed through my mind as I gazed down at the mysterious gift from Tarabai. A cloud of dust had risen from the dirty bag that held the gift. When it settled, I saw what this special gift really was and I was amazed. To the assembled farmers it was both precious and symbolic of their lives, their plight, and their love. What was the gift? Tarabai had sent hundreds of shells caked with dirt, each with a long, protruding stem. It was a pile of crude, freshly picked peanuts.

This was Tarabai's way of expressing her gratitude for our helping her son. Those peanuts were her prize crop that year. I pictured her walking miles every day with jugs of water to help them grow. The dirt on my floor was the precious soil that had finally nurtured her crop.

Peanuts. I'd heard it countless times when I was growing up: when someone hadn't been paid enough for a job or even when something was sold cheaply, "That's peanuts."

But my mother always emphasized gratitude whether she was given jewels or a simple flower. "It's the thought that counts," she said. My mother taught me that things couldn't bring happiness. Only love can do that. As a child, I couldn't appreciate that her words would one day be forever engraved on my heart and that I would come to share them with tens of thousands of people. Her words were actually my first lesson in bhakti. Those dirty peanuts covering my floor were a treasure in devotion.

For many days I shared, with no explanation, those dirty peanuts with my friends and students—the rich, the middle class, and the poor. I believed that those who ate them would be enriched by the kindness and generosity they contained. When I cracked open the shell of one myself and ate the raw nut, my tongue seemed to move out of the way and I tasted the nut with my heart.

By the way, after earning his master's degree, Tarabai's son Jñanadev became a professor of mathematics at a leading university in Mumbai. I had the honor of speaking at his marriage and later naming his first child. From his mother's tireless example, he has learned the value of hard work, dignity, humility, gratitude, and love for the Supreme Being.

In the character of one with a pure heart, be the person a famous orator, a career professional, or a simple village woman, we discover the true wealth of life: love for the Supreme. That love is naturally accompanied by integrity and genuine compassion. Although so many prayers sing of peace and harmony, religions have managed to divide human beings throughout an atrocious history of enmity and bloodshed. Yet behind the veil of egotism and hypocrisy, at the essence of all true spiritual paths, lies the inherent beauty of the pure soul and its relationship with the Supreme. If we're touched by that beauty, we'll realize the inherent unity of all beings and all creation and we will find ourselves willing to serve as an instrument of that unity.

One name of the Supreme is Hari, or "one who steals." Hari is all-beautiful, and his infinite sweetness steals our hearts from their fleeting pleasures and pains and submerges us in a limitless reservoir of pleasure.

He is also known as Ghanashyam, or one as beautiful as a blue monsoon cloud, because he showers the heart parched by the blazing fire of illusion with endless torrents of grace.

Another name is Bhakta Vatsal, or one who is irresistibly conquered by pure love and who irresistibly conquers the heart with grace.

*My dear Lord, you have made yourself accessible to*
*everyone in your countless names. In each of these names you have*
*invested your divine potency to cleanse the heart and awaken*
*prema, ecstatic love. If one is sincere, there are not even hard and*
*fast rules for chanting your names.*

—SRI CHAITANYA, *CHAITANYA CHARITAMRITA: ANTYA-LILA* 20.16

## A MATCHLESS GIFT

When Prabhupada, my beloved guru, first came to the United States, he rented a small, rundown storefront on the Lower East Side of New York City in order to teach a message of divine love. It was a meager beginning, and he didn't even have money to pay the second month's rent when he signed the lease. The previous tenant had run a trinket shop named Matchless Gifts, and the sign still hung above the front window when he took it over. When a student went to change the sign, Prabhupada smiled and said, "You may leave it as it is. Bhakti *is* a matchless gift."

## REALIZING THE HIGHEST LOVE

Enlightenment is a vivid, constant awareness of the world as inherently divine, of life as a loving partnership with the Supreme, and of every moment as a call to extend love to everyone around us.

The spiritual world is within each of us. It is not that we have to die to realize it. According to the Vedas, to the degree that we love the Supreme Being, to that degree we will realize his presence in others and ourselves.

Material existence is a mere reflection of an eternal reality, where the substance of the fulfillment we each seek is forever manifest. As our dormant love for the Supreme Being is awakened, we will have an intimation of that inner eternal realm. Still, bhakti texts and saints teach that the eternal world also stands apart: it is a tangible place, a destination that exists beyond the cosmic creation. The Sanskrit language gives this place many names, such as Vaikuntha, "the world free of anxiety," and Paravyoma, "the supreme abode." The Bhagavad Gita (8.20, 15.6) describes it like this: "There is another nature, which is eternal and transcendental to this manifest and unmanifest matter. It is supreme and never annihilated. When all in this world is destroyed, that nature remains as it is. That supreme abode of mine is not illumined by the sun or moon, nor by fire or electricity. Those who reach it never return to this material world."

People who have perfectly distanced themselves from selfish interests and live only to serve the Divine already dwell in this eternal realm. They see divinity around them everywhere, because everything reminds them of and brings them close to their Supreme Beloved. There is a great mystery to living simultaneously in this world and the eternal one, and those who achieve this deepest level of yoga know it well.

I would like to share with you descriptions of the spiritual world, beyond material existence, as they are found in the Vedic literature and as they have been realized and described by bhakti saints over the centuries. Although the purpose of this book is to present the universal nature of bhakti yoga's basic teachings and practices and how they are relevant to our daily lives, I feel these brief descriptions of the loving exchanges in the spiritual world may fascinate you as they fascinate me, for they provide a window into a spiritual reality.

According to Vedic texts, the material creation consists of innumerable universes, and among these many universes ours is but a tiny speck. These numerous temporal worlds together are like a single cloud in the endless spiritual sky called what many people think of as "the white light"—in Sanskrit, the *brahmajyoti*, an all-pervading spiritual existence. This divine light is the destination of those who achieve enlightenment focused on God's impersonal, all-pervading, undifferentiated oneness.

Within the eternal spiritual sky there are spiritual planets. The Supreme Being expands himself to personally reside in each of these planets. Life on those planets never ends because there is no matter; nothing decays or dies. The beings inhabiting these worlds are all situated in pure spiritual consciousness and they have spiritual, not material, bodies. The one Supreme Lord lives with these beings and reciprocates with each soul's specific, unique love for him. These spiritual planets are the destination of those souls who achieve enlightenment focused on the Supreme's personal nature.

For those in the beginning stages of spiritual practice, sacred texts generally emphasize approaching the Supreme in reverence to his greatness. This helps build a sense of appreciation for one's dependence on God and the need to follow his precepts. For those who are further along in their practice, however, the bhakti texts teach that although the types of relationships one can have with the Supreme are unlimited, they fall into five broad categories. The texts call these *rasas*, or "flavors of relationship."

The first rasa, and the most primary, is neutrality, a pure love of God steeped in awareness of his greatness and characterized by a kind of passive adoration.

In the second rasa, the mood of active, dynamic service is prominent. The servitors' love is imbued with reverence for the Supreme Person's utmost superior position, and they are fully devoted to serving their beloved's will.

The third rasa is love on the platform of intimate friendship, characterized by a free flow of spontaneous loving exchanges not distanced by awe or reverence. The realizations of the previous two rasas (neutrality and servitorship) are included in divine friendship with the addition of deeper intimacy.

The fourth is parental love. Rather than seeing God as master and father, the devotee sees the Supreme Being as his or her divine child. As mentioned earlier, small children tend to be self-centered and demanding, whereas the parent's mood is to give everything to the child; in this world, such love has no equal. So in addition to traditions that envision the Supreme Being as the heavenly father always being petitioned by his many children for favors, bhakti culture presents that the Supreme may take the role of child and reciprocate the love of those who wish to taste this rasa. A loving parent gives unconditionally to a child without expecting anything in return.

The Absolute Truth, the almighty creator, maintainer, and destroyer of the universe, can choose to appear as a small child. This ideal is realized in a special way in the Krishna conception of the Divinity. When Krishna is naughty, his parents, with limitless selfless love, scold him. Conquered by their love, which exceeds awareness of his power and sees him only as a dependent child in need of correction, Krishna feels great satisfaction, even though as God he is already Self-fulfilled.

Finally, the fifth is a conjugal love, an unbridled, complete surrender of the soul who approaches the Supreme as a Divine Lover.

We experience a limited, temporary reflection of these familiar relationships in the material world, but the origin of all of them is our love for and relationship with the Supreme Person. The beauty and pleasure of relationships are the basis of happiness. That happiness reaches its highest fulfillment when we realize our inherent spiritual love.

These five relationships can be further divided into two categories. The first is love based on an attitude of awe and reverence, a love motivated by a conscious awareness of the Supreme Being's unprecedented and infinite power and greatness. In the second category, awareness of the Supreme Being's sweetness and beauty eclipses awareness of his supreme power and allows a far greater intimacy with him.

I find this truth to be one of the salient gifts that the practice of pure bhakti has given the world. Anyone on a spiritual path can benefit from embracing, at least theoretically, the idea that to accommodate an intimate love, the Supreme makes himself approachable. He is especially approachable when we focus on the charming and disarming power of his sweetness.

Of divine love's many varieties, it is this awareness of the Supreme's sweetness and beauty—in Sanskrit, *madhurya*, or the feeling of tender affection for him—that several bhakti traditions hold in the highest esteem. Knowledge of the Supreme Being's majesty is included in madhurya, but it remains in the background and subordinate to the more spontaneous expression of love for a Supreme Beloved filled with infinite charm. The more intimate our love is, the more the Supreme Beloved steps outside his formal role as universal master in order to reciprocate with it. An example is given of a high court justice. In court he is addressed as "Your Honor." Out of court, his friends joke with him, his children play with him, his parents scold him for not taking care of his health, and his wife reminds him to take out the garbage. The same person assumes appropriate roles to cultivate these many different relationships.

There is an energy in this world that creates countless illusions to facilitate those who want to forget God. Similarly, for those who love him, there is a "divine illusion" that veils our perception of his majestic power simply to facilitate loving exchanges. The illusions in this world are affected by *maha-maya*, "great illusion," whereas the divine illusion is called *yoga-maya*. Yoga means "to connect or unite," so yoga-maya refers to the energy of the Supreme that makes possible our loving union with the Abode of Love.

The Supreme Being is often described as a kind of Divine Judge who rewards the pious and penalizes the impious. Bhakti texts like the *Bhagavata Purana* explain that that's only a part of the Supreme Being's multifaceted personality. God in his personal form has eternal loving exchanges with his devotees in the spiritual world. There, he delights not in exhibiting his Godhood but in sharing varieties of love.

In Krishna's pastoral paradise on earth, Vrindavan, yoga-maya covers the perfect devotees' vision so that they are no longer conscious of Krishna as the all-mighty supreme origin and controller of all existence. Rather, they see him as the most special object of their love. And he plays that role to perfection. For example, with those who love him in parental affection, he becomes an endearingly naughty child who sometimes steals butter from their houses. The women complain to his mother, Yashoda, but Krishna artfully feigns innocence and Yashoda is mystified until the telltale butter on Krishna's lips exposes him.

So celebrated are Krishna's Vrindavan pastimes that numerous philosophical treatises and hundreds of thousands of enchanting poems and songs have been composed about them, and millions of Krishna bhaktas delight in them. Here's a stanza from a bhakti poet of the thirteenth century:

*My dear Lord, O best of thieves, You who are celebrated*
*as a butter thief in the glorious land of Vrindavan. Please steal away all*
*my selfishness and delusion, which has accumulated over many lifetimes.*

— BILVA MANGALA, THAKUR

Skeptics who ask why the Supreme Being steals are missing the essence of the pastime: love. Besides, being the Supreme, Krishna owns everything, so there's no question of his stealing anything. Yet Krishna "steals" to have fun-filled loving exchanges with his bhaktas. When our hearts become as soft and sweet as fresh-churned butter, Krishna will steal them. Bhakti is the churning process.

As dramatic as Krishna's pastimes are, they are expressions of the highest reality—the reality of intimate love between the Supreme Being and the soul—where Krishna is simultaneously the master and yet enjoys being controlled by his bhaktas' love. Vrindavan is an especially extraordinary world, and the play between Krishna and the souls who have chosen to be with him there show us another dimension of the saying "God is love."

In that world of love, Krishna's friends feel themselves his equals and play with him free of formality. They amuse Krishna with their jokes and games, and Krishna amuses them. In the sports they play, Krishna sometimes defeats them with his love, and at other times Krishna is defeated by the love of his friends. These loving exchanges fill both Krishna and his friends with divine pleasure. Giving pleasure *is* his pleasure.

As the Supreme Lover, Krishna shares a pure, selfless love wholly free of selfish desire or lust. It is a love untainted by physical cravings; such love is impossible when there's any trace of false ego. Pure conjugal love of the Divine can be expressed only by completely liberated souls. Over the centuries, saints, scholars, and enlightened sages have proclaimed this ultimate expression of affection to be a completely pure, all-inclusive form of spiritual love that can be realized only through grace. The gopis, or cowherd girls of Vrindavan, are perfect examples of conjugal lovers of the Divine.

The pure, selfless reciprocation of love between Krishna and the gopis is epitomized in the *rasa-lila*, the joyous festival of song and dance vividly described in the Tenth Canto of the *Bhagavata Purana* and in a number of other texts.

The rasa-lila is performed in the eternal Vrindavan in the spiritual world and in the earthly Vrindavan in the material world whenever Krishna descends. Krishna held his rasa-lila in Vrindavan on a charming full-moon autumn night, calling the gopis to him by playing his celebrated flute under a banyan tree on the bank of the Yamuna River. The gopis responded immediately to his call, leaving aside everything else. The Bhagavad Gita says that the perfection of renunciation is to surrender to the Supreme's will completely. The gopis demonstrated this selfless love by responding without concern for any infamy their actions might bring them or fear of banishment from the orthodox society of their times. It's not that they abandoned morality; rather, they transcended mundane conventions for the sake of selfless surrender in pure love for the Supreme. During the rasa-lila, Krishna and the gopis talked, sang, danced, and relished the ecstatic love of the soul. Although their dealings may resemble the dealings between worldly lovers, they are in a different category. Iron and gold are both metals, but iron is common and gold is precious. The nature of the gopis' unconditional love is that they would endure an eternity of torment if they could just give their Beloved a moment of pleasure. To do so is their greatest joy. And it is the nature of Krishna's infinite love to give the gopis the pinnacle of happiness. That is his greatest joy.

How can such pure love not conquer the heart of the beloved? Krishna feels so indebted to the gopis' for their selfless love that he tells them:

*Your service is so glorious that there is no way I can repay you. Even offering you all the wealth in the universe for millennia would not be adequate to repay your love. So please be satisfied by your love itself.*
— BHAGAVATA PURANA 10.32.22

In the realm of devotion, according to the nature and degree of love offered by a bhakta, Krishna reciprocates by offering his own love millions of times over. This is the summit of love, where that infinite, transcendental love conquers the heart of the bhakta and the selfless love of the bhakta conquers the heart of God, who is otherwise unconquerable.

The renowned fifteenth-century saint and scholar Sri Vallabha spread the spirit of this divine love far and wide. To this day, his teachings remain the foundation of a prominent school of bhakti that has tens of millions of followers. One such follower was my beloved friend Shyamdas, an American by birth who in the early 1970s became the first non-Indian to be initiated in Sri Vallabha's lineage. Shyamdas was a Sanskrit scholar, a master classical Indian musician, the author of numerous books, an extraordinary cook, and a loving, gentle man. I asked him to write a passage for this book to explain the essence of his tradition. Just before his passing from this world, he wrote the following:

> Sri Vallabha taught what he called the Path of Grace (*Pushti Marg*) wherein the highest knowledge could be known through love. Sri Vallabha focused on the *gopis* of Vrindavan and taught that by emulating their dedicated devotion one can attain spiritual perfection. His conclusion was: *Always, with divine feeling, worship Sri Krishna.*

He fashioned his teachings to fit into the world. Sri Vallabha saw the world as Sri Krishna's playground and urged his followers to offer him the best of everything, according to their means. This inspired incredible art, music, and poetry to emerge around his Path of Grace, and poets, artists, writers, kings, Muslim mystics, pundits, and even animals gained entrance into the nectar of devotion.

In the same golden era of bhakti in which Sri Vallabha lived, Sri Chaitanya personified the ecstatic state of spiritual perfection. Throughout his life and precepts, and through those of his loving followers, he opened the doors for everyone to realize the ecstatic states of pure love. He taught the art of transforming every aspect of one's life into a spiritual truth through devotion, and particularly emphasized meditating on and chanting God's holy names as a means to both open oneself to the soul's depths and to realize love of God. A core practice of bhakti is therefore devotional song (kirtan).

We have the rare gift to realize life's perfection. We can experience the infinite sweetness of God's love for us and ours for him. The bhakti texts proclaim this to be the pinnacle of liberation.

When a beautiful woman puts on costly perfume to meet her lover, everyone she passes experiences the sweet fragrance. Divine love for God is compared to the sweetest perfume. Its fragrance naturally extends to everyone, wherever we go. And on arriving at our destination, the Supreme Abode of Divine Love, we will know for sure that we have at last come home.

Bhakti is the natural offering of love to the Supreme. Through bhakti, we realize infinite grace and give our hearts in perfect trust to that grace. We at last discover the real ecstasy we have mistakenly sought in the fleeting mirages of the world. The potential to realize this love is present within all of us, and it is our most precious inheritance, waiting to be claimed.

# CONCLUSION

## Unity in Diversity

I awoke to the sound of distant temple bells chiming to welcome a new day. Looking into the still dark sky, I rose from the dusty, cold riverbank where I had slept and submerged myself in the chilly Yamuna River to bathe. Climbing out of the river, I sat on the bank in the predawn quiet. As the first golden aura of the sun gently lit the horizon, birds began to warble and coo their morning songs from the forest behind me. This is how I began each day in 1971, when I lived in Vrindavan, the holiest place for bhaktas of Krishna.

One day, a barefoot holy man stepped out of the forest and approached me from behind, softly chanting Krishna's names. He was perhaps sixty years old, had long matted hair and a beard, and wore the robes and markings of an ascetic devotee of Krishna. He sat beside me and spoke in a hypnotic tone that drew me in. Citing sacred Vedic texts and chanting timeless hymns, he spoke of the mystical beauty of Vrindavan and the esoteric teachings and pastimes that Krishna revealed at the very spot where we were sitting. I felt a universe away from anywhere else in the world.

He gradually stopped speaking, and we looked at each other in silence. As I gazed back into his eyes, I was in a state of profound peace. Then he softly broke the silence.

"I have something for you," he said. "I have carried this with me for more than forty years. It will inspire you to deepen your love for Krishna, as it has inspired me." Slightly nodding his head, his gaze still fixed on me, the stranger handed me a folded piece of paper. It was tattered, wrinkled, and yellowed by time. Then he walked away, into the dawn. My mind soared with curiosity.

Peacocks cawed, parrots chirped, and monkeys screeched as they woke to the morning. Women passed me with brass pots filled with river water on their heads. I tenderly unfolded the paper. Was it an ancient Sanskrit incantation? A secret meditation?

The paper was so worn that I thought it might dissolve in my fingers, but I could still see what was written on it. I was not *at all* expecting *this*. Smiling, I marveled at the incredible ways of Krishna. It was a familiar prayer, attributed to St. Francis of Assisi in the thirteenth century:

*Lord, make me an instrument of your peace.*
*Where there is hatred, let me sow love.*
*Where there is injury, pardon.*
*Where there is doubt, faith.*
*Where there is despair, hope.*

*Where there is darkness, light.*
*Where there is sadness, joy.*
*Divine Master, grant that I may not so much seek*
*to be consoled, as to console,*
*to be understood, as to understand,*
*to be loved, as to love.*
*For it is in giving that we receive.*
*It is in pardoning that we are pardoned.*
*It is in dying that we are born to eternal life.*

Throughout my youth, growing up in a village north of Chicago, this prayer was often by my side, inspiring me to reach beyond my human tendencies for a higher truth. Now in that holy sanctuary in northwest India I reflected on how fittingly this prayer expresses the universal spirit of bhakti, the yoga of love. The essence of any devotional prayer, whatever its culture of origin, is to ask God how we may serve with unconditional love.

A saint once wrote that it's not possible to describe the devotional path completely. Like a bottomless, shoreless ocean, the subject of loving relationships with the Supreme is so vast that no one can estimate its length and breadth. The most we can do is try to describe one drop. The content of that single drop, however, can flood the entire universe with grace.

In *The Journey Within*, we have discussed a search for our lost love, a love deep within all of us. When we find it, we'll realize it everywhere and in everything. As immortal souls wandering in a mortal world, we've forgotten who we are and our inherent potential to love and be loved by the all-attractive Supreme Beloved. Tasting that love again will be our ultimate happiness. And it will empower us with unconditional compassion.

I am deeply grateful to you, my readers, for allowing me to share with you the joy of my life, the bhakti tradition. I pray that *The Journey Within*, which is full of wisdom from ancient texts, saints, and life experiences, will help you on your own spiritual journey.

Life leads us on many journeys, and all are ultimately meant to lead us to the love that lies within us. Divine love lives in a place inaccessible to the mind, senses, or intellect. It resides in the soul. It's waiting for you like an ever-flowing river. There, beyond the fleeting pleasures and pains of material life, is the infinite beauty, sweetness, and love of our Supreme Beloved, who is calling us home.

# GLOSSARY

*advaita*: Nondual.

Age of Kali (*kali yuga*): An age characterized by forgetfulness of the true self and subsequent quarreling and hypocrisy. We are currently in this age.

*ahankara*: False ego.

*ahimsa*: One of the regulative principles of yoga. Literally "nonviolence"; it means causing no harm to any living being through our actions, words, and as far as humanly possible, our thoughts. It also means to act positively: to be kind, to love others, to want their spiritual and material well-being, and to be compassionate. The biblical equivalent is "Do unto others as you would have them do unto you."

*ananda*: Spiritual bliss.

*annamaya*: Consciousness, or the distinguishing between the self and the "other."

*aparigraha*: One of the regulative principles of yoga. It means not to fall prey to the obsession of over-accumulating material possessions. "Simple living and high thinking" is a motto for the yogic way of life.

*arati*: A ceremony performed in Indian temples wherein the worshiper offers various items that represent one's devotional intent. The arati is meant to be a reciprocation of love.

*archa-vigraha*: A deity form of the Supreme that has been established and is worshipped on an altar according to the guidelines of Vedic texts, sacred traditions, and with the blessings of enlightened people. Revered teacher A.C. Bhaktivedanta Swami Prabhupada used the English word "*deity*" to refer to this sanctified form of the Supreme in order to differentiate it from an idol.

*asanas*: Yogic postures.

ashtanga or raja yoga: Known as "the path with eight limbs." It includes asana practice, breath control, and meditation.

*asteya*: One of the regulative principles of yoga. It means the "avoidance of stealing."

*atma*: The individual soul—the ever-existing, indestructible, conscious essence, the nature of which is blissful awareness. There is a difference between the material body we inhabit and the atma. The atma is not one with the body but it is the observer living inside it; the "I" who is experiencing.

avatar: One who descends. Refers to when the Supreme Being descends or incarnates into the world to extend compassion to all beings.

ayurveda: A Vedic system of holistic health that includes lifestyle, diet, natural tonics, and medicine.

Bhagavad Gita: "The Song of God"—often simply referred to as the Gita. The Gita is a 700-verse Sanskrit text that is a part of the Mahabharata epic and is considered the essential summary of all the Vedas.

*bhagavan*: The "Supreme Being" or "the source of excellences." The Vedas list those excellences as beauty, strength, knowledge, wealth, fame, and independence.

Bhagavan: The all-beautiful, personal, loving, and Supreme Person—God when he is fully himself.

bhakta: A practitioner of bhakti yoga.

bhakti: The word bhakti means "unconditional love for the Supreme Being and deep compassion for others." This love is so complete that it inspires love not only for God but for everyone and everything connected to him. In other words, bhakti is expressed in a dynamic, practical way by loving God, showing kindness to others, and caring for the environment, knowing that it is God's sacred energy, essential to the well-being of all life.

bhakti yoga: The yoga of love. The path of integrating loving service to the Supreme Being into every aspect of one's life. It is a practice of sincere compassion to all beings. It highlights practices such as hearing sacred topics and the prayerful chanting of God's names. Bhakti yoga culminates in loving service to God, unmotivated by desires for personal enjoyment, miraculous powers, or even our own liberation, which is a natural consequence of love of God.

*brahmacharya*: One of the regulative principles of yoga. It is a practice that helps one to control the mind and senses in order to better engage in spiritual practices and encourages acting in ways that lead us to Brahman, or spiritual unity. It generally refers to sexual regulation or, in some cases, abstinence.

Brahman: The omniscient, omnipresent truth of Absolute reality—the divine energy that permeates everything. Liberation is to recognize oneself as of the same essential quality as Brahman.

*buddhi*: Enlightened intelligence.

*chit*: Divine knowledge.

dharma: From the Sanskrit root *dhri*, meaning "to hold, maintain, or keep," and, in its noun form, meaning "that which cannot be taken away [because it is firmly part of something]." Think of dharma as a person's or a thing's inherent quality or purpose. Dharma commonly refers to one's spiritual duties.

*dhyana*: Meditation.

*diksha* guru: The initiating guru. The diksha guru gives initiation into a *parampara* for a student who has been practicing for some time and wishes to deepen and formalize his or her commitment to the path.

*gopis*: Cowherd girls. Refers to the cowherd girls of Vrindavan, simple village girls whose unconditional love for Krishna is honored by saints and scriptures as the quintessence of pure, spiritual love.

*gunas*: Defined as "ropes" because of their binding nature. Gunas are invisible influences, often referred to as "qualities" or "modes," that drive us to act in certain ways. According to our frame of mind and our choice of words and actions, we tune into a particular guna or a combination of gunas and come under their influence. The three gunas are *sattva* (goodness), *rajas* (passion), and *tamas* (ignorance).

guru: A spiritual teacher or master, a person capable of guiding others to awaken to their eternal spiritual self. In one of its meanings, *gu* signifies "darkness" and *ru* "to remove"—thus, gurus remove the darkness of ignorance. The guru's responsibilities include instructing the student, caring for the student's spiritual well-being, and guiding him or her on the path toward liberation from bondage and suffering.

*ishvara pranidhana*: One of the regulative principles of yoga that leads one to complete surrender to the Supreme. From the perspective of bhakti yoga, all forms of yoga culminate in this surrender. It means to dedicate one's actions, words, and thoughts—and ultimately, one's essence—to the will of the Divine. On the bhakti path, surrender is the art of dedicating our abilities, resources, family—whatever we have—with love to the Supreme Being.

*japa*: A private form of meditation on a mantra. It is an intimate and personal practice. During japa meditation, the practitioner recites the holy names softly to him- or herself, either out loud, sofly, or silently while focusing his or her attention on the divine sound vibration.

jnana yoga: The yoga path of cultivating spiritual knowledge.

*kama*: Refers to either intense spiritual desire (love) or passionate material desire (lust).

karma: Action. India's spiritual traditions consider the law of karma a natural law, similar to the law of gravity. Think of karma as an aspect of the universe that realigns itself in response to how we live in the universe. That is, for every action, there will be a corresponding reaction. The law of karma acts like a fever. Karmic reactions purge what is unhealthy in the world, just as a fever in the body burns up harmful bacteria. Because life is a long continuum of actions and reactions, our results include both joy and suffering. Spiritual teachings that give us insight into the law of karma urge us to improve the quality of our lives by taking responsibility for the choices we make.

karma yoga: The yoga path of knowledge in action.

*karuna*: Active compassion for the body, mind, and especially the soul. Karuna goes beyond sentiment and into thoughtful, committed, and directed action for the overall well-being of other beings, the environment, and for ones own true self. Karuna Sindhu is a name of God, and means a limitless ocean that an ultimate source of all compassion.

kirtan: A revered practice that leads to an ecstatic love for the Supreme. Kirtan is the chanting of hymns, prayers, or the holy names of God. According to the bhakti tradition, the Supreme Being manifests himself in his names, and he reveals his beauty, sweetness, power, and love to those who chant these names sincerely.

*laulyam*: The intense yearning to love and serve the Supreme.

*madhurya*: God's all-attractive sweetness that ultimately captures a devotees heart, lifting him or her beyond all material pleasures or sufferings. The awareness of the Supreme's sweetness and beauty awakens a feeling of tender affection for him and a will to serve. Several bhakti traditions hold this experience in the highest esteem.

*maha-mantra*: Literally "the great mantra." The Vedic literature especially recommends the maha-mantra as the perfect process for spiritual perfection in the troubled age that we currently live in. The maha-mantra serves as a prayer: "O Radha, O You who bestows grace, O Krishna, O Rama, please engage me in Your loving service."

> *Hare Krishna Hare Krishna*
> *Krishna Krishna Hare Hare*
> *Hare Rama Hare Rama*
> *Rama Rama Hare Hare*

*Mahabharata*: A classical Sanskrit epic narrating the famous story of the Kuru kingdom. It includes various philosophical treatises, ancient histories, and devotional narrations. The heart of the Mahabharata, a 100,000 verse poem, the Bhagavad Gita. The Mahabharata is often considered one of the two great epics of Sanskrit literature, the other being the Ramayana.

*mala*: A strand of beads, often used in conjunction with chanting or meditating.

mantra: In the Sanskrit language, "mantra" refers to a sound vibration. The word *mantra* comes from two Sanskrit root words: *manas*, which means "mind," and *trayate*, which means "to deliver" or "to free." Repeating a mantra frees the mind from anxiety and illusion.

*maya*: Divine energy. Generally refers to the energy that covers the awareness of one's true self, causing the eternal, blissful soul to identify with a temporary material body and objects related to the body (I and mine). The material atmosphere in which we are now living is commonly called maya, or illusion (that which is not).

*nada-brahman*: Divine sound vibration. *Brahman* refers to the Supreme, and *nada* literally means "a stream"—in this case, both a stream of sound and a stream of consciousness. Sanskrit texts often describe spiritual sound as the most effective way to awaken divine consciousness.

Navadwip: The birthplace of Chaitanya Mahaprabhu and therefore a sacred place of pilgrimage. Navadwip is situated in the Nadia District of West Bengal, India.

*niyamas*: Disciplined yoga practice.

*paramatma*: God as the inner guide. Also known as the "Supersoul" who is seated in the hearts of all living beings.

*parampara*: A lineage of saintly teachers. There are four such devotional lines of succession in the Vedic bhakti tradition that trace their roots back to the dawn of creation.

*prana*: The essential energy or breath of life.

*pranayama*: Yogic breathing practices that cleanse the mind and body and connect one to the prana.

*prasada*: Divine mercy. Refers to sanctified vegetarian food. By cooking food with the thought in mind of preparing it for the Supreme as an act of love, and then asking God to accept it, the food is transformed into prasada. Sharing sanctified food with family, friends, and guests, or distributing sanctified food to the needy, is a sacred form of charity.

*prema*: The ultimate and fullest realization of the souls innate love. The nature of prema is that one becomes so ecstatically immersed in love for God that one loses oneself in the happiness that springs from this love. The self is never actually lost; what does disappear is the illusion that we were ever separate from our Supreme Beloved.

*puja*: Puja commonly consists of offering physical objects in a specific order and with specific prayers to the object of worship. Puja is not ritual in the way many people imagine rituals—that is, routine worship without much internal participation. When properly understood and performed, puja leaves deep, positive impressions within the mind. A well-designed ritual takes the practitioner's body and mind through a series of steps that are simultaneously aesthetically pleasing and spiritually purifying. In its most enlightened form, puja translates the idea of devotion into an action of devotion. The spiritual energy we generate during puja can stretch beyond the limits of time and space and transmit blessings and grace into the world.

*rajas*: One of the three gunas. Rajas is the mode of passion, which compels us to work hard and achieve as much as we can. This guna increases our taste for challenge and reward. Rajas impels us to satisfy our passionate desires.

*Ramayana*: A classical Sanskrit epic written by Valmiki that narrates the story of the heroic avatar Rama. It articulates and explains philosophical concepts of duty, righteousness, truth, and ultimately pure spiritual love. The *Ramayana* is considered one of the two great works of Sanskrit literature, the other being the *Mahabharata*.

*rasa-lila*: The joyous festival of song and dance wherein the pure, selfless reciprocation of love between Krishna and the gopis is epitomized.

*rasas*: The flavors, or variations, of ecstatic spiritual relationships reciprocated between the Supreme Being and the liberated soul.

*samadhi*: A liberated state of unshakable peace.

*samsara*: The repeated cycle of birth, growth, dwindling, and death. The wheel of samsara revolves endlessly until one is liberated.

*samskaras*: Habits and thought patterns that inform how we act. Negative samskaras can be transformed into positive ones by creating new healthful habits. In another context, samskara also refers to ceremonial rites of passage that purify the self and attract blessings at transitional stages of ones life.

*santosh*: Peace or contentment. One of the regulative principles of yoga.

*sat*: Eternal truth.

*sat-chit-ananda*: Eternal and full of spiritual knowledge and bliss.

*sattva*: One of the three gunas. Sattva is the mode of goodness. The Gita describes it as "illuminating," meaning that people strongly influenced by this mode lean toward purity, knowledge, peacefulness, and happiness.

*satyam*: Truthfulness. One of the regulative principles of yoga. It teaches us to speak what is true with a simple and well-wishing heart.

*Shakti*: The feminine, motherly aspect of the Supreme Being. The divine, activating energy that nourishes, forgives, and empowers a soul with compassion. The feminine and masculine aspects of the one God are described in an analogy of the sun — shakti is the sunshine (the energy) given off by the sun (the source). Shakti (divine feminine) and shakti-man (divine masculine) can never be separated.

*Shaktiman*: The source of all that exists and the generating power of all material and spiritual existence, the masculine aspect of the one Supreme Being. Shakti (divine feminine principle) and shaktiman (divine masculine principle) can never be separated.

*shaucham*: One of the regulative principles of yoga. It is the practice of cleanliness in body, words, and mind.

*shiksha* guru: The instructing guru. The shiksha guru inspires and teaches disciples by his or her instructions and exemplary lifestyle.

*shravana*: A practice of dedicating quality time to reading sacred literature and listening to talks that discuss spiritual teachings and inspire devotion. Shravana refocuses our priorities, purifies the heart, and attracts divine grace.

Sri Chaitanya Mahaprabhu (1486–1533): The avatar of divine love. He is Krishna and descended to the earth to play the role of a devotee and taught us how to love God by his own example. Sri Chaitanya is the combined form of Radha and Krishna. He was known in his younger years as Nimai. He reformed and resuscitated the bhakti tradition by distributing love of God to one and all without discrimination and by inaugurating congregational kirtan, particularly the chanting of the Hare Krishna maha-mantra.

Supersoul: See *paramatma*.

*svadhyaya*: One of the regulative principles of yoga. It means self-study or introspection.

*tamas*: One of the three gunas. Tamas is the mode of ignorance and pulls one toward envy, hate, anger, apathy, indifference, intoxication, and depression — and in its more lethal stages, madness and suicide.

*tapas*: Austerity or sacrifice. One of the regulative principles of yoga. It means to accept what is favorable for spiritual progress and avoid what is unfavorable, even if doing so is difficult.

Upanishads: A collection of Sanskrit philosophical texts.

Vedas: Refers to a large body of ancient Indian texts, written in Vedic Sanskrit. The Vedic literature includes instruction on multiple arts and sciences, including martial arts, architecture, astronomy, astrology, medicine, philosophy, psychology, yoga, the social and spiritual duties that apply to people of various natures, and the ethics and guidelines for government and family. All of these subjects, and many more, are aimed at an evolution of consciousness (both individually and collectively) and ultimately, at liberation through knowing and loving the Supreme.

vedic: Relating to the Vedas and the teachings therein.

Vrindavan: The sacred place of pilgrimage where Krishna performed his loving youthful pastimes. Vrindavan is situated approximately 6 miles away from Mathura in Uttar Pradesh, and 90 miles southeast of Delhi, India.

*yamas*: Ethical disciplines of yoga.

yoga: Connection or union. Yoga is a practice relating to various systems of knowledge that originate from ancient India. The term accommodates a large range of schools and encompasses various physical, mental, and spiritual disciplines.

*yoga-maya*: The Lord's divine spiritual energy, which affects people in a liberated state.

*Yoga Sutras*: Compiled by Patanjali. The *Yoga Sutras* are comprised of various texts describing all the different components of the ashtanya yoga system.

# ACKNOWLEDGMENTS

I extend my sincerest gratitude and affection to all my friends and well-wishers, who have helped to make this book possible. Amy Hertz first conceived the idea of the book. She and Joshua Greene were there from the beginning as a source of wisdom and encouragement.

My dear friend Raoul Goff has been a wonderful inspiration; he opened the doors of his Mandala Publishing along with his staff, including Phillip Jones, Arjuna Van Der Kooij, Vanessa Lopez, Courtney Andersson, Gopika Misri, Pandita Wong, and Hanna Rahimi. Their encouragement and expertise have made everything about this project a pleasing adventure.

I am especially grateful to Kaisori Devi, who kindly extended herself to share her devoted heart and her visionary and editorial gifts. Kyra Ryan once again came forward to provide her true brilliance.

His Holiness Giriraja Swami blessed my effort with his priceless encouragement and profound insights. Rukmini Devi showered on me her motherly grace and divine intuition. My dear friend Vaisesika Das provided invaluable wisdom and inspiration.

My dear well-wishers Rajiv Srivatsam, Hrishikesh Mafatlal, Dr. Narendra Desai, Kusal Desai, and their families and Ajay and Swati Piramal were of invaluable support and inspiration.

Sharon Gannon and David Life, gracious and empowered activists of compassion, moved me to include special passages on compassion.

Rev. David Carter and Marguerite Regan taught me so much about writing with my heart.

Among those who shared their precious wisdom and literary skills were Kaustubha and Gita Priya, Carl Herzig, Graham Schweig, Radha Vallabha, Gadadhara Pandit, Gaura Vani, Chaitanya Charan, Radhey Shyam, Rasanath, Hari Prasad, Mahamuni, Dr. Abhisheka Ghosh, Gaura Gopal, Vraja Behari, Govinda, Gauranga, Balaram, and Kishori Lila.

The affection of my beloved father, mother, and brothers and my family, friends, and other well-wishers have made this humble effort a truly meaningful experience.

And, I thank all of you, my readers, for your open and beautiful hearts.

# ABOUT THE AUTHOR

Radhanath Swami was born in Chicago in 1950. At age nineteen, he traveled overland from London to India, where he lived in Himalayan caves, learned yoga from revered masters, and eventually became a world-renowned spiritual leader in his own right. His acclaimed memoir, *The Journey Home,* has been translated into over twenty languages and published in over forty countries worldwide.

Radhanath Swami presently travels throughout Asia, Europe, and America teaching devotional wisdom, but can often be found in Mumbai, where he works tirelessly to help develop communities, food distribution initiatives, missionary hospitals, schools, ashrams, emergency relief programs, and eco-friendly farms.

www.radhanathswami.com
www.facebook.com/radhanathswami

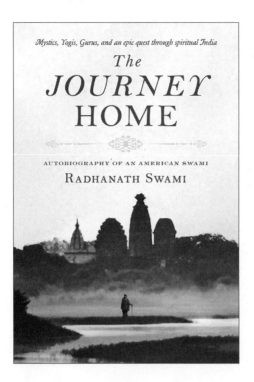

*Mystics, Yogis, Gurus, and an epic quest through spiritual India*

The
JOURNEY
HOME

AUTOBIOGRAPHY OF AN AMERICAN SWAMI

RADHANATH SWAMI

# THE JOURNEY HOME

Within this extraordinary memoir, Radhanath Swami weaves a colorful tapestry of adventure, mysticism, and love. Readers follow Richard Slavin from the suburbs of Chicago to the caves of the Himalayas as he transforms from young seeker to renowned spiritual guide. *The Journey Home* is an intimate account of the steps to self-awareness and a penetrating glimpse into the heart of mystic traditions and the challenges that all souls must face on the road to inner harmony and a union with the Divine.

Through near-death encounters, apprenticeships with advanced yogis, and years of travel along the pilgrim's path, Radhanath Swami eventually reaches the inner sanctum of India's mystic culture and finds the love he has been seeking. It is a tale told with rare candor, immersing the reader in a journey that is at once engaging, humorous, and heartwarming.

*Available wherever books are sold.* | $16.95 | 978-1-60109-056-0

MANDALA
PUBLISHING
www.mandalaeartheditions.com